3/20

# *The Last Negroes at Harvard*

# *The* Last Negroes *at* Harvard

THE CLASS OF 1963 AND
THE EIGHTEEN YOUNG MEN WHO
CHANGED HARVARD FOREVER

KENT GARRETT

*and Jeanne Ellsworth*

Houghton Mifflin Harcourt
Boston New York
2020

hmhbooks.com

*Library of Congress Cataloging-in-Publication Data*
Names: Garrett, Kent, author. | Ellsworth, Jeanne, 1951– author.
Title: The last negroes at Harvard : the class of 1963 and the 18 young men who changed Harvard forever / Kent Garrett and Jeanne Ellsworth.
Description: Boston : Houghton Mifflin Harcourt, 2020. | Includes bibliographical references and index.
Identifiers: LCCN 2019014973 (print) | LCCN 2019021933 (ebook) | ISBN 9781328880000 (ebook) | ISBN 9781328879974 (hardback)
Subjects: LCSH: Harvard University—Students—History—20th century. | African American college students—Massachusetts—Cambridge. | African Americans—Education, Higher—Massachusetts—Cambridge. | Harvard University—History—20th century. | Discrimination in higher education—United States—History—20th century. | BISAC: HISTORY / United States / 20th Century. | EDUCATION / Higher.
Classification: LCC LD2160 (ebook) | LCC LD2160 .G37 2020 (print) | DDC 378.1/982996073—dc23
LC record available at https://lccn.loc.gov/2019014973

Book design by Emily Snyder

Printed in the United States of America
DOC 10 9 8 7 6 5 4 3 2 1

Photos from Class of 1963 Register, Class of 1963 Harvard Yearbook, and Class of 1963 Radcliffe Yearbook used with permission by Harvard Yearbook Publications, Inc. All other uncredited photographs courtesy of the author/Kent Garrett Productions LLC.

*For Jack Butler*

# Contents

# *Preface*

*For most of my life, I've claimed that I rarely thought about Harvard.* As evidence, I would eagerly tell you what a lousy alumnus I've been. I hadn't given the school a nickel, hadn't gone to a class reunion or walked in any Commencement procession but my own. I never joined an alumni group, didn't pitch in to raise money, organize an event, or interview prospective students. I hadn't once submitted a photo or boasted of my achievements in the class books that are published every five years, nor did I buy any of the books and read up on my classmates. See what I mean? I hardly ever thought about Harvard—and of course, I protested too much. My partner and coauthor, Jeanne Ellsworth, likes to remind me that I managed to drop it into our very first email exchange and wedge it into the conversation on our first date. So I admit to being proud of it, and I acknowledge that the Harvard imprimatur has opened doors for me. Maybe even hers, she teases.

At the same time, I don't usually make too much of my Harvard degree, and I especially don't want to be associated with the college's elitist, clubby reputation. Apparently that ambivalence (or false modesty?) is part of it. Malcolm Gladwell says it well when he describes meeting Harvard alums: "Don't define me by my school, they seemed to be saying, which implied that their school actually could define them. And it did." Gladwell goes on to describe the reputation that I have always shrunk from—the backslapping camaraderie, the "tales of late nights at the Hasty Pudding," the royal roommates, the houses in the South of France, and the reverence with which the name Harvard is uttered.

In the summer of 2007, I was in my last days as an organic dairy farmer in upstate New York. I made an unlikely farmer for that place: a retirement-age Black man with a Harvard degree and a previous life in network television news. My back-to-the-land moment had come in 1997, when I left *NBC News* and New York City after almost thirty years as a television news journalist. In 1968, I had started my news career writing, producing, and directing for public television's groundbreaking *Black Journal,* an hourlong weekly national news magazine that was for, about, and produced by Blacks. After *Black Journal,* I traveled throughout the world working for *The CBS Evening News with Dan Rather* and then *NBC Nightly News with Tom Brokaw.* I covered all the wars, real and not so real—the war in Vietnam, the War on Poverty, the war in Grenada, the War on Crime, the War on Drugs, the War on Terrorism. At age fifty-five, I left *NBC News,* fed up with the rat race, office politics, and the intense commercialization of the news. Farming was hard, but it was good for the soul and the ego. The cows didn't care that I had been a big-time producer and had won three Emmys. They shit on me anyway.

But dairy farming is a young man's game. I was sixty-five, with knees and back wearing out, and I wanted to stop before something incapacitating happened. My marriage of over twenty-five years had also come to an end, and I had no idea where I would go next. One of those bittersweet last days on the farm, I pulled my prized Belarus tractor into the barn after spreading manure on one of the higher hills and clomped down to the mailbox. Among the bills and junk mail I found the latest *Harvard Magazine.* You might forget about Harvard, but Harvard never, ever forgets about you. I receive relentless pitches for donations and, every two months, my copy of the alumni magazine. It's slick and expensively produced, and it toots the Harvard horn and champions a world where every problem seems on the verge of a solution thanks to some illustrious Harvard grad. The magazine is sent out free of charge to every domestic Harvard alum, and it somehow managed to reach me no matter how much I moved around from house to house, from city to city.

On that morning, as usual, I flipped immediately to the obituary page, and read with sadness that Booker Bradshaw had had a heart attack in his home in Los Angeles and was gone. Booker was a year ahead of me at Harvard, a tall, handsome, light-skinned, popular Black guy. I remembered that after graduation he'd gone on to find some fame in Hollywood, and I learned from the obit that he had played somebody called Doctor M'Benga in *Star Trek* on television. Sparked by my coming life changes and the loss of Booker, I found myself wondering what had happened to the Blacks in my class, the class of 1963. Who had done what? Who had been happy? Who had been successful? For that matter, who was still alive? We were all pushing seventy, getting set to leave the planet, and it would be interesting to know what our fellowship and our individual experiences at Harvard had meant to us, how it all looked from fifty years' distance.

I spent the following year getting off the farm, selling the cows and equipment, and finding a place to live. The tasks and challenges of reordering my life squeezed out all thoughts about the Harvard project. The next year I met Jeanne via an online dating service, and when we had dinner one evening I told her about my ideas. She was about to retire from university teaching—her field was the history of education in the United States—and she was fascinated by the possibilities. From that first conversation, we've been on this quest. Indeed, we became partners in life and in *The Last Negroes at Harvard* project.

We would spend the next eight years tracking down and talking to my classmates, starting with no more than a list of names that I pulled from my memory and wrote on a yellow legal pad. I knew where a few of them lived, so I started by getting in touch, and little by little the list took shape—counting me, it totaled eighteen. We eventually found and met with the fourteen who were still living, in person at least once, and most more than once, following up with emails and phone calls. We also talked to some of our white classmates, to Blacks from classes ahead and behind ours, and to relatives of those who'd passed away. I interviewed my own father and sister. Jeanne and I drove all around New York and New England, to California twice, and to Georgia, Minnesota, and Michigan—some of our best ideas came in the car. And we flew to Austria and St. Thomas, Virgin Islands. Jeanne interviewed me more times than we can count, pulling out stories and feelings that I'd never have come up with without her relentless questioning. We spent endless hours transcribing tapes. We talked and read and studied and talked some more as the stories emerged and the ideas for this book slowly took shape. From the very beginning, this was a labor of love for us, and though we did other things over the years, singly and together, this project has been at the center of our lives, the stuff of countless and often contentious conversations. We even joke that once it's finished we may have to tackle something else or risk drifting apart.

We imagined in the beginning that Jeanne, with her academic background, and I, a journalist and also the "star" of the book, would have complementary roles in the writing. At times that was true, but far more often we worked together. When we actually sat down to write, however, we decided for reasons of clarity that the book would be written in the first-person singular, in my voice. It's important to both of us that readers know that there is hardly a word or idea here that isn't the product of our collaboration.

As we talked with friends about the project, we realized that most people expected eighteen rags-to-riches stories about eighteen geniuses who were plucked from the ghetto and plopped down in the wonderland of Harvard, where bratty aristocrats shunned or despised us. I knew from the start that it wasn't that way, but as the project went along the story became richer and more complex than either of us imagined. Then again, there is no one "real story," no single truth to how we experienced our four years at Harvard. We have tried to present all the guys' stories faithfully, and I think we have done that. We apologize for any errors we may have made. At the heart of it, this book is my story, the interpretations are my interpretations, and some of them I'm sure will not be endorsed by all the men you will meet here.

We eighteen, and all of our generation, were just starting high school in 1954, at the beginning of the modern phase of the long struggle for civil rights for African Americans, when the doctrine of "separate but equal" was overturned by *Brown v. Board of Education*. During our high school days, Rosa Parks and others would challenge segregation with the Montgomery Bus Boycott, Eisenhower would call out the National Guard to integrate Central High School in Little Rock, and the Southern Christian Leadership Conference would be organized. We came to Harvard in September 1959, on the very brink of the tumultuous 1960s.

We came from north and south, from the urban projects and from the upper echelons of the Black elite. We came with little in common except our youth, our academic ability, and our culturally defined "color." Like all young people leaving for college, the eighteen of us packed our hopes and fears along with our books and clothes and looked ahead to countless new experiences. Unlike others, however, we were going to have those new experiences in an institution that, for most of its long history, employed and enrolled men who openly despised and abused our ancestors. We would be attending a school that was founded and funded on the backs of our enslaved forebears, that had been virtually closed to our fathers and grandfathers unless they were pushing brooms. We were about to spend four years at the intellectual home—in some cases literally in the former homes—of people whose words and actions had oppressed and maligned our race and, by extension, us. We were headed for a campus where, until about eighty years before, each student was given a personal Negro servant, a campus that in the 1920s barred Negroes from the dormitories and had a branch of the Ku Klux Klan. We were headed for a college where just seven years earlier a couple of freshmen had burned a cross on the lawn of a dormitory that housed several Negro students and the administration decided that the act was "meant only as a prank." We were the largest group of Negroes admitted to a freshman class to date.

During the years we would spend at Harvard, the civil rights movement would heat up and reach the beginning of a more strident and violent phase. The historian Taylor Branch writes of that time that society was on the brink of "many changes including the extraordinary one in which the entire society shifted from 'Negro' to 'black' almost overnight." We would be the last Negroes at Harvard, and this is our story.

*The Last Negroes at Harvard*

# 1 *New Boys: Fall 1959*

*Arrival Day, September 18, 1959. The new boys trudge along with their* suitcases; attentive fathers carry trunks, mothers in flats and autumn coats tote desk lamps and portable typewriters, and kids trot along carting bags and boxes or just kicking through the first of the fall leaves. Harvard Yard is a verdant quadrangle of well-tended but simple elegance, boxed in by fine old American buildings, sequestered behind sturdy ivied brick walls and wrought-iron fences of fine design. Even on a busy day like this, the Yard is serene, as if over three hundred years of arrivals have inured it to any disturbance. Proud parents walk confidently into the epicenter of the American aristocracy, in the footsteps of some of the most illustrious feet in American history. Half of this year's boys have gone to private schools, and they watch out for familiar faces, letter sweaters, or school ties. For the many fathers who are Harvard alums, this is a ritual and a homecoming: they greet old classmates with backslaps and inside jokes. Other fathers tip their hats, secure in the knowledge that as of this day, through their sons, they have joined one of the most elite clubs in the world. Mothers exchange the polite smiles of privileged sisterhood.

Just after one o'clock that afternoon, another family comes across the Yard. Heads turn, eyes widen, a mother whispers behind her hand, a father shushes a child. Now treading on the Puritan soil and patrician pathways of Harvard Yard are eight dark-skinned, Sunday-best Negroes, one of them a tall thin boy carrying a suitcase. That boy is me, and this is the Garrett party; this is my family, my very Negro family, stepping onto the very white, very Old New England, very exclusive grass and gravel of Harvard Yard. We know we are being looked at. We stick closer together, say less, and walk more stiffly than the other families, maintaining what we hope looks at least like composure, if not aplomb. Aside from my fourteen-year-old sister and me—who were born in Brooklyn—the others in our party, my parents and aunts and uncle, were all born and grew up on sharecropper farms in Edgefield, South Carolina. They lived more than half of their lives in the rural Jim Crow Deep South. They were just two decades distant from driving mules and picking cotton, from the indignities of segregated schools, parks, buses, and water fountains, from violence and hatred, degradation and fear. They had clear memories of having stuffed Cousin Emery into the trunk of a car to escape the Ku Klux Klan. Considering their beginnings, their struggles, and the history of Harvard and of the United States, my family's arrival in Harvard Yard that cool early fall day in 1959 was one of incalculable dimension.

The wide lawns of Harvard Yard say to the privileged few who have been chosen, *You belong here, you are important, you are granted a generous share of space and time in this world,* while my family and just about everyone I had spent time with in my seventeen years on earth had been told, *You don't belong here, you're not very important, and what little you are granted we will begrudge you.* The trees of Harvard Yard rise confidently into a leafy canopy that keeps both the sun and the outside world from beating down too harshly on its chosen, while my family and our forebears slaved under the sun and the whip for more than three hundred years as generations of trees grew and died in the Yard and new ones were planted. Thousands of white Harvard boys and men had sat under the trees smoking, chatting in clusters with their hands in their pockets, considering the questions of the ages and dreaming the big dreams, or they had horsed around, singing drunkenly, considering the questions of the moment and dreaming the little dreams, while my family and our brothers and sisters in blackness had walked mean streets and dark country roads, trying to dream any kind of dream at all.

But I wasn't thinking about those incongruities on that day in September 1959. I was seventeen, awkwardly and tentatively confident. I hadn't thought much about Harvard at all, in fact, except that it was a good school and famous. The only connection I had to the place was a distant cousin of my mother, Ida Thomas, who worked in one of the kitchens. Had I wondered how many Blacks would be here? I don't think so. For that matter, had any of the white boys who were arriving that day thought about having Black classmates, or even roommates? Not likely. But here we were all together, and some of those white boys and their families no doubt were shocked to see me.

I was by no means the first Black at Harvard. That was Richard Theodore Greener, who graduated in 1870. From then until the mid-twentieth century, there were sometimes one or two in a class, and often none. Through the first half of the twentieth century, Harvard continued to have a trickle of Black students, more in the graduate divisions than the undergraduate. "The official view," according to one history of the university, "was that African Americans who had the grades and money to come to Harvard were welcome, but that there was no call to do anything more . . . African American students during the 1930s and 1940s were a not unwelcome sign of Harvard tolerance, as long as they were small in numbers and of acceptable demeanor. But by the mid-1950s, genteel liberal integrationism was the norm." A white member of the class of 1959 remembered that, in the midfifties, "there was no Black visibility in the college at all, save for an occasional boy from Boston Latin who commuted between Roxbury and Harvard Square. If you were Black at Harvard in the late 1950s, you kept a low profile, did your work, and moved on quietly to the business of real life."

That was pretty much how I had managed school—keeping a low profile, doing my work. I had grown up with little need or desire to have contact with whites outside of school, and so I didn't.

Nor did my family—I don't recall a white person ever setting foot in our home, in the homes of our relatives or anyone else we kept company with, or at our church. I encountered white kids only in school or Boy Scouts, and almost the only white adults I ever spoke to were teachers and shopkeepers. That day at Harvard I was facing four years of not only going to school with almost exclusively white people, but also living day-to-day, elbow-to-elbow with them. If I had paged through the introduction booklet I'd received over the summer, I would have had some clues as to what to expect. The black-and-white photos showed dozens of students, and they were all white, as were all the men in the photo of a faculty meeting. Maybe I was convinced by the booklet's claim that "the experience of living for four years with students having a wide variety of backgrounds, interests, and points of view is wonderfully broadening and maturing." More likely, I had skimmed the booklet and found it not very helpful, since it offered only grand statements like that and little practical information about what I really needed to know—like, *How will I know what to do? Will I make it?*

The summer before I left for college had gone by in a steamy blur, with New York City hot and humid as usual. I spent a lot of time up in my bedroom, slouching around, thinking about girls, listening to Lloyd Price sing about his girl who "walked with personality, talked with personality." No such luck for me—by my teenage reckoning, it was the light-skinned boys who got the girls and brains were useless for my social life. I was a studious, dark-skinned, gangly kid who did well in school and was still a Boy Scout. Others rose on the neighborhood social ladder by expressing disdain, or at least a jokey tolerance, for square boys like me. Even though I had trained myself to walk pigeon-toed like my hero, Jackie Robinson, those other guys were cool, and I was not.

The day came to leave for Harvard, and as if signaling the changes to come, the heat broke and we were up at dawn on a morning that felt like fall. Two cars full of family were going up to Cambridge to see me off. My parents; my sister, Velma; and I would ride in our Pontiac, and in the other car would be three of my mother's sisters—Aunt Estelle, Aunt Mag, and Aunt Carrie

Lee—with Aunt Estelle's husband, Kaiser-Bill, behind the wheel. I had rolled my eyes at the prospect; the thought of going to college and having the aunts pinch my cheeks or call me Butch, as they typically did, was a horrifying prospect for a boy who already felt hopelessly uncool. But all my complaining had proved useless. On that early morning, the men debated the pros and cons of various highways and settled on a route. The women wrapped sandwiches in waxed paper and packed them into shoeboxes. It was unlikely that we'd be turned away from a roadside restaurant, as we would be if traveling in the South, but we could be deliberately made so unwelcome that we'd wish we hadn't gone in. We would find a shady turnout and enjoy our sandwiches there.

I had one trunklike suitcase besides the clothes on my back. I had managed to pack my clothes without the name tags that my mother wanted to sew in, as she had done for every single shirt and pair of BVDs that I took to Ten-Mile River Boy Scout Camp two summers earlier. I'd won the rare argument with my mom, insisting that the other boys at Harvard would not steal my clothes, although I didn't really have any proof of that. The men and I put on our church clothes—dark suits, crisp white shirts, and sleek ties—and the women wore smart hats and high heels. We were a degree or two more formal than the relaxed insiders we would encounter that day.

Velma and I slid onto the slick leatherette backseat of our beautiful white 1959 Bonneville, with the sneering grill and the space-age fins that made us feel more affluent than we actually were. The caravan wound through the narrow residential streets of Queens and then turned north in first daylight over the East River on the grand suspension of the Whitestone Bridge, into and out of the Bronx, then through the leafy unknown territories of New Rochelle, Larchmont, Rye, and Port Chester. Finally, we were out of New York altogether, cruising on through Connecticut and Massachusetts, the farthest north I had ever been. Things were pretty quiet in our car: Velma was lost in her own teenage reveries, and my mom fussed nervously in the front seat. We had had countless car breakdowns and missed events in the past, so even now, in this new car, she and I were mildly plagued by "what-ifs." Mom had learned to drive less than a year before, and the experience included a panicked slam on the brakes that had sent me flying and gave me the chipped front tooth that I still have today. All of this had left her a nervous rider, but Dad was patient with her suggestions about his driving. I'm sure both of them were worrying about leaving their only son among strangers in an alien land, far from Queens, in a place they'd never seen before and didn't fully understand. As we rode along, Dad would now and then direct me to check to see that the other car had kept up, and I'd swing around and reassure him that, yep, they were still right behind us. It looked like they were having a lot more fun than we were. Uncle Kaiser-Bill was singing along with the radio, doing the snazzy finger-pop that I could never imitate, with the aunts sometimes chiming in and otherwise keeping the chatter going.

*Kent and his dad unpack the Pontiac.*

Early that afternoon, we were nearing the campus, driving past the ivy-covered Harvard Stadium at Soldiers Field, then across the Charles River and right on up to the Harvard campus. We joined the line of cars along Massachusetts Avenue, which forms the southern border of the Yard. Upperclassmen did their best to direct cars in and out and pointed us toward the freshman dorms. Since the early twentieth century, all freshmen had been required to live in one of the Yard's red-brick, ivy-covered Georgian-style halls: Wigglesworth, Weld, Grays, Matthews, Lionel, Stoughton, or Thayer, all named after Brahmin New England families. They are handsome but plain, reflecting the kind of Puritan stoicism thought best suited to the scholarly life. George Santayana described their style as "the architecture of sturdy poverty, looking through thrift in the direction of wealth." The little black-and-white photos of the campus that I'd seen did this place no justice. I had seen the neighborhoods of New York City, mostly from bus windows, and I'd seen all kinds of cities and towns and countrysides from the windows of trains, but to actually be walking into Harvard Yard with the thought of soon going into one of those fine buildings—we might as well have landed on the Champs-Élysées, or the moon.

We made our way cautiously across the Yard, passing between the two halves of Wigglesworth Hall, behind enormous columned Widener Library, toward the white spires of Memorial Church to Thayer Hall South. I located the room on the first floor that corresponded with the number on my room card, shook a key out of the tiny envelope tied to the card, and fumbled the door open. The eight of us filed in and stood there. Aunt Mag planted her fist on her hip, her eyes scanned the room from floor to ceiling, corner to corner, and she humphed theatrically, "What is this?" The tension was broken. I thumped down my suitcase, and we were alone to smile and breathe—dear sassy Aunt Mag had gotten the jump on any judgment Harvard might make on us! It was true that my room, especially after the grandeur of what we'd seen so far that afternoon, looked pretty old, small, and bare. We associated high status with oversized, ostentatious luxury, and the idea that the Spartan might be chosen for its own sake, or that simplicity could be more prestigious than extravagance, was simply not part of our concept of social class, which had been shaped by life in the rural South and in the poor districts of New York City.

*Kent Garrett, 1959*

I was born in 1942 in Brooklyn. Both of my parents were born and grew up in rural Edgefield, South Carolina, on small farms. Dad's father worked in a coal mine and preached in his own small church, and my grandmother and their fourteen kids ran the farm. My mother's family had a smaller farm nearby, and they were poorer, since her father didn't work off the farm. Both my parents went to the local Negro elementary school and then moved to nearby Aiken to go to Schofield Normal and Industrial High School; since there was no Black high school near enough for them to commute, they boarded with family. After they left for Aiken, neither of them lived full-time on their family farm again.

I have a wonderful photo of my parents at about eighteen, standing outside the school. I like to think that it was the day he asked her to marry him, but I don't know. My father faces the camera looking like a man who'd just heard "yes," one arm around his fiancée's waist, the other holding her hand. My mother is wearing a polka-dot dress and smiling at someone outside the frame who seems to have teased her into a smile just before the picture was snapped. When we sat down and looked at the picture together seventy-five years later, I asked my dad about that smile and he laughed and said, "She was happy to be with me." When she pasted

*Mother and Dad, 1939, Aiken, South Carolina*

the snapshot into the album, my mother wrote on it in fountain pen: "1939, Alonzo + Willie Mae, Schofield School, Love Days."

On his summer vacations, my dad, who went by his middle name Alonzo, traveled north to work as a busboy, and later as a waiter, in big hotels on the New Jersey shore, in Cape May and Wildwood. During the summer of 1940, he had a chance to go up to New York City and visit the World's Fair, where he walked around seeing the wonders right along with white people, and he made up his mind to leave South Carolina for a good job and, equally important, for freedom from Jim Crow. He'd relocate to California, he decided on a whim, with his new wife by his side. But first they would visit my mother's Uncle Charlie in Brooklyn and see the sights of New York City. Dad bought tickets for the curtained-off back section of the bus—Greyhound was still segregated. He bought three tickets because, as it turned out, my Aunt Mag wanted to come too. In singles and pairs and trios, many of my parents' siblings had already gone north, and eventually every one of them would leave South Carolina.

That first stop in Brooklyn turned out to be my folks' last stop, because Dad found a job in a restaurant owned by another of my mother's uncles, and very soon thereafter he got a much better job at the Brooklyn Navy Yard. Like virtually all the Blacks hired for World War II work at the Navy Yard, my father was hired as a "Class I Common Laborer," on a "duration and six months" contract. The new job allowed my parents to leave Uncle Charlie's and take a series of short-term rentals while they waited for the opening of a new apartment complex built specifically for war workers. Though officially named the Fort Greene Houses, the buildings were not houses at all but thirty-five boxy, high-rise brick apartment buildings, the city's largest public housing project to date, and the first to lose sight of the principles of design that maintain a sense of community and connection to the city. Before Pearl Harbor, the Fort Greene Houses had been planned to meet the shortage of affordable city housing for blue-collar workers, but by the time they opened just a few weeks after I was born, the thirty-five hundred apartments, like so many Americans themselves, were conscripted into war work, housing military and shipyard personnel.

Dad worked hard and took extra training in order to get an electrician position, although, as a Negro, he was eligible only for the position of "Electrician Helper." He is still proud of his inside-out knowledge of the USS *Missouri* and the other battleships he worked on.

By the spring of 1946, when "duration and six months" was up, thousands were out of work. My father was among the lucky ones who found other work right away, first at a foundry and then with the New York City Transit Authority, where he started working as a subway conductor. When the job of motorman was opened to Negroes, he studied, took the test, and passed. He was rightfully proud of being a motorman, driving the trains in the New York City subways, the important and stable job that sustained him and our family until he retired. Still, it took years before the white subway workers would eat at the same table with him in the break room.

At first, as my dad has reminded me, the Fort Greene Houses were well maintained, orderly, and pleasant. I was very much an ordinary Negro boy, a bit precocious, perhaps, but just one of hundreds of kids who streamed noisily down out of the buildings

*Kent Garrett, 1946, Fort Greene Projects, Brooklyn, New York*

in the morning for school. I did well there, despite the fact that my parents didn't have the resources, intellectual or financial, to spend time reading to me and my sister or carting us to theaters and museums for "enriching" experiences. I had tropical fish, though; my father would take me to a wonderful store in the Wall Street area, where I wandered around and chose the few freshwater specimens I could afford. I always noted the species names, which were as enchanting as the fish themselves (even the lowly guppy, or *Poecilia reticulata*). For a few years I loved to dazzle classmates, family, and teachers and even complete strangers by announcing that when I grew up I was going to be an ichthyologist.

Or maybe a cowboy. My best friend, Mickey, and I practiced every day, with holsters and cap pistols flapping at our sides, as we ran around under the scrawny trees of our asphalt prairie. Mickey played the stocky sidekick to my spindly imitation of Hopalong Cassidy, and we shot 'em up outside our building every afternoon until my mother leaned out of my sister's bedroom window and called, "Junior! Get on up here now." Mickey and I studied our cowboy roles eight blocks away at the Peerless movie theater on Myrtle Avenue. On as many Saturdays as possible, we would walk up there on our own, feeling big and free. My father admitted to me more than fifty years later that he followed us to the movie theater to make sure we got there okay.

As we got a little older, Mickey and I watched more television, imbibing advertising's fantasies of white family life and the wealth of material happiness that seemed to await us outside of Fort Greene. We noticed, too, the mysterious and seemingly glamorous lives of the middle-class Blacks we saw in *Jet* and *Ebony* magazines. We gawked and elbowed each other over the "Beauty of the Week" and pretended disdain for the photos of cotillions and other Black bourgeois social events.

We hung on there in Brooklyn, scrimping and saving, as the Fort Greene Houses turned into the projects, with all the bleak baggage that phrase carries nowadays, and neighborhood life became increasingly ruled by the Fort Greene Chaplains, a Black gang, and the Mau-Maus, a Puerto Rican gang. By the late fifties, the Fort Greene Houses were described in the press as "a testament to the failure of public housing; another million-dollar barracks with shattered windows, elevators used as toilets, and utterly no sense of belonging or responsibility." One day came the news that Mickey was moving away. After the going-away party the neighbors threw, I flung myself on my bed and bawled out my grief and envy. I wanted my own going-away party to come. I longed for a house that had a shower instead of a tub and a back door where the milkman would leave two or three bottles of milk every morning. I wanted to have a house with an upstairs bedroom and to hear my mother say, "Junior, now go upstairs to your room!" like TV moms did.

After losing Mickey, it seemed that I was going to lose my whole crew, my homies. When I was in the sixth grade, someone at my elementary school, PS 20 in Brooklyn, recommended to my mother that I take the test for the New York City Board of Education's Special Progress (SP) program. Promising students were chosen from all over the city to attend one of several schools where the three-year junior high curriculum was accelerated into two years and students were prepared to enter the college-prep city high schools. My parents insisted that I take the test, I did, and I was admitted to SP. That meant leaving the neighborhood, my local school, and my friends: I would have to spend three hours a day commuting via two buses, traveling clear across Brooklyn to John Marshall Junior High School 210. Plus, I would be one of the few Black students in the SP program. I didn't want to go into SP. But the decision wasn't mine to make, and off I went.

As consolation, I promised myself that this would be a temporary, two-year thing, and that afterward I would get back to "normal." Learning and knowledge were part of the white man's game, and to be Black and intellectual was to be not, to my mind, normal. The normal kids were back in the neighborhood. The few friends I made at JHS 210 lived all over the city, so I couldn't hang out with them and do the normal things, like playing stickball, talking about girls and records, and just hanging around the 'hood, keeping clear of the gangs.

My parents would see to it that getting back to "normal" never happened. After the SP program, when I was recommended for Boys High School, again I had no choice but to ride the buses away from my Fort Greene community and clear across town. Boys High was a grand, gabled, red terra-cotta school in the Bedford-Stuyvesant section of Brooklyn, with a reputation in my day as a "hard school." Boys High was mainly college preparatory, with a rigorous traditional curriculum; often called the "school of scholarships," it boasted various notable alumni. I went because I was an obedient son, and also because little by little the idea of being intellectually capable had been growing on me. Maybe I would be an ichthyologist after all.

And then there were the summers, when I was a country boy. Every year, the day after school ended, my mother and my sister and I traveled by train to South Carolina to stay on the farms of my parents' families. From New York to Washington, we rode the *Silver Meteor* in the same car with the white families. But unlike the white families, we ate out of the familiar shoebox; the dining car was off-limits to us, of course. As we approached Washington, the conductor came through the car with the nod that meant it was time to gather up our things and make our way forward to the Colored Car. Back of the bus, front of the train—the custom for the train developed in the steam days, when the forward cars were the most prone to blasts of coal dust. My sister and I didn't ask my mother why we had to switch—the twenty-five-hour trip was exciting no matter where we sat. Plus, there was a lot to look forward to. Being on the farms was a welcome change from the projects: my father was one of fourteen siblings, my mother was one of nine, so there were cousins everywhere. We had our chores, of course—slopping the hogs, picking cotton, and fetching water from the well—but we also went barefoot, stayed up late, and ran around outdoors six days a week. Sunday was all church, all day, and my paternal grandfather, as the Preacher, saw to it that we were all in attendance.

*Kent on Emma, Wagner, South Carolina*

The big old plodding mules, Emma and Kate, were under my care, and I could even ride them around and dream my old cowboy dreams. My dog was a brown-and-white hound that I creatively named Spot, and I remember him most for fiercely defending me against the hogs when it was my turn to slop. Like many rural kids, I learned about suffering and death on the farm. We all stood clear, up on the porch, when Cousin Luther's gunshot smacked down an eight-hundred-pound hog, and we squealed and pretended to gag at the bloody blotch on the dirt. And on one sobering day, I cried at the bloody blotch left when I shot brave old Spot with a .22 rifle, after he limped back to the farm with his leg irreparably splintered by a hunter's trap.

More threatening than anything on the farm was the grim reality beyond our acres. I don't remember going often to town—that is, to Aiken—and when we did go, the adults kept us on a very short leash. As the Preacher's grandchildren, we were a notch above other Black kids when we were in town—not because my grandfather commanded more respect, I believe, but because he was useful to whites as a conduit to the Black community. Despite our minuscule bit of status in Aiken, my sister, Velma, heard the n-word for the first time when a store clerk yelled out, "We need somebody to keep an eye on them niggers." Our elders had imparted to us a visceral sense of fear that kept us wary, close at hand, and obedient. They grew up knowing about lynching, including a time when a local white woman accused one of four brothers of some real or imagined inappropriate action; when the mob found out that she wasn't quite sure which brother it was, they lynched all four.

I didn't know much about lynchings, beyond the bits and pieces of hushed grown-up conversation I could latch onto now and then, until I was thirteen. Shortly after getting off the *Silver Meteor* that had rattled us back to Brooklyn that year, I settled in one afternoon to check out the pictures in the latest *Jet* magazine. I was casually paging through the September issue, seeking news of a movie or recording star or ads for the 1956 cars that were just hitting the showrooms, when a photo grabbed my eye. As it swirled into focus, I was knocked breathless . . . a hideously deformed man? . . . something from the latest horror movie? "Close up of lynch victim," I read. The room closed in around me. I bent closer to the page and saw the word "castrated." I had heard the word with reference to calves and pigs, but . . . people? A boy?

The boy was Emmett Till, who was a year, almost to the day, older than I was. I had been in the South too, on the very day of the murder, and just like him, I had been a northern city boy visiting southern relatives. That moment didn't feel like the coming-of-age that it probably was; it just made me sick and afraid, feeling like nothing would ever really be the same again. I did what I always did when I was bewildered and scared—I hid in my room with the pillow over my head. Maybe I cried—probably I should have—and I want to cry now, thinking of that boy.

A more auspicious sign of my growing up was that I got my first job, albeit with my own father. As long as I could remember, my dad had spent most of his time off waxing floors for wealthy Long Island white people, scheduling the appointments around his varying subway shifts. He started taking me with him, and before long I was helping out. The linoleum in the suburban kitchens of the fifties needed waxing once a week, so we had a regular route around the upscale Jewish neighborhoods of Woodmere. It wasn't a bad job—once we hauled the heavy machine into the house and got set up, I could daydream into the bright geometric patterns, to the whirring hum of the buffing pads.

I liked the sense of accomplishment. What I didn't like was chatting with the housewives. I was unnerved by my father's deference, how he played the jovial Uncle Tom role, nothing like the strong and serious man I knew. The degree to which that was about race would vex me only later in life; at the time, to my adolescent sensibility, it was puzzlingly embarrassing to see him act so undignified. My unnamable distress sometimes came to the surface as anger, misdirected toward my father.

Researching for this book, I talked to my dad about our family history several times, but it took me a while to get up the nerve to ask him why he acted so damn "jolly" with those customers. "We-ee-lllll," he said, looking up at the ceiling and drawling the word out as he does when he'd rather not talk about something. I pushed, so he explained: we were coming into men's homes while they were at work, while their wives and daughters were "unprotected." *Of course,* I thought. We needed to show them that we were weak, harmless, comical, insignificant. Of course.

Beginning the spring when I got my college acceptance letter, however, we had a real zinger for his customers: Dad managed to work Harvard into every conversation. I could see by their reactions that this was something impressive. Pretty soon, I was doing it too; now and then there would be kids my age in a customer's house, and I made it a habit to ask where they were going to college. "Oh, Skidoodle College, that's a good place," I'd say. Pause. "And you?" my polite foil would ask. I expect not everyone believed us, but nonetheless Harvard was a magic word that landed with a big satisfying splash and rinsed away our humiliation—a little bit anyway.

The floor-waxing business paid off too: sixteen years after my parents said good-bye to South Carolina, and two years before I left for Harvard, we got out of the projects. My parents bought a story-and-a-half house on 140th Avenue and 170th Street in the Springfield Gardens/Jamaica section of Queens. Once the home of mostly Irish immigrants, Jamaica was experiencing white flight in the late 1950s, leaving modest homes to be bought up by people like us. Planes roared over our little house at all hours of the day and night, taking off and landing at Idlewild, and no doubt the noise was one reason that the house was affordable for a Black family escaping Fort Greene. The new house was light brick, on a small corner lot that gave us tiny front and back yards. There were two bedrooms on the first floor, one for my sister and one for my parents, and to my great delight, I had a bedroom upstairs under the eaves, the perfect hideout for an adolescent boy. The milkman left bottles of milk in our own tin milk box. Pretty much like my dreams.

Back in Thayer Hall South in Harvard Yard, the hour had come for my family to start back to Queens. It was early yet, but my parents and aunts and uncle were too fresh from the South to be confident traveling after dark. They couldn't easily forget about the "sundown towns" where to be Black after dark was to be in danger of your life. The Aunts had finished making and installing the fine set of curtains I would one day pass on to the next freshman duo. The women kissed and hugged me, probably even pinched my cheek and called me Butch. Kaiser-Bill shook my hand and then gave way so that my father and I could have a moment. "Your granddaddy," my father said. "One of the things he always said to us was that we had to think for ourselves, nobody has the power to think for you, think for yourself. And always listen, listen, listen, and don't say too much, and think before you speak." We were not a family who went around saying "I love you" all the time—in fact, pretty much never—but he shook my hand in both of his. And then they were gone.

*Kent's sister, Velma; Kent; Aunt Estelle; and Kent's mom, in front of Thayer Hall South*

By early afternoon, most families had had similar scenes and left their sons with roommates whom they'd never laid eyes on before but would live with for the next ten months. Over the summer, deans had sat sorting through roommate forms, matching interests and trying to create well over five hundred roommate pairs that would, at the very least, not cause any family to march over to administration in horror. Toward that end, there was a box to check if you would accept a roommate of another race, and apparently a few white boys had checked the box. One of them was Ron Blau, a Jewish boy from East Orange, New Jersey, who came to his room to find a trunk marked JOHN GORDON BUTLER. Until he actually saw his roommate, though, he didn't know that he'd been paired with the new boy who'd be one of the most visible and politically active Negroes on campus and my best friend at Harvard, Jack Butler. Pat Tovatt from Indiana had checked the box on his roommate form; although he grew up in a pretty bigoted town, his family were progressive intellectuals. Pat walked into Thayer Central and met his Negro roommate from New Jersey's excellent Peddie prep school, Lionel Deckle McLean, whom everyone just called Deck.

*Ezra Edward Holman Griffith, 1959*

I already knew my roommate, Ezra, so I was spared the suspense. We'd been classmates at Boys High, and when we found out that we were both going to Harvard, we decided to room together. Ezra was Barbadian, and for the first fifteen years of his life he'd lived the outdoor life in a tropical climate—playing cricket and soccer, zipping around the island's roads and paths by bicycle, swimming in the sea, and enjoying breadfruit roasted on a beach fire. His childhood was shaped by colonialism, race, and racism, but Ezra's parents were usually able to sweep poverty and racism under the rug of a loving home and their love for Barbados itself.

Ezra was educated at the excellent, integrated Harrison College, patterned after British prep schools. In May 1956, when Ezra was fourteen, his family decided to seek a better life, and they left their beloved island home for Brooklyn. Ezra found himself thrust into a world of heavy coats, crowded subways, gangs and derelicts, and the other gritty realities of Brooklyn's urban poverty—the world that I, ironically, was just escaping, though only for another part of New York City.

We hadn't been close friends at school, even though we were almost the only Blacks on the scholarship track. Ezra had his own social group of West Indians, centered on their similar cultures and, in particular, on soccer. Ezra and I were both quiet boys who didn't seek too much socializing, at least not in school. But right then, he felt like my best friend, and I was awfully glad to know that he was on his way. I took a deep breath, sat down on my narrow bed, took off my dress shoes, and waited for him.

Fifty years later, almost to the day, I would set out on what I'd begun to call my "journey": trying to find Ezra and all the other Black boys who arrived at Harvard that day. As far as I knew, there were at least a dozen of us, based on a list I'd jotted down from memory.

Hobie Armstrong was one of us, and he was now living in

*Hobart Glenn Armstrong Jr., 1959*

Kingston, New York, just an hour's drive from my home. So, on a gray afternoon in the fall of 2009, I got my recording gear together and made the drive. I pulled up to Hobie's house on a quiet street across from an enormous cemetery, and there he was, doing yard work. I could see that he had a full head of white hair and still had an athlete's body. Sports were always a central part of Hobie's life: as a child, he set records on his Little League baseball team, and in high school he led the football team to three consecutive unbeaten seasons. Hobie also had a sterling academic record, so a number of colleges were interested in him; he remembered that, even as a junior, he heard from West Point, Rutgers, Syracuse, Ohio State, Notre Dame, and USC. Kingston High was an ordinary small-city school, the kind that rarely sent any kids to the Ivies, but Hobie's guidance counselor had a connection with Harvard, and Hobie got an invitation to come up to campus, where he stayed with a member of the football team. Then he was invited again the next year and stayed with a professor and his family. That visit sold him on Harvard, and the prospect of being one of a very few Blacks at a white school didn't faze him—he was used to it from high school. Hobie recalled, though, that as part of Harvard's recruiting pitch while he was visiting, an admissions officer had told him that they were trying to recruit more Black students and promised him that there would be twenty in his class.

*Twenty? Well, maybe so,* I thought. But I doubted there would be any way to know for sure, unless Harvard kept race statistics from those years. I had read that at one time Harvard required that a photo be submitted with every boy's application, so admissions officers must have known who was Black. But that practice had stopped before we got there. While these thoughts were rambling around in my mind, Hobie went to a bookshelf and pulled down a large-format, cloth-covered, predictably crimson book: *The Register 1963* was stamped in gold on the cover, below the Harvard seal — *Veritas.* I'd forgotten all about the freshman class book, and I couldn't wait to get my hands on it. Hobie and I parted with promises to stay in touch, and I left with *The Register* in my briefcase.

Back at home, I dug in. The flyleaf shows Harvard Yard in the springtime, with pale flowers on an elegant tree in the foreground. Thirty or so men and one woman—all white—stand in front of Widener Library, amid the huge columns on the wide granite steps, in candid, assured poses; everyone seems to be looking up. Following the gaze of the people in the photo, I noticed two men up in the flowering tree, apparently involved in some kind of prank. That's Harvard, epitomized in a photo: ever looking upward toward wealth and prestige, with the freedom to climb up in trees just for fun. I turned a few pages and then there we are, the freshmen. Sixteen photos per page, from Frederick Johan Aalto of Ashokan, New York, by way of Phillips Exeter, all the way to Burton Zwick, a public school boy from Herrin, Illinois, on page 82. There, in glorious black and white, is every member of the class of 1963, staring out from a passport-size photo, his address, high school, and intended college major printed below. There are sons of the WASP aristocracy, many of them the sons of the rich, or the famous, or the rich and famous, including Marshall Field V, a Rockefeller, a Vanderbilt, and also, from the family with a boy at Harvard in every generation since 1659, a Saltonstall. There too are the heirs to the fortunes of Borden's milk and Corning Glass, right on the same pages with boys from farms and cities and a few foreign countries who grew up in modest homes and of modest pedigree. Some of them look like kids, and others strangely like old men. Many wear the owlish glasses of the day, with their dark plastic rims; all of the boys have very short haircuts, some sporting the stiff brushed-up crew cut, and all wear jackets and narrow ties. There is a sameness to these photos that makes anything different jump out—and from the third page, top row, out jumps Hobart Glenn Armstrong Jr., his dark face serious, nearly expressionless, imperturbable, as I've always known him to be.

Flip, flip, flip . . . white, white, white, and more white. Finally, on the tenth page, I found John Gordon Butler, Jack to the many who knew him, with his dark-rimmed glasses and characteristic wide smile showing off the dimple girls loved, the boy who would be my roommate for three years at Harvard and a good friend for life. More pages, more faces, some that rang a faint bell. Here and there a face caught my eye—did I know him?—and then, on page 23, the next Black face, Lowell Skinner Davidson, whose gaze is directly at the camera, chin slightly upraised, a hint of defiance on his face. Lowell Davidson, whose life and death would turn out to be glorious, tragic, and mysterious.

I closed the book that day with a list of seventeen, some of whom I remembered very well, others less so. They had all been there in the Yard that day; all had arrived from their hometowns and cities with their families, sat for their pictures, found their rooms, met their roommates, and very likely been stared at by white families. As I traveled through the country and across the seas collecting their stories, I would come to know something about each of them and to realize that our backgrounds and life stories reflect the diversity of Black life in the mid-twentieth century. It was at Harvard that we had come together for a brief but important four years, and it was the Harvard experience that would bring us back together in our retirement years.

*John Gordon Butler, 1959*

Among them, Jack Butler was the only one I'd kept in contact with through the years, although I'd hardly been the faithful friend I should have been. Jack was by far my closest friend at Harvard; without him, I would likely have missed a lot of fun and some of the most important events of our four years there. Jack was a light-skinned guy with brown eyes and hair. Confident and ebullient, he was always on hand with an idea or a plan, ready to kick up a lively debate or stir up a controversy, and hanging out with him was an education in itself. A few years before I started the journey to find my Black classmates, I'd been to his home in New Paltz, New York, for a holiday gathering. It was our first meeting in years, and I learned he was in remission from multiple myeloma, a cancer of the plasma cells. It was time to go back and see him again.

I found him still looking great, still in remission. I'd been the stringy partner in our college days, eager to bulk up a little, while Jack always seemed to be trying to shed a few pounds. Now, in our late sixties, we had evened up, each of us looking a little thick around the middle. Though I knew a lot about his background, he went over it all for me. He grew up in Pittsburgh, the son of well-educated, upper-middle-class parents; his father was a physician educated at the historically Black Lincoln University and Meharry Medical College in Nashville, the first medical school for Blacks in the South. Jack's mother was a teacher at the secondary and college levels, with degrees from Oberlin and Ohio State. The family home stood on a small lot on Iowa Street in Pittsburgh's Hill District, in the heart of the downtown area known as the educational center of the city; Jack's younger brother remembered that it was considered the best part of town for Blacks: "Everybody said, 'That's Sugar Top up there. That's where life is good.'" Jack could see all the way out across Pittsburgh from his bedroom window to the steel mills and, in the nearer distance, the campuses of the University of Pittsburgh and Carnegie Mellon and the lights of the Pittsburgh Pirates' Forbes Field.

Residential segregation was a way of life in Pittsburgh. Daily life was largely segregated by tradition and mutual understanding, so few Jim Crow laws or WHITES ONLY signs were necessary. The rules were clear, especially for Blacks, and whites were on hand to see that those rules were enforced—hence the beatings endured by the young Blacks who thought they would swim in the Highland Park "public" pool in 1931. During Jack's boyhood years, activists made concerted efforts at desegregation, starting with the city pools. The peaceful integrators were pelted with rocks, but prevailed nonetheless, and they took their fight to the city schools next.

Jack's father couldn't quite approve of these public protests; his younger son remembered him as "definitely a guy who came up in the Booker T. Washington mind-set—if it was good, it was white." Jack's brother remembered that the family's life in those days "was all about cotillions, bridge clubs, and all that kind of shit." But everything changed when Jack was nine: his father abruptly left the family and moved to Detroit, leaving his wife and children in shock and disbelief. That was the end of bridge clubs and cotillions. It was not solely a matter of money, but of mutual rejection. Divorced women couldn't last long in the bougie world, and Jack's mom had never been comfortable with the Black social life that had been so important to her husband. Jack's mother, an intellectual who would go on to found the Black studies program at a state university, was now head of the family, and it was her values that prevailed in the home.

Like me, Jack was into scouting and had gone all the way to Eagle Scout when he came to the attention of Gwilym A. Price, head of the Westinghouse Corporation and a Harvard alum, who became his mentor and sponsor. It was Price who suggested that Jack apply to Harvard, Dartmouth, and Carnegie Tech. Jack's white high school counselor was not supportive, insisting that those schools did not accept many public school kids and that their school, Schenley High School, was not a premier high school. Admitted to all three colleges, Jack chose Harvard because it offered the best financial aid and work-study package. So he was Cambridge-bound on September 18, 1959, too.

On that same day, our soon-to-be classmate George Jones was completing a three-day road trip to Cambridge. He'd been traveling with two white boys, Eric and Lyman Johnson, the sons of

*George Henry Jones Jr., 1959*

a prominent physician in Muskogee, Oklahoma, where George Jones was born and raised. Muskogee was a segregated town with a vibrant Black middle class that went all out to support the all-Black Manual Training High School. The school's name was misleading—it had a strong college-preparatory program and excellent, super-dedicated teachers. It was one of those legendary activist Black schools that sent unprecedented numbers of its graduates to colleges all over the country. Although he had a fine education and the will to succeed, George wasn't sure he would get into Harvard, but he took a chance, applied, and was accepted. The doctor's sons, one about to join the class of 1963, the other a year or two older, had heard that George was headed for Harvard and offered him a ride. They'd started out rattling along the old US Route 66 in the Johnson boys' old Rambler. The trip was going along well, and they had even inadvertently integrated a Big Boy restaurant along the way—or so it seemed to one white man, who leaned over to George and told him he was the first Negro to eat there. Whether or not the man was right, the boys were lucky to have made it through the journey without a racial incident, but they did encounter problems of a different kind.

Somewhere around Angola, Illinois, they stopped to pay a toll, and when Eric shifted into first gear, nothing happened. Reverse, also nothing. The boys got a tow to a mechanic and found out that the Rambler had a broken axle. One of the Johnsons called their father. To George's astonishment, the doctor told them it wasn't worth the expense and the wait to have the Rambler fixed, so they should just go and buy a new car. George knew that they were a prominent family, but the idea of just buying a new car, like that, was beyond his imagination. They rolled into Cambridge in a brand-new Chevy.

Like Ezra and me, George had not visited Harvard before, hadn't gone to a private school, wasn't a legacy. Like me, he was dark-skinned and not used to privilege. So, like me, he was in awe looking around the campus, wondering if he would make it through the first few days, let alone four years. Our classmate Freddy Easter was more confident. After all, Freddy was from Harlem.

*Wilfred Otis Easter, 1959*

Fred had come up to the Harvard campus a week early to work on the Dorm Crew, whose job it was to tidy up the rooms after the summer school students had departed. During that first week, he had gotten into a poker game with some of the other boys and had come out on the losing end. Fred would tell people for years that the first thing he learned at Harvard was "just because you know three of a kind beats two pair doesn't mean you can play poker."

The Easters, like my family, lived in the projects. Unlike Fort Greene, the Harlem River Houses complex was designed with lower buildings and common areas that would foster a sense of community among the residents. Fred was precocious and earnest, and he had been skipped ahead two grades by the time he finished high school in 1957. He then spent the next two years at The Gunnery, a prep school in Connecticut, so that he would be prepared for the rigors of Harvard. When it came time to leave for Cambridge, the family bookie offered his services. Everybody in Fred's neighborhood played the numbers, and Al was the guy who came to Fred's building and handled collections and payouts. He had an Oldsmobile 88, a newer and bigger car than the car owned by Fred's father, who in any case had never driven as far as Boston, so Al took Fred and his father and mother up to Cambridge. Only a few other boys were arriving that day, but at least one must surely have scratched his head at the sight of three Black men leaning confidently on a sharp new Oldsmobile 88 parked in Harvard Yard, while a Black woman snapped the photo that Freddy would keep for the rest of his life.

*Freddy Easter, New York City, 1958*
COURTESY OF FRED EASTER

We all had a lot to learn about the nuts and bolts of daily Harvard life, and the college had all manner of meetings and activities to get us acclimated. We had to stand in line to sign papers and fill out forms and get the "bursar's card" that would admit us to meals and events, allow us to check books out of the library, and so on. At dorm meetings, we met our proctors and learned the rules, including the two that were perhaps most often complained about: that we wear a jacket and tie at all meals (inconvenient and irritating) and that girls were allowed in the dorms only during official "parietal hours" (always far too short). We also heard about the consequences of failing to follow the rules, one of which was to have your bursar's card taken away until you'd had a conference with a dean or starved to death, whichever came first.

Other meetings were more uplifting and encouraging—Harvard spared little effort and expense to ensure that students felt they truly belonged to the college and to their class, that being "Harvard '63" became a central part of their being. Much of the week's activity was aimed at cementing that new identity, that feeling of having joined an exalted group. One of the first things on our agenda was an assignment to report to Memorial Hall to have a freshman photo taken. Our photos would be hastily assembled and published in *The Register*—the freshman class yearbook that allowed everyone to know everyone else from the first few days of the semester.

Late in the afternoon of Arrival Day in 1959, we'd gone to meetings, introduced ourselves and strained to remember at least a few names, and eaten a nervous late lunch at the Freshman Union, some of us more nervous than others, to be sure. Our next assignment would take us to a formal greeting in Memorial Hall, just across Cambridge Avenue from my dorm. Here we would officially become the class of 1963. Memorial Hall's dramatic high Victorian Gothic beauty topped everything I'd seen that day, even without the tower that had burned a few years before. Built to honor Harvard students who had fallen in service to the Union in the Civil War, the building was meant also to serve as the central meeting place on campus, where boys "might be inspired by the pictured and sculpted presence of her founders, benefactors, faculty, presidents, and most distinguished sons."

We gathered in Sanders Theater, which put me more in mind of a church than a theater. Richly paneled in dark walnut, carved and gabled, the space was studded with twenty-two stained-glass windows, statues of famous orators in togas, portraits in oils of past presidents, benefactors, and famous sons, and scrolled with quotations in what I assumed to be Latin. It was hard not to be impressed or overwhelmed. I looked nervously around me, the way everyone did: we were all intensely aware of each other, some of us sizing up the competition, others simply looking for signs that everything was going to be okay.

Maybe I was searching for Black faces. Had I been able to see them all, I would have found out that Ezra, Freddy, Hobie, Jack, George, and I had twelve more Black classmates from around the country. Two were from the Upper Midwest: John Woodford, a doctor's son, from Benton Harbor, Michigan, and Kent Wilson, the son of a single mother, from Springfield, Illinois. Two were from the Washington, DC, Black bourgeoisie: Lowell Johnston and Wesley Williams, who would soon rise to the top of our class and stay there. Four boys came from cities in the South—Travis Williams from Durham, North Carolina; Henry Exum from Frankfort, Kentucky; Charles Frazier from Mobile, Alabama; and Bobby Gibbs from Atlanta, Georgia. There were two more boys, besides Ezra and Freddy and me, from the New York City area: Deck McLean from Jersey City, New Jersey, and Larry Galindo, most recently from Manhattan but born and raised in Havana, Cuba. And one young man, Lowell Davidson, had simply crossed the river from his home in Boston, where he'd attended Boston Latin School.

I'd found seventeen by paging through the freshman *Register.* But there were eighteen, I know now, thanks to the always active Harvard alumni network. Our class puts out a newsletter called *Joint Jottings,* and in the 2007 edition I posted a request for reminiscences about our class, particularly about the Black members.

I received a few replies from classmates, one of whom startled me with the news that there were two more Blacks in our class—and he named them. I went back to the *Register* and realized that it had been stupid of me to believe that my "scan for Black faces" approach would work. I might not even have been able to find Jack Butler, Lowell Johnston, or Deck McLean had I not known them well. I flipped to the photos corresponding to the two classmates my classmates had told me were Black—they didn't look any more or less Black than some of my other classmates. *So,* I thought, *now what?*

I decided to use the quickest and easiest approach I could think of: I called them. After a minute or two of pleasantries, I made a quick explanation of my mission and then popped the question: are you Black? A doctor in San Francisco said no. But Gerry Secundy, whom I reached at his home in Pasadena, California, said yes. So there were eighteen of us. We constituted 1.595 percent of the freshman class that arrived at Harvard College in 1959, more than any freshman class had included since the institution's founding in 1636.

In those last weeks and months before we had all left home for Cambridge, the Little Rock high schools reopened after being closed for a year to avoid continuing to integrate: the segregationists were out of tricks. Americans already frightened by the Cold War learned that the Soviet Union could launch ballistic missiles from submarines, and Khrushchev was visiting the United States. *Explorer 6* sent us the first pictures of Earth from orbit, and the first two Americans were killed in Vietnam. In Washington, the US Commission on Civil Rights issued its first report, which detailed abominable situations in voting, education, and housing that were by no means limited to the South. C. Wright Mills had christened the new era "postmodern." Miles Davis recorded *Kind of Blue* and was beaten by police outside his workplace. Mike Wallace profiled the Black Muslims in *The Hate That Hate Produced,* a series of half-hour documentaries that introduced Malcolm X, shocking white America and tripling the membership of the Nation of Islam in New York.

There in that beautiful theater in the grand hall on the sacred ground of American power and privilege sat eighteen Negro boys —many more than had ever been in a freshman class. We were surrounded by over a thousand white classmates and innumerable ghosts of Harvard's white past—John Kennedy had sat in this hall, as well as Robert Oppenheimer, Robert Frost, William James— presidents and Rockefellers, world-shakers and empire-builders. We had made it through the needle's eye of admission, and on that day in 1959 we had made it onto campus.

Above the stage at Sanders Theater is a triptych inspired by the Harvard shield: three open books, each inscribed with a syllable of the college's simple motto: VE-RI-TAS—"Truth." The first two books, shown right side up, are said to represent existing knowledge, while the third, inverted, stands for what is yet unknown. It was into that unknown that we were bound. Some of us were downright afraid of the unknown; I know I was. The last speaker had spoken, we were officially the class of 1963, a spatter of polite applause rose and died out, and then with the scuffling of two thousand feet and the rising buzz of conversation, we stepped out into the last of the September sun and went forth.

# 2 *Curiosities*

*The drive to Cambridge today, via sleek and efficient thruways, is a* pleasurable one. At the clean bright rest areas, I walk in without fear, and I see drivers and passengers of all colors; my coffee is poured by immigrants from Senegal, Haiti, and Eastern Europe. After talking with several of my classmates, I realized that I should make the trip and get my feet back on sacred Harvard ground again, to see what has changed and let the place spark old memories. I pictured having my photo snapped standing in front of good old Thayer Hall and maybe getting a nostalgic bite to eat at the Freshman Union. Turning off the Mass Turnpike around noon, I navigated through more traffic than I am used to these days, the GPS intoning "bear left" and "stay right" to land me safely in the parking garage under the Charles Hotel, new to Harvard Square. Parking anywhere near the campus looked next to impossible—imagine my father just sailing right up Mass. Ave. all those years ago. Besides Velma and me, my wiry old dad was the only surviving member of that Arrival Day entourage, and he was not only alive but chirpy and sharp, a cane the only concession to his nineties.

Once out of the parking cavern and on foot, I started to recognize street names. Somehow I dredged up a remarkably accurate mental map of the area around Harvard Square, despite the fact that so much had changed: Club 47 on Mount Auburn Street—where we heard Joan Baez, Mississippi John Hurt, and our classmate Tom Rush in his early performing days—was gone. The Hayes-Bickford Cafeteria, where we could grab greasy diner food until the wee hours—gone. Elsie's, the best delicatessen in the world, where a Black guy named Smitty made sandwiches with blinding speed and took special care of us brothers—gone. Still there on the Harvard Square traffic island was the Out of Town newspaper stand. The Harvard Coop had made it through the years as well, but now it sold not only textbooks and necessaries but also a dizzying array of Harvard-logo'd clothes and trinkets: Harvard sweaters and T-shirts, Harvard ties and pajamas and key chains and decals, Harvard headgear of all kinds, not only for your own head but for the heads of your golf clubs. I bought a black baseball cap with a modest H on the front, asked the clerk to snip the tag off, and wore it out of the store.

Across the street, everything started to look very familiar. On through the gates, and there it was, the Yard itself, unchanged. Harvard cares about beauty, but maybe even more so about tradition and continuity, so no matter how much money they get, or how many more things they can buy or build or acquire, the Yard remains the Yard and presumably always will be the Yard. I stopped when I saw Thayer Hall South: it looked pretty much as I remembered it, but completely shorn of its Ivy League outfit. All of the climbing ivy was gone from all of the buildings, removed in the 1980s, I later learned, because the tendrils did so much damage to the mortar and the windowsills. It set me to pondering whether those tendrils and their removal had a deeper meaning: was the polished mystique of the Ivy League already cracking by the time we were there? Did it start crumbling, in part, because we were there? I had my picture taken standing on the stoop of the side entrance to naked Thayer South, then sat on the stone steps and let the memories seep up.

The skinny seventeen-year-old me is walking toward Straus Hall, keeping my head down and my step swift. I am a bona fide Harvard boy, crossing Harvard Yard—but not at all as I'd imagined it. I'm not walking proudly, carrying a few books, and wearing a nice jacket and tie like everyone else. The actual picture makes me cringe even today: I'm in dungarees and an old flannel shirt, with a toilet-cleaning canister slung across my back, in one hand a sack of toilet paper and in the other a bouquet of rubber gloves and rags. Of all the images I might have presented to my white classmates—many of whom have rarely seen a Negro in any other role than servant, let alone as a peer—this is the worst. Ironically, I'd wager that any boy who saw me like that back then would have assumed that I was a janitor, and so he would have paid me no mind, assuming I was not a "fellow Harvard boy," but "boy."

I can see myself ducking into Straus Hall and trudging up the four flights to begin my work in the top-floor suites. Following the instructions that my upperclassman boss gave me, I knock on the first suite door. If a boy answers, I am to ask, "May I come in and clean your bathroom?" "Do you need toilet paper?" Something about that moment is always excruciating—for both of us, I suppose, but far more so for me. On my luckier afternoons, most of the residents are in the library or doing sports, so I don't have to suffer the humiliation of asking, or even of being seen. Especially on Friday afternoons, many of the boys are out and about, and I can go in and do the job alone: aim the nozzle at the toilet, spray the smelly stuff all around, look away and swish with the brush, then flush, wipe up the drips, and go on to tend to the sink and mirrors, taking care never, ever to let a toilet rag touch a sink or mirror, and leave a roll of toilet paper. Then a quick pass on the floor, trying not to notice that some of the boys are really slobs, and finally, get the heck out unseen.

Although I had hardly imagined my first days at Harvard, I know I didn't picture this. But there was simply no way around it: this was my campus job and I needed it. I had a scholarship, but my family had to come up with almost one-third of the cost of attendance: the total annual cost of tuition, fees, and room and board was over $2,700, and $800 was our share. That was about one-fifth of my father's gross income at the time, so he would have to keep on waxing floors. The money I made on Dorm Crew was applied toward that balance and also to books and school supplies. To add to my financial worries, I'd read in the student newspaper that an increase in the meal rates was in the works. The job was a must, and I knew that very well.

The Harvard Dorm Crew was part of a nonprofit company run by student managers that provided income for the influx of poor and working-class students who'd become a real presence on campus after World War II. Fred Easter and I worked on Dorm Crew our freshman year, but so did some eighty white guys, so it was not a racial thing—most of the Dorm Crew guys were white, and not all Blacks who had student jobs wound up on Dorm Crew. Luck simply hadn't been with me when I went to the Student Employment Office on Brattle Street a few weeks earlier: Dorm Crew was the only job left that would work around my course schedule. Other guys, including some of my Black classmates, had landed more genteel jobs, like working in one of the libraries. For years that had been all I expected from my education—to wind up working in a jacket and tie, not getting dirty.

And now here I was. For several hours a week, I was a Negro doing Negro work—I was in my place. I had a gut-level awareness of being just another chapter in the long history of Blacks serving Harvard's white faculty and students as janitors, custodians, cooks, and waiters.

By Friday afternoon, I've cleaned my last toilet for the week. I gather my rags, sponges, and rubber gloves, swing the stinking canister up on my back, and retrace my wary steps back to Dorm Crew headquarters in Weld Hall. I drop the equipment in the closet and head back to my room in Thayer South, where I rinse off my resentment along with the disinfectant smell in a hot shower. Fall weekends mean football and the quintessential American college tableau: bright foliage against a crisp blue sky, clean-cut, Ivy League young men strolling through their domain in the garb that marks them as a breed and bears their name to this day. Boys have tossed their sack jackets and slim ties on the bed in favor of costly but casual Harris tweeds, perhaps from the Andover Shop on Harvard Square, comfortable flannel slacks, and white bucks or penny loafers. Some might be lucky enough to sport a letter sweater, from Harvard or one of the feeder preps. Girls are in the picture too, in their own Ivy uniforms—a plaid wool skirt or perhaps the stylish new fall Bermuda shorts, sleek sweater sets, flats. They stroll on the arms of or hand-in-hand with those young men, mostly upperclassmen, who show off the campus to their dates and their dates to the campus. There are football-eve parties—scenes, in my imagination, of drinking, carousing, maybe even orgies. But few public school freshmen of any color get invitations to parties of any kind.

Freshman boys, especially those who had come to Harvard without the ready-made prep school friendship circle, looked at each other, made small talk, and began to naturally coalesce into friendship groups. But even without my toilet-cleaning gear, I had learned in my first few days on campus that being noticed, at least in the way that I was noticed, could be unnerving. There was the sidelong glance, that half-second when my color registered, and then the quick shift of gaze to the ground or the sky, to the left or right, anywhere but at me. Boys High certainly hadn't been without racism, but seeing a few Black guys around the school was no big deal for New York City kids. I felt more conspicuous on the Harvard campus than I had in high school, but it was the opposite for my Black classmate Wesley Williams, who had had tough times as the only Black kid in his high school.

*Wesley Samuel Williams, 1959*

Wes grew up in the Washington, DC, elite Negro world, where his parents, like mine and Ezra's, shielded him from racism for the most part. But then they sent him to the Taft School in Connecticut, where he would be the only Negro in the place for four years, and he endured some harsh racism; as he puts it now, it "hit me like a ton of bricks; it was hurtful and it made me ache." Many southern boys attended the school, he tells me, and there was "name-calling, exclusion from activities, marginalization." Often when Wes would walk into a common lounge or the dining room, boys who had been casually chatting would go silent, get up theatrically, and leave the room. He responded by ignoring such behavior, persevering, making a few good friends, and, especially, excelling at everything he did. He carried that practice through to Harvard, where he set out from day one to meet as many of the boys in our class as he could, even using the *Register* to keep count of his progress.

I went along shyly and cautiously during those early days. One day I heard that the campus daily newspaper, the *Harvard Crimson,* was having an open call for writers. Back at JHS 210, I had become a news junkie. My social studies teacher, Mrs. Rutledge, the only Black teacher in the academic areas at 210, assigned regular reports on "current events." After my first essay triumph, about a Korean War draftee, I was hooked. Mrs. Rutledge encouraged my interest, and even played up the competition between me and a Puerto Rican classmate to keep us both on our game. I began to read every newspaper I could get my hands on.

Having access to a free daily newspaper was one of the delightful discoveries I had made while checking out Harvard in the early weeks. I read the *Crimson* every day, starting with their thick preregistration issue, where I'd seen advertisements for all the many things one could buy at the nearby stores eager to capitalize on the new fall crop of boys, many of them flush with spending money: everything from pens to sport coats to an undoubtedly very useful "sofa-bed" for $52.50. I'd read also that "politically moderate liberals" predominated on campus; that the "lecture system," while impersonal, really was outstanding; that I should consider Old

Spice aftershave if I wanted to get a girl; and that the star of the varsity soccer team was an African national named Larry Ekpubu.

Besides the ordinary stories about sports and campus events, the *Crimson* staff took on some real news, and that interested me: for instance, someone had done an in-depth piece on Fidel Castro's plans for Cuba, and another student writer had a story on the United Steelworkers of America strike. According to a front-page *Crimson* item, all students were invited to a meeting where you could "get your foot on the escalator" by working on the campus paper. This was no idle boast either: *Crimson* alums have included Presidents John F. Kennedy and Franklin D. Roosevelt and the writers Cleveland Amory, Daniel Ellsberg, David Halberstam, and Frank Rich.

The *Crimson* meeting was sure to involve some demonstration of ability, I reasoned, and not having done much writing, I worried that I would embarrass myself. And the whole thing was a little mysterious, starting with the photo that accompanied the meeting announcement: two slim blondish boys, each nonchalantly holding half of a naked female mannequin. What could that mean? Years later, Fred Gardner, a white classmate who did join the *Crimson,* would tell me that "the whole thing was jive and elitist." It seemed to me at the time that those boys were clever in a way I never felt clever, already sharing private jokes that I wasn't in on. The notice for the meeting announced that "old myths will be exploded, new ones created in this second and last day of the Bacchanalia." I'd apparently missed day one of whatever Bacchanalia was. The article's last line read, "The only thing you have to fear is fear itself." That's exactly what I had, fear itself, and I didn't go. I was hungry too, so, fumbling with my narrow tie en route, I trotted over to the Freshman Union.

The oak-paneled Great Dining Room had two-story-high ceilings, four cavernous fireplaces, and chandeliers crafted from the antlers of animals shot by Teddy Roosevelt. Over the doors were taxidermied heads from a huge collection of hunting trophies that he gave to the college. The sad stuffed heads looked down on photos and paintings of famous Harvardians, the supply of which seemed unending, and beyond them onto us boys. One of the dinner ladies nodded at my bursar's card, and I picked up my tray—which was no ordinary cafeteria tray, but a "Gropius Tray." The special trays were designed for Harvard and Harvard alone by the Architects Collaborative, headed up by the Bauhaus School founder and Harvard professor of architecture Walter Gropius. The trays were an unappealing beige plastic, round with pie-shaped compartments of various sizes; today they evoke an artsy midcentury modern style, and style is something that matters very much at Harvard. Malcolm Gladwell has rightly observed that Ivy League schools are not merely educational institutions, but also "luxury brands" that must provide the customer with an exceptionally high level of functionality and an equally high-class aesthetic experience. Most of us would have gladly skipped the aesthetic experience, though, since the food compartments were so shallow that inevitably gravy leaked into the salad or salad dressing splashed the Jell-O. Holding my Gropius tray as level as possible, I looked out over the sea of freshman heads in search of . . . yes, there it was: the Black Table.

Almost from the first day, we Negroes started noticing each other, making mental note of who and where the brothers were. There were five of us in Thayer South—Ezra and I, Freddy and his roommate Lowell Johnston, and Jack Butler—and we had unintentionally become the Black Table, with a fluid membership not always limited to Negroes. But for this one Negro, with so little experience of white people, it was something of a refuge, a ready-made friendship group where I would be understood and liked. And there was something comforting about the rhythm and style of conversation at the Black Table in that tricky freshman year. As Fred would remind me, if one of the guys said, "I'm fittin to go to study," instead of "I'm getting ready to go study," no problem, nobody looked askance, and everybody understood you. The Black Table kept you in touch with the Black world, its politics, culture, trends, language. After a visit home to Harlem, Freddy might come back and give us a few tips on how to stay cool: "A record used to be a side, now it's called a cut; guys are saying 'bad' to mean good . . ." Much of the time at Harvard, some of us had to modify our behavior and our speech and be careful about not perpetuating any Black stereotypes, to speak only what was then called "proper English." Today the Black comedian Deon Cole calls it "managing your Blackness" to avoid frightening the whites. We were all adept at it, but it could grow tiring; at the Black Table we could be ourselves and quit "managing our Negro-ness."

As we got to know each other, we tossed around ideas about what had brought us all there. We seemed to have had a gut feeling that something was up—it looked like there were more of us in the class of 1963 than in all the other classes combined, and we couldn't quite buy that as coincidence or some sudden flowering of ability in Black high schools. There were three or four Black guys from the South—maybe a coincidence. For both Ezra and me to have come from lowly Boys High—that seemed suspect. Freddy thought maybe Harvard was using us as some kind of celebratory symbols because we would graduate in the centennial year of the Emancipation Proclamation and the college could show how far it had come. Or maybe, as John Woodford half-jokingly theorized, we were "part of some sort of sociological experiment while being simultaneously turned into 'normal' Harvard men."

We were visibly not "normal Harvard men," and we could see that some of the white guys were just itching to find out more about us. At times we surely did feel like curiosities or anthropological specimens. One day Freddy was at the Union early, and by the time the Black Table convened, he was deep into conversation with a white classmate in the rotunda. After they'd passed their empty trays through the window, Fred came over to join us. "I was just reading my mail," he said, "and this guy came over and asked could he sit with me, and I said of course." It was an unwritten rule that you never refused. "I kept eating and reading my mail, and then he looks right at me and says, 'Do you mind talking to me?'" Fred made a "What the heck?" face. "Then he says, I swear, 'I've never talked to a Negro before.'" We looked up. "It wasn't insulting or anything, I mean it was all in a kind of academic inquiry way. His name is Gordie Main and he's from Minnesota. He's a hockey player and, well, the sport sounds interesting—on ice, you know? I'm getting tickets for the next game."

A perpetual topic of discussion at the Black Table and just about everywhere was girls and how to find them. About half of us hadn't gone to school with girls since elementary school, so we hadn't had the daily encounters that might have put us more at ease with them. When I went out at all in high school, it was with Ellen, my next-door neighbor in Queens. Our parents were friends, we went to the same church, and so we had been drawn into an easy familiarity—it was almost expected that we would date. My dad was generous with the Pontiac, and Ellen and I went to movies and the occasional concert—I could invite her out in a comfortable, informal way. But how was it going to happen here?

The guiding principle of the college's policies with regard to our libidos was to try to hold down the fort. First off, they would simply keep the sexes separated as much as possible, hence the parietal rules that set specific times when girls were allowed in the residence halls. As I recall, that was Sunday afternoon and Saturday afternoon and evening until eleven, except on football weekends, when girls had to exit by eight in order to keep partying under control, or at least out of the houses. Repeated pleas and campaigns to increase the hours met with democratic patience followed by stout refusal. But even the most lenient parietal hours are useless if you don't have a girl.

Of course, there was Radcliffe, the female side of Harvard, at the time sometimes referred to as "the Annex." Until World War II, the sexes were pretty strictly segregated, but the war had created a temporary shortage of professors, and so Radcliffe women were allowed to come to male territory and take classes, right along with the men. That privilege wasn't revoked after the war, so we had women in many of our classes; women could also use Widener Library but not Lamont. They couldn't go into the Union or, outside of parietal hours, into any house or dormitory or dining room. Back on their own campus, they had strict curfew hours. Reportedly there were some women who never came to the Harvard campus, but there were always a few women around—enough to remind us daily that they were indeed real living things.

*Cornelia Elise McDougald, 1959*

As for Negro women at Radcliffe—the proportion there was even lower than our class's measly percent-and-a-half. There was precisely one Negro girl in the Radcliffe class of 1963. Her name was Connie McDougald, and she was a pretty, lively, and super-smart girl from an aristocratic Black New York City family. Having grown up amid Negro high society, Connie had already met Lowell Johnston and Wesley Williams by the time she got to Harvard. She was interested in languages, and a few of us were in classes with her. Most of us knew her and liked her, and she told me she went out with some of the guys, but no romance came of it.

For our convenience, there were what amounted to catalogs of girls, with photos. Radcliffe put out "the Z-book," which they sold to Harvard boys, with photos and contact information for all the girls. The nearby girls' schools, plus Boston University, Tufts, and Boston College, published their own versions. Copies of these books were circulated on the Harvard campus, and we would comb through them in search of Negro girls. But alas, those little black-and-white photos could be deceiving. Then the process got tricky, but leave it to Freddy to come up with a solution, one that he reminded me of when I interviewed him. "These women did not often leap off the pages at you, they were not always to the eye African American, plus there were always six or seven names with no pictures. So, you could call around to people who lived in their town, saying, 'Look, here is the name of someone and here is her address in Kansas City,' or wherever—'Is that likely a Black person?' And they'd say yes, or probably, or no, not living over there."

Not totally blind to our desire for female companionship, Harvard, like most single-sex colleges and prep schools, held "mixers"—stilted affairs with members of the opposite sex shipped in for the occasion. Then commenced the mingling, choosing, presenting oneself, small talk, and insanity. Radcliffe optimistically called these dances "jolly-ups," but a Cliffie remembered them years later as "horse fairs at which prospective buyers carefully examined the horseflesh before purchasing." As if this wasn't bad enough, the whole thing was wildly more complex for us Negroes, because the "mixing" intended was strictly boy-girl, not white-Black. Dating at the time had one official purpose—marriage. In a 1958 poll, fully 96 percent of white Americans reported that they disapproved of interracial marriage, and it was illegal in about half of the states. Many integrated colleges had specific policies against interracial dating, to the point of reprimanding students who did it and sending their parents warning letters. This put the organizer of a mixer in a sticky situation—there simply weren't many Black girls in the local girls' schools, and frequently there were none at all. I suppose that in generations before ours, Negroes simply weren't invited or allowed to come to the mixers, if they even ever considered going. But these were the days of integration, so "arrangements" were made. One Black graduate remembered overhearing one of the "arrangers" when she "announced triumphantly, 'I finally got somebody for *him*.'"

Freddy's introduction to "arrangements" had come in prep school. "I would sign up," he said, "because if it was going to have girls, I wanted to be there. And they would match you to dance and so forth. They called ahead to tell the girls' school that 'we have a Negro,' and they'd see if there were any volunteers. None of them volunteered, so one girl would have two dates—me and another guy." Wesley Williams, too, had been stung by the mixers: he remembered "the agony we went through at Taft when they had their little tea dances and they matched up the students. One faculty member would always explain to me why I was not matched up with anyone: because 'it would not be fair to the girl.'" Wesley said he got over it and joined the dance band, "so I didn't need a date. I got to watch all the silliness."

That was high school, and it didn't seem likely that they would do any matching up at college mixers, so we'd have to take our chances. Given pretty much no other choice except to be monastic for nine months a year, most of us decided to chance it and went to the very first freshman mixer in the Union in September 1959. Nobody remembered much of it, but Jack met a young woman named Leslie Hansel that night. She was only fifteen years old, and her mother had reluctantly allowed her to go to the mixer so that her cousin, a student at Boston University, wouldn't have to go alone. Leslie and Jack dated a few times, and it ended with Jack thinking, "I'm not interested in a platonic relationship." But Leslie would come back into Jack's life years later.

I remember going to a mixer later that fall, this time with Kent Wilson, a fellow Negro freshman from Springfield, Illinois. Somehow, we had drummed up the courage to go. He probably didn't have a lot of drumming up to do, given that he had Belafonte good looks, with the singing voice to match. Kent was a perennially sociable and cheery guy—one classmate would say that he had an "almost magical power to win himself new friends"—and he seemed to actually like mixers. So, at the Black Table one Friday afternoon, when someone passed along the news that a mixer was scheduled at a girls' school over in Boston and there would actually be Black girls there, Kent pounced on it and persuaded me to come along. We managed to borrow a VW Beetle, puttered over there, parked, and unfolded ourselves into an autumn evening. We pushed down our pant legs and made a cursory swipe against the wrinkles, and we each took a deep breath. Ahead, a set of double doors stood open onto a brightly lit room where we could see girls in pastel shirtwaist dresses. Twisted crepe paper streamers swayed limply out to the corners of the room, and a few couples were dancing, also limply, to some out-of-date-sounding music. We tried our best to look relaxed as we stood in the doorway, scanning the scene. From behind a table, two white girls wearing name tags dipped pinkish punch into tiny cups and set them in rows. White boys picked up the little cups and passed them to girls and then stepped away, maybe with a hand tentatively at a girl's waist or elbow, making what I assumed to be brilliant small talk, but also sneaking glances at the crowd themselves. It was an intimidating scene even before we were spotted. And then we were.

*Kent Wilson, 1963*

We were used to being seen, used to waiting for the moment when it registered on people that something unexpected had just happened. I imagine that even a few years earlier, the crowd might have taken a collective inbreath and gone quiet, the band would have stopped playing . . . but that night the band didn't stop playing and the moment of recognition came and went. Although I'm sure there were some shocked and dismayed partygoers, the heads that had turned toward us turned conscientiously back to their conversations, and a chaperone couple stepped toward us. The husband shifted his pipe to his left hand and stuck out his right to shake each of ours in turn; the wife made a welcoming sweep of the arm toward the punch table.

And then we saw them: two or maybe even three Negro girls. My mind must have been spinning, because everything that happened afterward is hazy. We had a few dances and a little chitchat, and I learned a new word when my dance partner told me I had "scintillating shoulders"; whatever that might mean, it didn't sound bad. She was nice; her name was Pat, she was from New Jersey, her father was a dentist, and I left with her dorm phone number. In the next few weeks, thanks to Boston public transportation, we went to a few movies together. Hardly the stuff of which dreams are made, for either of us, but a few nice evenings in that first difficult year.

On the vast majority of evenings, though, there were no girls, no mixers, no movies or parties. My typical day on campus, after classes and toilets and dinner, included some early evening studying followed by what we called a "bull session." Thayer South, particularly Jack Butler's room, was a common meeting place. We talked about girls and classes, of course, but we also spouted off on the "meaning of life" and tackled all kinds of issues, from the mundane to the transcendental, from the immediate to the global. One of our first contentious topics was the Black Table—or more broadly, the tensions of integrating and self-segregating there at Harvard. There were those who argued against any kind of separation, self-imposed or not, believing that we should almost always mix with whites; those making this argument included a couple of boys from the South, who thought we needed to show them that Negroes were not only human but intelligent and decent. We middle-of-the-roaders thought that the Black Table could do no harm and that our coalescing was almost incidental. After all, we had some things in common to talk about. A few guys actually expressed doubts about the wisdom of integration, and that surprised me. I knew enough about the civil rights movement to know that integration was what we Negroes wanted—or what we were supposed to want, right? Now all of a sudden here came someone like Jack Butler, saying that integration might not be altogether a good thing—or at least he now and then took the lead in arguing against it. I was beginning to see that Jack was a powerful force who loved to argue against the current, or even to switch sides in the middle of a debate just for the fun of it. But when the talk turned to matters of race, he wasn't fooling around.

My family didn't do much integrating, that's for sure, but I didn't see that as a political statement. Nor did I see the Black Table as any kind of statement. I came to Harvard knowing little about Negro thought and history, nor even suspecting that things like that existed, at least not in the same way as American history and European literature and Western civilization. Even the most rudimentary elements and hollow symbols of Black history and philosophy were absent from my education, and of course from my entire family's. Even though I was now a Harvard boy, I'd never heard of Harvard's most famous Black alumnus, W. E. B. Du Bois, who earned his first undergraduate degree in 1890 and five years later became the first Black to earn a Harvard PhD. He could neither live on campus nor find board with one of the white families who offered it to Harvard boys. He had no white friends at Harvard, was mistaken for a waiter, and was rejected by the Glee Club. He succinctly described his time at the college as being "in Harvard, but not of it."

It's easy to assume, as I did when I first encountered the "in but not of" quote, that Du Bois meant that he was abused, maligned, and excluded by his white fellow students. But actually, he didn't wait around for anything like that to happen. Instead, he chose to set himself apart; he would write of his Harvard days in his autobiography: "I sought no friendships with my white fellow students, nor even acquaintanceships." Du Bois chose to seek a social life among the "colored folk of Boston and surrounding towns." He chose segregation deliberately, despite knowing that many of his fellow Blacks "saw salvation only in integration at the earliest moment and on almost any terms in white culture." But Du

*W. E. B. Du Bois*
W. E. B DU BOIS PAPERS (MS 312). COURTESY OF SPECIAL COLLECTIONS AND UNIVERSITY ARCHIVES, UNIVERSITY OF MASSACHUSETTS AMHERST LIBRARIES

Bois, as he put it, "was firm in my criticism of white folk and in my dream of a self-sufficient Negro culture even in America," and he found encouraging evidence of a growing solidarity that crossed class lines: "The group of professional men, students, white-collar workers, and upper servants, whose common bond was color of skin . . . together with a common history and current experience of discrimination, formed a unit . . . , so that increasingly a colored person in Boston was more neighbor to a colored person in Chicago than to a white person across the street." In another version of the same account, Du Bois wrote: "I had my 'island within,' and it was a fair country."

At the Black Table and in our bull sessions and all around the campus, despite what little we might have had in common otherwise, we were Negroes and there was some natural impulse that drew us together in a "common bond"—that "fair country" that Du Bois found. These were the first conversations I'd ever had on the subject of my race, or of our race and our place. I'm not saying we sat around talking about Du Bois; the "bull" part of these sessions was often piled high and deep, but we did spend quite some time trying to figure out what we should do and how we should manage our Negro-ness at Harvard. And then, after working up an appetite shooting off our mouths for a while, and not having eaten in a few hours, it was off to Elsie's on Mount Auburn Street for their signature roast beef sandwich, the best in the world.

After my afternoon of reminiscing on the Harvard campus, I would gladly have gone over to Elsie's and bought one or two or even a few weeks' worth of those great sandwiches. With Elsie's long gone, there was still the Freshman Union—surely, I could get a bite there—so I set out diagonally across the Yard, passing Weld Hall to my right, wondering whether the infamous toilet-cleaning supplies closet was still there. I walked on past the libraries—imposing Widener and old friend Lamont, plus a new one named for "our" president, Nathan Pusey. I crossed Quincy Street near its intersection with Harvard and Mass. Avenues and was abruptly disoriented. The Freshman Union, where we ate and laughed and convened the Black Table . . . Oh, no! Gone too? I blundered around until I spotted the rotunda sticking out from one side of the building, and that gave me my bearings. I found the main entrance that we had used back in the day and went in—only to become disoriented all over again. Maybe I should have realized that those old Teddy Roosevelt taxidermies would long ago have become too moth-eaten or outré for the times and been removed. After all, they were already in shoddy shape, I remembered, when Pat Tovatt hauled an enormous moose head to Thayer Hall and enlisted Deck McLean to help nail it to the wall in their common room—only to have it come crashing down to the floor, where it would serve for the rest of the year, antlers up, as a hideous ashtray.

I was jolted out of that memory by a Hispanic security guard who asked if I needed any help. I explained myself and he assured me that yes, this used to be the Union, and he showed me where the tables and service counters used to be. He said that the building, now called the Barker Center, had been altered some years ago to take on its new role as the humanities center. He laughed at me and with me: "It's all about change, brother, change!" I thanked him and meandered back out into the terra cognita of the Yard.

It was a busy time of day as students crossed in all directions, dodging the tour groups taking selfies with the John Harvard statue. I made it a point to look at the young people and to notice the Black kids in particular. I admit it could have been my imagination, or the new invisibility my advanced age has given me, but I didn't get that brief second of recognition and eye contact that Blacks have with each other when we are in a mostly white place, something that we all did back in our time on campus. *Maybe,* I thought, *that convention has changed among the young.* Nowadays there are as many as 150 Blacks in a class—is there some critical number of the "other" in a group beyond which you don't need to or just can't give that little look, the micro-nod of brotherhood? Looking at their faces, I thought, *these kids are different.* They know something about Black history. They have heard of guys like W. E. B. Du Bois.

What a difference it would have made to know about him back when we were freshmen. Or, in fact, to have literally *known him.* We could have. Du Bois was still alive in that fall of 1959, when my classmates and I were in our first unsure days at Harvard. He was ninety-one years old in 1959, just returned to the United States after a trip to Eastern Europe, the Soviet Union, and China, where he had been showered with accolades and honors from the socialist world. Vilified in the United States for his faith in communism, and suffering from ill health, he was nonetheless very active and working. During our first days at Harvard, Du Bois was writing the postlude for his autobiography. He was living in New York City, not that far from Cambridge, so he could have decided to take his own nostalgic trip back to Harvard.

I like to think of Du Bois ambling on over to the Freshman Union to have a look at the class of '63 freshman boys. I like to think that he'd stand there with his Gropius tray, looking out across the sea of faces, spot the Black Table, and sit right down with us, and that afterward he'd stroll across the Yard to see our dorm rooms, right there on campus, some of us sharing with white boys, and join in one of our bull sessions. I'm sure he'd have had a thing or two to tell us.

# 3 *Integrators: Spring 1960*

*The 1960s began in typical New Year's Day style in the Garrett home. I* had my pillow clamped down over my head, now swimming with a whole semester of Harvard learning. But a pillow is little defense against the worst stench known to humankind—boiling chitlins. Velma and I always dreaded this day, although at least in our Queens house the smell was more dispersed than in our tiny Projects apartment in Brooklyn, and we didn't have to risk being pointed out as the family responsible for stinking up the entire floor. Besides the smell, there was also the idea that chitlins are pigs' intestines—it was probably one of my elder cousins who had let me in on that delightful fact, since I don't recall that any of the cousins could stand them. Mom and Dad didn't force Velma and me to eat the stuff, though, even though their usual rule was that we ate what was put in front of us. Chitlin-eating was a generational divide that they tolerated, maybe because they were assured that we could get a full year's good luck from the rest of the meal—rice, hot sauce, and black-eyed peas. For our part, Velma and I adopted the New Year's tradition of finding excuses to be away from the house for as much of the day as possible.

We had had our Christmas, with the usual rounds of family visiting, and I'd suffered through dozens of questions about Harvard, most of which were blessedly unspecific, owing to the fact that the inquirers had virtually no idea what to ask about. I slept a lot and possibly even did some studying for my very first round of college exams, which I would face when I went back to school.

The trip back to Cambridge was routine and unmemorable this time, with just my parents and Velma in one car. While I'd been catching up on my sleep during that semester break that spanned the last days of the 1950s and the first days of the '60s, Cameroon had lowered the flag of colonial Britain and raised its new national banner, President Eisenhower and his advisers began considering what to do about Fidel Castro, *CBS Sports Spectacular* debuted with a Harlem Globetrotters game, and Harvard alumnus John F. Kennedy announced his candidacy for the presidency.

On campus, too, we could see signs of the decade to come: the college's 1001(f) Committee was organizing to stand up to the requirement in the recently passed National Defense Education Act that recipients of federally funded education grants not only swear allegiance to the nation but also disclaim "membership in, belief in, or support of subversive organizations." Ground had been broken for a new million-dollar computing center, the college's old Mark I computer was retired, and a few instructors announced that they would not be requiring an end-of-semester exam, on the grounds that such exams limited creative thought and synthesis. At the same time, college life for the spring 1960 semester began in completely typical ways—the Chess Club was having a brilliant season, Lamont Library announced a policy of spot-checking bursar's cards, our classmate Hampton Howell III was elected captain of the squash team, and the Fogg Museum added Picasso's 1901 *Woman in Blue,* the gift of Mr. and Mrs. Joseph Pulitzer, to its already impressive art collection.

On the damp wintry afternoon of Saturday, February 27, the Woolworth's five-and-ten-cent store on Brattle Street at Harvard Square presented a scene that would soon become emblematic of the new decade: a protest picketing. Woolworth's wasn't a typical destination for many of Harvard's middle- and upper-class students, though it was okay for picking up, say, a monogrammed handkerchief for your uncle's birthday, a copy of the latest *Look* magazine, a sink stopper, or a tin of oxblood shoe polish. Your mission accomplished, you could finish your shopping trip with an inexpensive coffee and pie at the lunch counter. But on this afternoon, two dozen or so nicely dressed and well-comported students were out in front of Woolworth's, looping a long oval on the sidewalk and carrying hand-lettered signs: END EATING BIAS IN THE SOUTH and SUPPORT SOUTHERN STUDENT PROTEST.

Shoppers craned their necks and squinted as they noticed the picketers from a block or two away, then dodged the kids or shuffled by in their haste, some frowning or shaking their heads. This being liberal Cambridge, some stopped to chat eagerly; a few actually turned around and shopped elsewhere or even joined the picket line. Most locals, though, ignored the kids, since they were accustomed to seeing students doing all kinds of things around the square, and usually there was not much to it. According to a *Crimson* poll, the prevailing stereotypes of Harvard students included that they were "goof-balls," "fairies," and "vandals," "going around with foolish beards," wearing "crazy Egyptian shoes," and forever acting "like they're supreme over everybody else." None of the locals that day was particularly importuned by the protest, and the *Boston Globe* barely mentioned the picketing, which was going on at several dozen stores in the area. There was as yet little inkling that in two short years the politics of integration would bring out eight thousand to march through the streets of Roxbury in an early phase of the fighting that would last for decades and bring Boston to the national stage with the violence of forced busing.

If you could make out the faces of the picketers under their scarves and earmuffs and caps, you would see that among them were two very young Negro boys. John Woodford, my classmate from a middle-class midwestern home, handsome and well built but not tall, would have been less likely to step up and engage you; he'd leave that to the more gregarious Travis Williams. If you paused too long, looked interested, or were just too polite to refuse, Travis would step up and push a limply fluttering paper into your hands: "Don't Buy in Northern Woolworths as Long as Southern Woolworth Segregates."

Looking at you from his six-foot height, through thick glasses that he frequently had to shove back up his nose with his index finger, Travis would explain further: Unlike you, Negroes in the

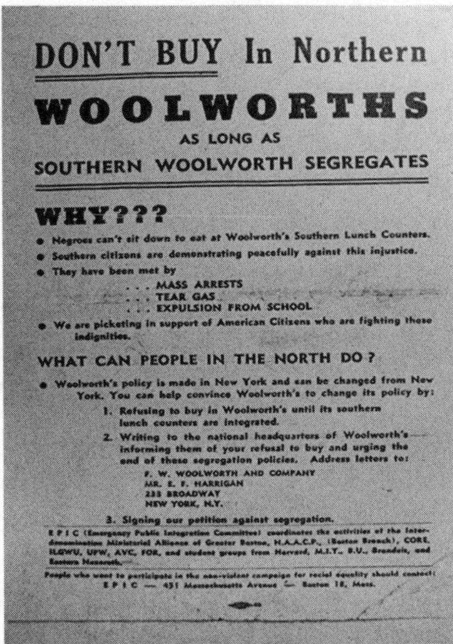

DON'T BUY In Northern

**WOOLWORTHS**

AS LONG AS

SOUTHERN WOOLWORTH SEGREGATES

**WHY???**

- Negroes can't sit down to eat at Woolworth's Southern Lunch Counters.
- Southern citizens are demonstrating peacefully against this injustice.
- They have been met by
  . . . MASS ARRESTS
  . . . TEAR GAS
  . . . EXPULSION FROM SCHOOL
- We are picketing in support of American Citizens who are fighting these indignities.

WHAT CAN PEOPLE IN THE NORTH DO?

- Woolworth's policy is made in New York and can be changed from New York. You can help convince Woolworth's to change its policy by:
  1. Refusing to buy in Woolworth's until its southern lunch counters are integrated.
  2. Writing to the national headquarters of Woolworth's — informing them of your refusal to buy and urging the end of these segregation policies. Address letters to:
     F. W. WOOLWORTH AND COMPANY
     MR. E. F. HARRIGAN
     233 BROADWAY
     NEW YORK, N.Y.
  3. Signing our petition against segregation.

E P I C (Emergency Public Integration Committee) coordinates the activities of the Inter-denomination Ministerial Alliance of Greater Boston, N.A.A.C.P., (Boston Branch), CORE, ILGWU, UFW, AVC, FOR, and student groups from Harvard, M.I.T., B.U., Brandeis, and Eastern Nazareth.

People who want to participate in the non-violent campaign for racial equality should contact:
E P I C — 431 Massachusetts Avenue — Boston 18, Mass.

*EPIC's Woolworth flier*

South could not finish off their shopping day with that lunch-counter pie and coffee, because of segregation. Negro students in the South were standing up—no, they were "sitting in"—for their right to be served at the lunch counters in the five-and-dime stores. Their peaceful protests had been met with "mass arrests, tear gas, and expulsion from school." Here, today in Harvard Square, northern students were showing their support for those "American Citizens who are fighting these indignities." The flier went on to say that anyone could contribute to that fight by boycotting Woolworth's, writing to the national headquarters in New York City, and "signing our petition."

"Our," explained the fine print at the bottom of the page, referred to the Emergency Public Integration Committee (EPIC), the group that was coordinating the efforts of various religious, civil rights, labor, and student groups around Greater Boston. The "emergency" in the group's name suggested an urgent need—in this case, the need to show solidarity with the students who were demonstrating to force integration at department store lunch counters. The sit-ins had begun on February 1 at Greensboro, North Carolina, when four Black college freshman boys took seats at a segregated lunch counter and propelled the civil rights movement in a new and dramatic direction. Before that day, there had been some protests, fund drives, and student versions of the adult civil rights groups, for instance, on college campuses, but that first hastily organized sit-in in North Carolina took hold in a way that the historian Taylor Branch would later call a "quickening." Greensboro, he said, "helped define the new decade."

As of February 1, 1960, the Harvard third-year graduate student Michael Walzer had been writing for the politically left *Dissent* magazine for about four years, since his undergraduate days at left-leaning Brandeis, where, in his words, "the '60s started in the '50s." As soon as his editor heard about Greensboro, he dispatched Walzer to cover the story. Walzer met with students on that campus and others, and he also spoke at churches, where almost spontaneously he announced that he brought a message of solidarity from Harvard. So he came back to Cambridge with not only his story but also a promise to fulfill: he would have to mobilize. He hooked up with another ex-Brandeis grad student, Harvey Pressman; the two enlisted the participation of unions and other community groups, and the result was EPIC. Pressman took charge of college campus recruiting and organizing contact persons in the local colleges, including Brandeis, MIT, Boston University, Eastern Nazarene,* and Harvard.

Pressman wasn't going to have an easy time of it. As the new decade opened, the majority of Harvard students were described as supportive of general liberal aims, but "apathetic toward any type of political activity" and "suspicious of all political organizations." One observer commented that "the thing is *not* to be enthusiastic. It looks bad at cocktail parties." A *Crimson* poll in the spring of 1959 concluded: "Safely perched in the 'middle-of-the-road,' many of [Harvard's] 'moderate liberals' hold fast to their

* Misnamed on the flier as "Eastern Nazareth."

comfortable philosophy of 'don't-give-a-damnism.'" But on Friday, February 26, the *Crimson* had announced the picketing scheduled for the next day and editorialized enthusiastically about this "welcome sign of resurging political interest and activity." It was in this climate that picketers John Woodford and Travis Williams had arrived for their freshman year back in September, each with a tendency to give a damn.

As I continued my journey, talking to my former classmates, I found that everyone remembered John Woodford. Looking at his photo in the freshman *Register,* you can almost see why: most of the boys are staring at the camera, some grinning, others looking a little gun-shy, in photos that are just a notch above mug shots or passport photos. In contrast, John is looking off toward some distant thing over his right shoulder, his skin almost glowing and his eyes dreamy. Freddy remembered John like this: "Woodford was a thing apart. He was a different man, he was brilliant, and intellectually, in terms of just brain power, he seemed to be something that I know I wasn't."

I remember John as a lively intellect and a person who suffered neither fools nor authority gladly. He was independent and critical-minded; he also skipped a lot of classes and was ready to

*John Niles Woodford, 1959*

challenge rules that he judged to be petty or arbitrary, including the dress code; he would write later, in a chapter that he contributed to a book about the days of protest, that his attitude at the time was that he "hadn't accepted admission to become a gentleman and I probably had a much different definition of what constituted a gentleman than did the Harvard types who didn't care where their money came from."

Freddy Easter reminded me of another event that made John legendary: the "fence posts incident." Every year before winter sets in and the ground freezes, the Harvard maintenance crews put green wooden fence posts and rope lines on each side of the walking paths that crisscross campus to guide the snowplows. One night John had the impulse to attack the posts, for kicks. Freddy said, "Here is Woodford going through those stakes and cross-body-blocking them . . . one after another. The ground was frozen, and every time he hit one of them it would snap. Soon as he got one, he'd get up and go after the next one. He must have snapped off, I don't know, maybe fifteen or twenty of those things." The prank would one day be memorialized in the Class Poem—one of many things, of course, that went on at Harvard during those years that transcended race, politics, and intellectualism and boiled down to just plain old adolescent, boundary-pushing fun, breaking rules, and, occasionally, breaking things.

John was living in Ann Arbor when we reconnected, and I set out on a road trip across the southern tier of New York counties, through Pennsylvania's little panhandle and all the way across the northern ledge of Ohio along Lake Erie and around the lake's western end into Michigan. At dusk on day two, I pulled into John's driveway alongside the modest arts-and-crafts-style house where he had lived for years with his wife, Eliza, a Cliffie he met way back in our freshman year. We exchanged hugs, laughs, and bullshit: "You haven't changed a bit in fifty years."

John came to Harvard from the small town of Benton Harbor, Michigan, where he was one of the very few Black students at Benton Harbor High who was college-bound. His father was a physician, and an uncle had gone to Harvard. The family had a casual friend who had also gone to Harvard and thought John would like it, so he applied and was accepted. When he got to Cambridge, as he recalled, he wasn't in awe of the place so much as just thrilled to have been "liberated from being in a little town." In an essay about those days some years later, John wrote that "I'd entered a grand new world bustling with plenty more people and ideas than I'd been used to, not to mention the traffic. Right from the beginning, awaiting the arrival of my unidentified roommate in Matthews Hall North in the Yard, I began meeting a range of classmates who, to a man, were remarkable free spirits—friendly, energetic fellows."

Travis Williams, John's freshman roommate in Matthews Hall, a Negro boy from Durham, North Carolina, turned out to be one of those remarkable free spirits. The roommates, John remembered, "started out a bit edgy toward one another, as if the room assignment had deprived us of acquaintance with someone who might present a more novel outlook on life than a fellow Afro-American." But the two quickly found a connection in their intellectualism and their eagerness to get involved in campus political life. Before the Woolworth's picketing, that usually amounted to going to meetings and signing petitions, which they did despite the fact that John's parents had warned against it. While McCarthyism was in decline by 1959, many Americans remained supercautious about possible repercussions in the future. John told me that his parents had told him, "Those communists up there will want you to sign stuff and then later on you won't be able to get a job, so don't sign anything!" But John and Travis were not inclined toward caution; they signed and listened and read and talked, and the two were soon "as close as brothers."

John Woodford wasn't the only one with whom Travis Williams cultivated an early and enduring friendship—he was close with our white classmate Lance Morrow too. The two freshmen met in English: after class one day, Travis simply introduced himself to Lance and continued the conversation they had been engaged in during the class. "He was very, very smart," Lance told me, "and he had an eccentric range of interests. He read a lot of screwy things;

*Travis Jackson Williams, 1959*

for instance, he knew a lot about cabalism and magic. He would follow an interest like a hound dog wherever it took him. I think his reading was sort of hectic, chaotic, and unorganized. And his mind was a little hectic and all over the place too, and yet he had a very good mind and made connections intellectually."

Travis "was very funny," Lance added, "with a sense of the ridiculous, and he was able to disarm people with this." As an example, Lance remembered that English class again. "We were reading Camus's *Myth of Sisyphus.* Travis misspoke and referred to it as the *Myth of Syphilis,* and when he realized what he had said, he broke out in this terrific laugh." Lance paused, looked off, and then turned back to me. There was another side to Travis, Lance continued: Travis was gregarious and easy to know, yet "I'm not sure I knew him that well at all, even though we were best friends for nine years." I would later hear more comments like this from others who knew Travis Williams—that he was gregarious, that he had a sharp sense of humor that rose to the surface easily, and yet that humor almost seemed to come from a darker interior place.

Travis had come to Harvard from Durham, where he attended Hillside High School in the days when the state's high schools were completely segregated. He was exuberant and generous of spirit and made friends quickly with Blacks and whites alike, but there is no doubt that he had a keen and unforgiving hatred for racism and oppression, an anger that might not exclude violence. John Woodford told me that Travis had grown up knowing about Robert F. Williams and *Negroes with Guns.* The book would not be published for two more years, in 1960, but the events that Williams would describe had happened in the late 1950s in Monroe, about 150 miles across the Piedmont from Travis's home in Durham. From the mid-1950s on, Williams led the Monroe NAACP in campaigns to integrate public services; when faced with Klan terrorism, he chose "armed self-reliance" and came to advocate violence in self-defense. John was only guessing that such ideas were part of Travis's worldview, but he did recall that Travis had known some of the young people who had been involved in the first sit-ins down in Greensboro. "That kind of radicalized him," John told me, "and it had an effect on me, because he told me about all this and what they did and how they did it." Travis injured his leg during the winter of freshman year and wound up on crutches for most of the spring—and being incapacitated, John thought, may have simply given him more time to get involved in politics.

Out on that Woolworth's picket line, despite a gray February cold, the mood was bright; Mike Walzer would later say that among the EPIC volunteers, "along with moral idealism went the very real joy of participation and common work." Someone bought a *New York Times* over at Out of Town News and wrestled against a rising wind to read aloud the reports from the South: a bomb threat dispersed the Black protesters in Henderson, North Carolina, but the intrepid students had simply reassembled at a different store; students in Alabama were sitting-in at the snack shop in the Montgomery County courthouse, heedless of threats of expulsion from their school, all-Black Alabama State, and one of those picketers had announced that they would simply enroll at the all-white University of Alabama or Auburn. In Raleigh, North Carolina, seven hundred students turned up for the trials of forty-three of their sit-in brothers and sisters, forcing the authorities to postpone. The news was fortifying and exciting. There on Harvard Square, the excitement mostly took the form of impassioned theoretical debates. As the picketers paced around and around, Mike Walzer was explaining to an undergraduate the difference between hard Trotskyism ("they supported the Soviet Union when they were invading Finland," for instance) and soft Trotskyism (they opposed the invasion). That eager undergraduate was Frank Bardacke, a public school boy from California. Mike Walzer had recruited Harvey Pressman to coordinate EPIC outreach to the colleges, and Harvey, in turn, had recruited Frank to round up Harvard boys for the picket lines. Among his recruits were Travis, John, and a sophomore named Tony Robbins. Tony grew up in New York City, the son of two journalists, and he attended Greenwich Village's Little Red Schoolhouse and Elisabeth Irwin High School, the favorite of left-leaning and progressive parents of the day.

I don't remember hearing anything about that first day of picketing—most kids on campus were pretty oblivious to it, going about their increasingly comfortable routines. The first days of March 1960 were mild, and it seemed like spring semester might live up to its name any day. But on Thursday morning of that week, a heavy gray sky was down around my shoulders, shedding fat snowflakes into my eyes as I loped across the Yard to get a quick breakfast before my morning classes. When I emerged again from the Union, the snowflakes were smaller and denser, and the wind was pushing them half sideways. Boys stooped into the wind, wrangling unruly umbrellas, or sprinted across the Yard with their overcoats hiked up over their heads. Those of us who had come out without galoshes sat through classes with soaked trouser cuffs and wet socks. I had Spanish lecture and Chem lab that morning, and it was good to be finished with classes at noon and to be able to watch the snow pile up from inside Lamont Library.

One of my clearest memories of that first year at Harvard is of sitting there in Lamont. It was the newest, most modern-looking building on campus, right across the street from the Freshman Union in the southeast corner of Harvard Yard. Three levels of reading rooms were honeycombed with books shelved in alcoves, making it easy to browse and even just grab a book, which you couldn't do at huge, research-oriented Widener, where you had to request your materials. No girls were allowed in Lamont—I suppose we undergrads were judged too distractible—but I still loved spending time at one of the small tables on the first floor next to a bank of floor-to-ceiling windows that looked out on the Yard.

I was sitting in that favorite spot when I had what felt like a turning point in my life as a student. I was reading something assigned for class, and without fully realizing it, I'd put down my trusty note-taking pencil. I'd read past the point where I should have been writing something down, something that I could "study" later, commit to memory until the test came up, and then more or less forget about it. I had become engaged in whatever this book was telling me, as if it really meant something to me, as if it made sense in the context of what was going on in the course, and what the author was saying had carried me along. Something is lost when you're focused on taking notes—it was as if I had suddenly captured the meaning that slips away between brain and pencil. Sure, studying involved some hard work, often careful note-taking, and plenty of remembering. But it didn't always have to be mechanical, joyless, and boring. My epiphany was subtle but important to me, and to the way I thought about my academic work. It also made me feel more comfortable at Harvard: the relaxed but serious student immersed in a good book, hard at work, and serenely at home at a handsome library table at Harvard University—that guy was me.

Soon enough I had to face the storm again to go to work. This time I stuffed my pant legs as tightly as I could into the tops of my floppy black rubber boots and hoped for the best. I was still toting the toilet-cleaning canister, but I had become adept enough to avoid the icy trickle-down-the-back, most of the time. I could tough it out. I'd seen other guys doing it. And as always, necessity pushed hard on me: board rates had indeed gone up by fifteen dollars for the spring term and were scheduled to be increased by the same amount in the coming fall and again in the spring. But it wasn't only necessity driving me. I was going to classes and work and even socializing with a composure that sometimes almost felt like cool. That feeling of wanting to get back to "normal" had finally left me, replaced by a new normal: being smart and curious. Very intelligent guys, even "grinds," had actual dates, with actual girls, so brains might help me out after all.

My fall grades were two Bs, a C+, and a C; hardly the As that came so easily at Boys High, but enough to make me and my parents relax and, more important, to give me the feeling I could honestly stay in the game. My Dorm Crew boss told me that next year I could bequeath my canister and rubber gloves to some hapless freshman, so there would soon be an end to that job. I'd learned how to be fast, and if I cut a corner here and there, I could finish early.

By the time I had squirted and mopped my way down from the fourth-floor Straus suites to the last first-floor toilet and ducked out the door, it was obvious that this was a serious snowstorm. Boys slogged their way through a foot or more of snow by dinnertime, and at the Union we brushed and stamped off in the hallway and kept dripping as we slid our trays along the satiny wood of the serving counter. The dining hall women were taking shifts listening to the radio in the kitchen, and now and then one turned away from her tray of Parker House rolls to peer uneasily out the window—*How's it look out there? How are we going to get home?* The radio was using the word "blizzard," but we just loaded up our trays, insensitive to the hazards for the men and women who served us.

The heavy quiet of deep snow settled into the Yard; nobody was going anywhere that night, and probably not the next night either. Back in my room, I gave in to another round of thinking: what about that Humanities paper? It would be my first Big Paper. The course was Hum 3: "Crisis and the Individual in Drama and History." We had read Prometheus, Antigone, *Henry IV, Uncle Vanya.* The professor had said that as far as a topic was concerned, he would leave the door wide open—we could start with any question or idea that the readings had provoked in us, anything we wondered or cared about deeply. As the snow and the silence intensified, I couldn't seem to think of anything that had been provoked in me, nor anything that I cared about deeply, at least nothing suitably high-toned to write a college paper about. I stared at the walls. The walls had nothing to say.

By the time it stopped snowing late Friday night, the nor'easter had blasted everyone from Maine to West Virginia, with eastern Massachusetts seeing about twenty inches of snow and intense winds. A glass door in Lamont Library had blown out, but more glass was broken by enthusiastic snowballers than by the blizzard itself. The EPIC picketers told a *Crimson* reporter that they planned to go out to Woolworth's again on Saturday despite the weather, and early risers that morning were the first to see a fat snowman in the Yard holding a sign that read SUPPORT SOUTHERN STUDENT PROTEST.

As the semester went on, EPIC continued to drum up support and recruit more students for their actions. The small print on the back pages of the *Crimson* listed dozens of meetings ranging from the typical foreign language clubs, including Esperanto, to hobby clubs for enthusiasts of everything from flying to philately; clubs for lovers of jazz, opera, folk music, and string quartets; and political and religious groups across the spectrum of options. In the midst of it all were calls for "All Integrationists" to participate in the picketing, advising students who were interested to call Tony Robbins. A few days later, the Harvard Student Council took a stand on the southern sit-ins: after a "heated discussion" and a close vote (13–10–2) the representatives decided to send a supporting telegram to Diane Nash, the student movement leader at Fiske. Walzer, Bardacke, and Pressman sought and received administration approval for the establishment of the Harvard branch of EPIC, called the Lunch Counter Integration Committee (LCIC), which would not only picket, they announced, but also develop a letter- and postcard-writing campaign and raise funds for legal expenses and scholarships for southern Negro students who had been expelled from their colleges for their sit-in activities.

Meanwhile, Harvard administrators were wary: in Frank Bardacke's opinion, they were "one hundred percent tight-asshole people in those days." Dean McGeorge Bundy called Bardacke to his office to give him a warning: "You should think about your

*Franklin Joseph Bardacke, 1959*

future. I know it's hard when you are a young man, but I think you should know . . . the people who are running that picket line are Trotskyists!" "Well, yes, sir," replied Frank, "but they're soft Trotskyists, do you know the difference?" It's tough to imagine that Bundy was interested in the difference. Tony Robbins, too, faced a dean, who, he remembered, "basically read me the riot act." He was polite but firm, warning that "if any problems come out of this, your continued attendance at Harvard College is on the line." Tony listened respectfully to the admonishments, but he also knew that the dean had been an activist in his day. As Tony stood up to leave the office, he asked one last question: "What would you do?" Without missing a beat, the dean replied, "I'd go ahead and run the protest." This was John Usher Monro, a man I would later learn much more about and the person who had been instrumental in bringing us to Harvard.

The picketing continued on Saturdays through March, mostly without incident, though sometimes townspeople would holler out an objection, and a few high school boys called them "reds" and ripped up a sign. The police were on the whole very patient, but Mike Walzer did have his first view of prison cells when he was brought downtown to do a little "negotiating" with the local captain. Walzer would later tell me that on the picket line there was more conflict with the Trotskyists than with either the locals or the police: "They wanted to come to the lines with their own signs about world revolution, and we wanted to fight on the integration issue." Harvey Pressman, whom Frank Bardacke called a "PR genius," kept the *Crimson* well supplied with encouraging press releases; Pressman would later tell me that some of that genius amounted to creating the "illusion of a groundswell."

LCIC drew up a petition of protest to send to the national headquarters of Woolworth's, and to kick off the signature campaign, someone scored an impressive coup. On March 5, Eleanor Roosevelt spoke at Cambridge's First Congregational Church and, in talking about America's image in the world, she emphasized civil rights. Immediately after her talk, she signed the LCIC petition, a photographer snapped a photo, and the article made front-page news in the *Crimson*. Within a week, Pressman was announcing that around one-fifth of Harvard students had signed the petition and some twelve thousand signatures had been collected at picketing sites in the Boston area.

Student reporters picked up their own leads on the integration story and followed them. One writer, for instance, talked to Woolworth's managers and found that the economic impact on the stores was negligible; although a few were in general sympathy with the demonstrators, they reported, others thought "it stinks." Another reporter wrote a two-article series about the picketing, the second of which explored why coverage of the events was so sparse in the Boston newspapers—which was rather curious, since the *Globe* did publish three pieces about the demonstrations that spring. Pressman also saw to it that the story went further than Boston and came to the attention of the Negro press in New York.

The topic of integration swirled around in the Harvard intellectual community too. In early March, the psychology professors Gordon Allport and Robert Kellman declared in a talk that "picketing aids Negroes" and that their "moral influence" would speed integration. The history professor Oscar Handlin told a crowd at the Union Coffee House that civil rights would be a big issue in the 1960 presidential campaign, and he opined that pressure from

Negro voters, international opinion from newly independent African nations, and "basic economics" would lead to "a totally new situation in the South and the country as a whole in the next five or ten years." In fact, he would go on, equality in education and employment were due "very soon." However, another talk, this one by William Y. Elliott, a professor of history and political science and the author of "three feet of books," who had then been teaching at Harvard for almost forty years, sparked another round of controversy. The *Crimson* carried a summary of a presentation he had made in Roanoke, Virginia, to the Southern Humanities Conference, the theme of which was "What Lies Ahead for the South?" Elliott, born and raised in Murfreesboro, Tennessee, had recommended that, with regard to integration, "to make haste slowly is the voice of wisdom in the Negro's quest for equality."

Within a few days, the *Crimson* ran a long letter in reaction to Elliott, written by Spencer Jourdain '61, a handsome preppy Black student whom I would come to know in my sophomore year. Spencer countered that "most Negroes want speedy action," and that the gradualists' rhetoric was part of the ongoing "attempt to please and placate the two opposing groups in the traditional way which has long held out long-distance hopes, but has for so long delayed vigorous legislation and social action . . . Negroes refuse to continue unquestioningly to bear the burden of inferior political, economic, and social status merely because persons in authority do not wish to upset the temper of some unjust whites."

Spencer was one of a rare breed: a second-generation Negro Harvard man. His father, Edwin Bush Jourdain Jr., graduated from Harvard and went on to the graduate business school in 1921. He had spearheaded a campaign that led to the overturning of the ban on Negroes in the dormitories imposed by then-university president A. Lawrence Lowell.

Late that spring, EPIC would have one last big event. The occasion would be the sixth anniversary of the *Brown v. Board of Education* decision, and planning was under way for rallies in various cities across the country. In Atlanta, more than 2,000 would hear Martin Luther King speak before they were turned away from the capitol by police; about 100 University of Michigan students would march through Ann Arbor with a motorcycle escort, and the mayor would declare the day "Freedom Day"; Madison's march included 350 protesters from the University of Wisconsin and local high schools. New York City's rally was principally organized by labor groups, and a crowd of 15,000 Blacks and union supporters would hear speeches by Sidney Poitier and Harry Belafonte.

Planning for Boston's rally would include a march up Columbus Avenue to Boston Common, where a crowd of 3,000 to 5,000 was expected to show up to hear the Reverend Wyatt Walker, a leader of the Southern Christian Leadership Conference (SCLC) as well as the Congress of Racial Equality (CORE). On campus, a notice went out seeking LCIC "coordinators in every dorm and house" and asking volunteers to call Anthony Robbins. At an early meeting of EPIC, after somebody came up with the brilliant idea of capitalizing on Boston's fame as the "Birthplace of Liberty" and its prominence in the American Revolution, a plan gradually emerged: a group of students dressed as minutemen would fire "The Second Shot for Freedom" from the Old North Bridge in Concord. And the group of minutemen would be integrated. The shot, an EPIC representative said, "will be heard not only around the world, but even in the American South." Pressman, with his sharp ear for publicity, knew that the Harvard name would make that all the more likely, and he turned out to be right.

Nobody can quite remember how it all came together, but it did: on May 17, 1960, four young men in sport coats and ties, two of them Black and two white, three of them in borrowed tricorne hats that transformed them symbolically into "minutemen," stood on the Old North Bridge in Concord, the gracefully arched wooden bridge that was the iconic site of the first shots fired in the American Revolution. As a small crowd looked on, one of the boys, Travis Williams, stood uneasily on his crutches (which some people thought he was using for show); Frank Bardacke carried a replica rifle and introduced the performance with a short speech about nonviolent action; Tony Robbins waved a big American flag, and John Woodford read Ralph Waldo Emerson's poem "Concord Hymn." After the four staged a firing of the freedom shot, they then solemnly left the bridge, John carrying a wreath that he would lay at the monument to the minutemen. The famed photographer Alfred Eisenstaedt knelt at the far end of the bridge and snapped a photo.

At the same time, a crowd of some 1,500, largely comprising students from the area colleges, began marching down Columbus Avenue toward Boston Common, without incident and frequently to the cheers of onlookers. They assembled around the white Grecian columns of the Parkman Bandstand, dramatically lit from within as night fell, to hear Reverend Walker declare that, "if the road to freedom leads through the jailhouses of the South, then to the jailhouses we shall go."

A few weeks later, *Life* magazine published, above the caption "Integrated Minutemen on School Decision Anniversary," Eisenstaedt's photo of Travis Williams, Frank Bardacke, Tony Robbins, and John Woodford.

I wasn't there for any of it. I can't claim ignorance, because I

Life, *May 30, 1960*
TED POLUMBAUM / NEWSEUM COLLECTION

was a dedicated *Crimson* reader. Maybe I just had my head in the sand or in a book or in the clouds?

And what about my Black classmates? Most of us sat it out, and nobody seems sure why. Almost to a man, we have woven race and Black activism into our lives, and so we look back at our freshman year at Harvard and can only conjecture about why, with all that was going on, we stayed on the sidelines. Ezra Griffith, having grown up in Barbados, told me that he "was not engaged in the same kind of racialized thinking that people who had grown up in this country were distinctly attuned to," and he also reminded me that we were very young, adrift and uncertain in a new world. Freddy described us as "naive," but for his own part, he maintained, he was just plain busy with his studies and usually gave over his off-hours—and sometimes, in freshman and sophomore years in particular, his "should-be on" hours—to fun, like playing bridge and going to hockey games. He also explained his general lack of activism in his undergraduate days in true Freddy style: "Okay, for myself, if I had blown my chance at graduating from Harvard because I was dancing with a police dog in Birmingham, I would have beat myself half to death. I felt like, 'There will be sit-ins whether I show up or not. There will be freedom rides whether I'm on the bus or not. But I'm the only one who can be here trying to do this the best I can.' I was doing it for my mother. And it was important to me, and if you look at my career, I have been able to help more young people having gone through that than I think I would have helped going to a freedom ride."

Maybe we already knew what Deans Bundy and Monro had warned our white classmates about—that our futures, both at college and in the big world, could be endangered by getting into the fray. Maybe we had too much at stake: our presence at Harvard was precarious, and we were not about to make any waves or divert our attention from the serious task at hand. That was certainly my own situation—my head was not really in the sand, but in the books. George Jones, too, said that he didn't even date freshman year, so jealously did he guard his studying time and maintain his focus. George's home community and school back in Muskogee would countenance nothing less than success, having invested in him as they had. George was well aware of that pressure. Spencer Jourdain would tell a reporter many years later that "we were there to get an education and then to go out and be successful people in our chosen fields, not start a cohesive social movement." We had gotten to Harvard precisely by staying away from distractions, by sticking to the books and considering ourselves intellectuals. To a large degree, that's how we had made our names and scored our successes, and how we had gotten into Harvard. Not knowing Negro history, we lacked a sense of an unfolding story that applied to the "we," and so we focused on the "me."

In addition, some of the ideas that the white integrationists came up with were at best misguided, at worst insulting. Frank Bardacke had the idea, for instance, to try to integrate some all-white barber shops and asked his roommate Hobie to volunteer to get an "integrated haircut." Years later, we had a good laugh over the story, since I couldn't quite imagine having a white barber cut my Negro hair (back when I had hair), but Frank was still shocked at his own naïveté. He also saw a certain presumptuousness in the idea: "It was like I was trying to get Hobie to do something he didn't want to do, in the name of his own interests, when it was really my interest. I felt I was using him, I felt embarrassed, and I didn't blame him at all."

There was always a sense that the white activists were doing something *for* us and subconsciously, or semiconsciously, assumed that we couldn't do it for ourselves. George sometimes felt a little like Hobie when he talked to white students at Harvard. "Many of the conversations," he said, "as you might imagine, were condescending: 'What do we need to do to make you and your people better? What do we need to do to lift you people up?' I just stopped answering and steered the conversation in another direction. If someone asked me that question, I would say something like, 'What do you mean by "you people"?' And usually I could adopt some sort of stance that made them understand that I didn't want to talk about that."

To many northern Americans of the day, particularly those who viewed the daily indignities of racism from a distance, it looked like the race problem was on the way to solution. Through nonviolent action like sit-downs and letter-writing campaigns, the South would step forward into a new era of integration, they believed, and Negroes, with the help, support, guidance, and brotherhood of the white man, would take their place in the white American world. Maybe I, like so many others, also believed the race was almost run.

I know that, at Harvard, I didn't have the consciousness that Travis and John seemed to have. My family had played by the rules and kept their heads down and their minds on work and family. They had come too far from racist South Carolina to risk sticking out in a crowd or doing anything stupid like carrying a sign around town. I was just a young, hardworking, shy kid from that family who still ate chitlins.

# 4 *Bright Shadows*

*Warm weather finally arrived, the semester was zipping along, and we had* papers to write, pages to read, exams to worry about. Jack Butler's roommate spent many evenings that spring of 1960 running from room to room all over Harvard Yard interviewing people for a term paper that would earn him a big fat A from one of the best-known professors on campus: David Riesman.

Riesman had become famous for his book *The Lonely Crowd: A Study of the Changing American Character,* an academic tome that became a surprise bestseller and landed the author on the cover of *Time* magazine in 1954. This book described midcentury middle-class life and confirmed the discomfort felt by some Americans with the conformism they had started seeing everywhere. As an educator, Riesman was concerned that narrow and strict disciplinary lines of research simply didn't make for particularly meaningful teaching and learning. In response, he and five other instructors from various academic fields led a freshman seminar with forty-eight students divided into six groups purposely mixed among majors. The small sections met weekly with their leaders, and all of the sections came together at weekly dinners for what Riesman called "cross-fertilization." Once a month a famous guest would come in and tell his life story to the group: these included Dizzy Gillespie, the psychologists Arthur Maslow and Erik Erikson, and Edwin H. Land, an inventor and the founder of the Polaroid Corporation (and, not coincidentally, the disaffected Harvard dropout who secretly funded the seminars).

Riesman's seminar required a term paper, and students could pursue nearly anything they wanted to, ideally exploring their chosen topic from a variety of disciplinary approaches. Ron Blau had at first been stumped about what topic he'd tackle.

*Ronald S. Blau, 1959*

He and his roommate, Jack Butler, had exhausted innumerable subjects in their long and rambling conversations. Now Ron wondered whether Jack had any ideas for his paper. "Well," Jack suggested, "why don't you write about us? I mean, us, the Negroes in our class." Ron squinted at him—Jack couldn't be serious. Jack pressed on. Spreading his arms in a dramatic flourish, he ad-libbed a title: "The Social Life of the Harvard Negro." Jack went on to suggest that Ron do interviews during the week with the eighteen Negro men in their class, and then go to parties and social events with us on the weekends.

Ron was intrigued at this prospect, and his rising interest is palpable in a paragraph of the paper he would eventually write: "In September, long before classes had begun, these young men had penetrated into Boston Negro activities." "Consequently," Ron continued, "they went to dances and parties as a group, and during the week they traded lively tales of weekend experiences with each other often at the dinner table." At first, though, Ron still wasn't exactly on board, and he countered with "Why the Negro Freshman Comes to Harvard." Jack rolled his eyes and said that our reasons were no different from anyone else's; he urged Ron to reconsider the "social life" topic. But Ron backed away, saying that he felt a "sense of impropriety" about it. In the end, Ron decided to conduct preliminary interviews with a few of us and see what emerged. Just as well, because he would have been disappointed to learn just how much the "lively tales" of our social lives that he heard at the Black Table were enhanced by boasting, exaggeration, and wishful thinking.

Ron still had that freshman paper in 2009 when I met with him at his home near Cambridge, and he gave me a copy. I worked up a full head of indignation on the drive home. The nerve of it, I thought, to see us as specimens, as if we were some newly discovered exotic creatures. "Bright Shadows in the Yard" he called us . . . shadows of what? And the word "shadows" itself was way too close to the racial slur "shade."

My pique subsided when I turned from the title page to the first page, typed out in the old carbon-paper blur. There we all were, pseudonymously: Al, Bill, Booker, Donald, Doug, Ed, Harry, Herb, Joe, Pete, Ralph, Roger, Roy, Sam, Terry, Tom, and Walter. Each name was followed by Ron's brief description, and all through the paper, there were quotes and commentaries from us; Ron's paper was a gold mine of information about all of us, including things we said at the time, before our memories were clouded by the passage of fifty years. It was easy to develop a key to the pseudonyms. I was "Ralph," of the "lower middle class group" (not "lower class," as Ron takes care to note), whose father was a subway motorman and who, despite growing up in New York City, "did not learn much about city life outside his own home and high school."

Ron described "Al" as coming "from a small town in which few Negroes live. His unconcern for racial issues has made him apathetic toward the Lunch Counter Integration Committee, even though one of his roommates, who is not Negro, is a leader in this movement." Hobie had to be "Al" (and Frank Bardacke the not-Negro roommate). "Terry," I found on another page, was "truly a New Yorker, although he spent two years at a prep school in Connecticut. In the city, he was always more aware of what was going on around him than Ralph was." "Terry," then, was Freddy, and fair enough, he was indeed "more aware" than I was. Another pseudonym that was easy to identify was "Walter," since Ron says he "arrived in the United States from Cuba nine years ago." "Walter" was Larry Galindo, whom I would interview years later in Atlanta, on the same trip when I'd meet my Muskogee classmate George Jones at Emory University.

*Lazaro R.M.A. Galindo, 1959*

When I picture Larry from our college years, I see him in an immaculate three-piece suit or the perfect tweedy Ivy League look, as if he wanted to err on the side of formality for every occasion. Most of us—well, I at least—would often just fling on whatever looked the least wrinkled and show up as is. But Larry was fastidious and always well turned out. Fifty years later, in his luxury high-rise Atlanta apartment, both in our comfortable retirement duds, we fumbled into bear hugs and sheepishly talked about how we'd "put on a few pounds." Larry still had a slightly lazy right eye that could be a distraction in conversation, but only at first.

Over a fine dinner prepared by his wife, Lena, Larry told me about his childhood as a mulatto in hyper-color-conscious Cuba.

His father was an educator with political and social connections to the Batista government, but he believed that the only hope for his dark-skinned kids was for them to get an American education and then come back to Cuba. So, in 1951, when Larry was eleven years old, he was dispatched with his mother to the United States for school, and they settled in New York City's crime- and drug-infested Spanish Harlem. Like me, Larry was sheltered, went to a high school outside of his neighborhood, and was able to steer clear of the drugs, gangs, and crime that surrounded him. He tested into Cardinal Hayes High School, a Roman Catholic school in the Bronx, and that prepared him for Harvard.

The first serious challenge Larry faced at Harvard was not about race or academics, but about swimming. Starting in the 1920s, every freshman had to pass a swim test, likely a holdover requirement from the days when a real Harvard man was expected to be able to do everything from parse Greek to survive in the wild. Ironically, even though Larry was from an island nation, he couldn't swim and was afraid of the water. He took lesson after lesson, and we all gave him advice and encouragement. Larry and I amused Lena by describing some of our dorm room bull sessions in which we'd tried to help, going so far as to writhe on the floor demonstrating one stroke after another. Something worked, because after numerous attempts, he finally passed the test.

During his freshman year at Harvard, Larry said, he "really saw for the first time how race played itself out in the United States." He felt that his fundamental being was challenged: Who was he? What was his identity? Some white students and professors and even some Negroes considered him to be Negro, but others saw him as Latino. He had mostly been around Hispanics before Harvard, but he wanted to be considered a Negro there, telling Ron that he "would like to connect myself with their problems."

Larry wasn't the only one who told Ron he was not sure about being defined as an "American Negro." "Bill" had refused to participate at first on those grounds, but later agreed after Jack interceded. Ron noted that "Bill" was West Indian, so that was Ezra. I knew from our later acquaintance that he would always feel that he was at least as Barbadian as he was American—and back in 1960, he'd only been in the United States for a few years. Ron remarked in his paper that Ezra had been the only respondent to give "scornful" replies, although the only such reply Ron quoted was: "I pity the American whites, who are almost without exception anti-Negro." Ron also wrote that Ezra "does not make friends so easily" and remarked on his "bitterness." I believe that the "bitterness" and "scorn" that Ron perceived were probably just Ezra's exasperation at the assumption that his West Indian identity was irrelevant.

Some guys didn't consider themselves American Negroes, and others couldn't easily be identified as such, so how did Ron find us all? Jack was probably acquainted with all of us by the end of our first semester. And he presumably used skin color and physical features as his measure, as I had done when I leafed through the freshman *Register*, and made the same mistake I did—missing Gerry Secundy. None of us knew Gerry was Black. These were the days before "I identify as . . ." but Gerry had been saying that all his life, using other words.

*Gerald David Secundy, 1959*

"Hi. I'm Gerry Secundy, I'm a Negro." That's how he introduced himself throughout college. Gerry could pass for white if he wanted to, but "never in my life have I passed and never would I." By the time he got to Harvard in 1959, he'd seen plenty, having been "discriminated against on both sides my entire life." "Are you really Black?" Blacks would ask, and whites would forget that he'd told them he was Black. "So I heard every damn joke about the niggers this and that." He'd also endured the "kike jokes" told by those who were oblivious to the white part of his heritage being Jewish.

I drove across the country to meet with Gerry in his Pasadena, California, home. Clearly he had done well financially. His neighborhood was immaculate and serene, and all the houses were large and set well back from the street behind grand lawns, some with formal gardens and statuary, many boxed in by perfectly trimmed hedges, with guesthouses and sparkling swimming pools tucked into lush and shady backyards. As we were shaking hands and making the usual small talk, I apologized again for forgetting to include him as one of the Negroes in our class. But to be honest, even at that moment, my "Black-dar" didn't kick in—it was tough to stay convinced that he was of the brotherhood. It turned out that Gerry's mom was Black and his father was Jewish. He guided me through the older pictures in an array of family photos lining the staircase wall, and I could see that his mom was identifiably Black. I decided my "Black-dar" might need a tune-up.

When we sat down for the interview, I asked him if he still introduced himself as "Gerry the Negro." "I don't do that anymore," he said. "I stopped that probably after law school. I calmed down. I was not as angry, aggressive." He still, however, considered himself Negro—a word he said he preferred to Black because "it's just difficult for me to look at my skin and relate to that." Gerry reminded me that today it is becoming harder and harder, not only for people like him but for everyone, to define themselves by simply checking "White" or "Black" on a form.

When we got back to talking about Harvard, the subject of Dorm Crew came up—Gerry had cleaned toilets too! But he'd dealt with it much better than I had. He laughed and said that his experiences with discrimination had prepared him for the job: "It was a rotten job, but I had a pretty thick shell. It did not bother me when people made some disparaging remarks about it. I said, 'Hey, I'm making $1.39 an hour.'" Gerry became a student manager on the Dorm Crew the next year and stayed with them all four years, so like me, he actually cleaned toilets only that first year.

Gerry remembered seeing the Black Table for the first time. "I walked in and I'm looking around. There's a table with all the Negroes sitting at the table. I remember saying, 'What the hell are you guys doing? Why the hell are you all sitting at the same damn table?' I said, 'My mom didn't spend all this money to send me here to be segregated. This is ridiculous.' So I went and sat at another table with people I didn't know." I suspect that his choice was one reason why we all forgot about Gerry, who subsequently became sort of neither here nor there—a "Bright Shadow" but also not.

Having temporarily put aside how rankled I'd been by "Bright Shadows in the Yard," I found myself now silently thanking Ron Blau for not throwing out his paper years ago. I discovered that he had a keen perceptiveness, a remarkable ability to size up a guy. For instance, this character sketch: "Roy is the most polished, educated, and self-assured of the group, and the most self-conscious. Aware of his own position in any group, he is willing to work hard for all of the innumerable activities in which he takes part. According to his own estimate, made by leafing through the Register one evening, he knows over three hundred members of the Class of '63 well." Ron nailed him; I needed to know little else to write "Wesley Williams" on my decoding key next to the pseudonym "Roy."

As I deduced who was who, I noticed that "Harry" had given Ron some puzzling answers. For instance, he said that "a life of striving is just not worth the effort," that he would like to "spend his life as a 'parasite,' living from subsidy," and that his ambition was to "just hang around." Who was this "Harry," giving that kind of answer? Ron wrote that he judged those answers to be "insincere," and I finally remembered John Woodford telling me that he had purposely tried to confound Ron by giving some facetious answers, and that he and Travis had rolled their eyes and joked about the "study" in private. Sure enough, in another part of the paper I learned that "Harry's" father was a doctor. John later admitted that he was trying to have a little fun with Ron and goad him into coming to some crazy conclusions. But Ron and John had a good time nonetheless: "One night I interviewed Harry, who I had never met before, for about a half hour, ending shortly after midnight. Then we slowly drifted away from the topic of Negroes." (*Good idea,* I thought.) "We talked on and on until about four-thirty," Ron continued, "when we both decided that we had work to do. So, I used Harry's machine to type up the report on him, while he read a few pages in a novel. Strange circumstances to make a new friend!"

By a process of elimination, I determined that "Tom" was Travis Williams. Quoting "Tom" repeatedly in the paper, Ron characterized him as "the most courageous rebel" and reported "Tom's" statement that he had "since childhood valued his freedom above all other possessions." "But this year," Ron continued, "after finally breaking away from the south, he spent most of the time with his leg in a cast, once more deprived of freedom." I knew about the leg, but I didn't think Travis meant that kind of freedom as his valued possession. "Tom," Ron said, "is apt to become bitter when talking about any aspect of human relations, because he realizes that the world could be a much better place to live in than it is today, and he says that he loves humanity but hates most individuals." Given others' comments about Travis, I would have thought just the opposite—that he hated humanity but loved most individuals. Of course, these comments from "Tom" are taken out of context, both by Ron and now by me, but they do point to an extraordinary and complex young man.

The boy Ron Blau called "Roger" was the elusive Bobby Gibbs. Someone had told me that he was living in California, but for a few years I couldn't get any closer than that, despite trying to convince a Dr. Robert Gibbs, DDS, that he was "our" Bobby Gibbs. I was thinking about hiring one of those detectives who look for missing persons when I got a call from John Woodford. He'd found "our" Bobby.

*Robert Edgar Gibbs, 1959*

Bobby's freshman photo shows a light-skinned boy with a faint mustache and strong arched brows, looking very young. I remembered him as short, lean, and handsome, with a kind of glide in his walk. I called him at his home in Victorville, California, and he launched into his life story. He was from Atlanta, where he'd gone to all-Black Booker T. Washington High School, which counts among its notable alumni Martin Luther King Jr. Bobby remembered the school as rigorous: "By the time you were a senior, you had read all of Shakespeare. If you wanted to graduate you had to take two years of Latin and mathematics all the way up to analytical geometry." Now and then in our phone conversation, Bobby seemed to pause, as if he were very tired. I had many more questions, but they would have to wait. I told him that we would come to Victorville after meeting with Gerry in Pasadena.

When we got to Victorville, Bobby asked that we meet at the home of a friend of his, where I taped a short interview about his life after high school. Again, Bobby seemed not in the best of health, and I had a gut feeling there was something he wanted to say but couldn't. He was thrilled to be back in touch, though, and so I promised to come back.

It would be several years before I made good on that promise, but eventually I drove across the country again. I hit Victorville in late June—not the best time to visit the Mojave Desert, especially during a record-breaking heat wave. The previous night the town of Needles, California, just over the border from the southernmost tip of Nevada, had come within one degree of a record when the temperature hit 125 degrees. Two and a half hours west lay Victorville, looking like it had been lobbed onto the desert from on high, as if it didn't really want to be there. Bobby lived outside of town in a flat, gridded, 1970s-era subdivision of story-and-a-half, desert-pastel-colored ranch houses that had seen better days. The little vegetation that had been coaxed to survive around the homes was brown or gray. I stepped out of the car and said that it felt like 110. I was wrong: it was only 109 degrees. I'd called Bobby earlier that day, and he had said something about their electricity being out, what with all the drain from the air conditioning; to me that sounded not just unpleasant but life-threatening. Bobby had said that maybe we should reschedule, and I countered with a suggestion that I take him out somewhere to talk and cool off. He reluctantly agreed.

Dogs yapped wildly when I knocked on the door, and faint voices inside seemed to be trying to quiet them, unsuccessfully. At least I knew someone was there, but it was a long time before Bobby's sister opened the door. We introduced ourselves, and peeking inside, I saw that the room was dark and cluttered. The dogs kept at it. When Bobby finally ambled to the door, he was dragging two oxygen tanks. He had told me on the phone that he had chronic obstructive pulmonary disease (COPD), which I found out later is an umbrella term for a variety of unfixable conditions that restrict breathing. He had to carry an oxygen tank with him, and he got tired very easily. He looked awful, and I was ill at ease until he started telling me about his most recent treatment for COPD—large doses of Viagra. It was helping his breathing, he said, but it just "replaced one problem with another, if you know what I mean!"

Bobby again suggested that we reschedule, for some time the next week, when the electricity and air conditioning would be fixed and he could cook some of his famous fried chicken. I pressed him to go to a café and do the interview, but it was becoming clear that he didn't want me in his house and wasn't up to going out. When we talked by phone a few days later, Bobby sounded a little better, and he suggested that I talk to another of our classmates, Carter Wilson, who was his roommate in Winthrop House. Bobby and Carter had stayed friends through the years, and Bobby had discovered that we had a common interest in Chiapas, the southernmost state in Mexico, on the border with Guatemala. Jeanne and I had been spending a month or three there every year for some time, and Carter had done anthropological work in Chiapas in the 1960s, written two novels set there, and visited regularly in the decades since.

One email led to another, and it turned out that Carter would be in Chiapas at the same time we were, and in the same city—San Cristóbal de las Casas, the beautiful colonial city in the mountains. We made a dinner date. Carter had used "we" and "us" in his emails, and I imagined sitting with Carter and his wife, hearing stories about the city and the people from far before I even knew the place existed. Strolling down the cobbled streets of San Cristóbal, I passed a pair of gringos about my age—outsiders stand out there, because the vast majority of tourists nowadays are from the growing Mexican middle class. I claimed a table at Cocoliche, a small restaurant that made a great Thai curry. Minutes later, the two men I'd seen in the street came in the door—"Hi, I'm Carter. This is my husband, Thomas."

We went on to have a lively chat about Chiapas, Harvard, Bobby, dogs, and politics. At one point when Carter was talking about Bobby, he said something about how "he fell in love with this man." Well, Bobby was outed, and the problem was now, where would I go with this? I'd had the sense that Bobby was holding back with me, and I meant to respect his privacy.

I called Bobby from Mexico a few days later, and he was lively, talkative, and pleased to know that he'd hooked us up with Carter and Thomas. I eased into the gay question by saying that "the issue" of homosexuality might come up in my book, and how did he feel about that? "I have to be fine with it," he said, "because it ends up I'm gay." He sounded perfectly happy to have been asked, maybe almost relieved to have had it come out that way.

We didn't have long to talk that day, but I couldn't resist asking what it was like to be gay at Harvard fifty years ago. Carter had recommended that I read *Sons of Harvard*, a book that came out in 1977 about gays at Harvard in the class of 1967. I'd read some of it, enough to know that closet doors had been shut very tight at that time. Bobby's first few comments were concordant. He said that being gay at Harvard was "harder than I can even begin to describe to you. I could tell you ten thousand stories that would curl your hair. Primarily, I was afraid to let any of my Black brothers know that I was gay." Bobby said that he had one gay friend in high school, and that no one else, including his family, knew. "It wasn't easy," he said, "but having been born in the South, you could not have that hanging over your head or you were ruined socially, and academically, and every fucking thing else. So it was totally undercover. Completely."

As I read more about homosexuality at Harvard, I wound up back at A. Lawrence Lowell, president of Harvard from 1909 to 1933. During the early 1920s, President Lowell presided over what one writer called a "savage purge of campus homosexuals" that involved a secret court and closed-door interrogations. Harvard not only expelled several students and fired a professor but also had the gall to banish them from Cambridge. Reputations were ruined, families were torn apart, and a dentistry student three weeks from his graduation took his own life. Before the purge, and apparently during our day and beyond, Harvard's position was "Be what you will, but keep it private." I went on to read in another book that in my own Eliot House in the late 1940s, one gay man recalled three incidents of expulsion for getting "caught," one of which ended in yet another suicide. I had been completely blind to any kind of gay life that may have existed in Eliot or anywhere else on campus and had no idea about Bobby Gibbs.

I had just one more pseudonym left and one more guy to pair it with; "Joe" could only be Lowell Johnston. But one sentence of Ron's description gave me pause: "Joe is proud of the fact that he has not lost many fights since his height shot up eight inches a few years ago." Yes, Lowell was tall—but fighting? I just couldn't picture it.

*Lowell Douglass Johnston, 1959*

Lowell grew up among the elite Negroes of Washington, DC, but had been a New Yorker almost since leaving Harvard. He was now retired and living in a beautiful old restored farmhouse in rural Columbia County, New York. I found him outdoors with his German shepherd, filling a bird feeder with sunflower seeds. He was, as he had been as a youth, tall, slim, light-skinned, handsome, and dignified. Not a person who would be getting into fights—not physical fights anyway. That day he told me his life story and about his journey to Harvard.

Interviewing—for both the questioner and the subject—can be more tiring than one might imagine, and after an hour or so, we needed a break. I'd noticed when I came into the house that the wall going up the stairs held an intriguing bunch of photos, many of them from decades past. I asked Lowell to walk me through and comment on them, and he gladly did so. There was a picture of his father in uniform—he'd fought in World War I—and of his mother around the same time. In a photo of the Virginia State College band, Lowell's grandfather was playing cornet in the back row, and another from Virginia State showed Lowell's namesake.

Then Lowell showed me a picture of his grandparents and his father as a young boy. Still looking at that photo of his father as a boy, Lowell went silent and then said quietly, "He died." He paused again, then repeated. "He died. I never told anybody, but he killed himself. He was fifty-nine, and I was fourteen. It was 1955, and I was in my second year at Kent School."

I stumbled for words—Lowell's life had seemed to me almost charmed—but I gathered my journalist's wits about me and asked about the circumstances. "It must have been depression. He had been treasurer at Howard University, and in 1948 the Supreme Court decided the *Shelly v. Kraemer* case." Then as now, Washington, DC, had suffered deep racial divisions and tensions, and many Blacks were restricted to the least desirable homes and properties by means of restrictive deed covenants. When those covenants were struck down in *Shelly v. Kraemer*, many believed that the real estate market would open up for Blacks, so Lowell's father left his position at the university and opened his own real estate office. It did not do well. Lowell described his father as a "traditional male who expected to support his family. He had been opposed to my mother becoming a public school teacher because he thought he should take care of her, but she ended up supporting us at times. He eventually went into a deep depression." Lowell didn't know a lot more: "The family never talked about it after he died. He didn't succeed, the world didn't change, and on a Sunday afternoon, August 21, 1955, he went out and shot himself with a gun he had gotten in the First World War." Two weeks later, the influential Black newspaper the *New York Age Defender* reported that "the former Howard Treasurer was found fatally shot in his car near the school by a passing motorist. A .45 Caliber pistol was found in the grass near the car and two notes left on the car seat indicating he was despondent over financial matters."

Understandably, his father's suicide, and the part that race played in it, affected Lowell deeply. At the time, when he was so young and off alone at boarding school, he was "really kind of preoccupied, obsessed with the loss of my dad and what he must have gone through to do something like that." And still today, he said, "it's constant, it's something I spend some time each day thinking about, and it bears on my whole sense of race. It was a motivator for me to go out and challenge segregation and try to make the world better."

Reading Ron's paper brought back so many memories, including a hazy one of having been interviewed. But I didn't remember any specific questions Ron had asked, and when I came to this one, I got riled up all over again: "If you were to be reborn tomorrow, either as a white or as a Negro, which would you choose?" I was relieved and proud that we had all chosen "Negro," although one of us added that the question was "psychological nonsense," and Hobie Armstrong hedged, saying, "I'd like to try being white for a year and then decide." That was Hobie, always cautious and thoughtful about his life decisions and more practical than philosophical.

"Terry," aka Freddy, had answered the reborn question, "Being white would be a lot less trouble, but being Negro would be *nice*." (Ron underlined the word "nice" in his paper.) That was so Freddy, and I smiled as I pictured him saying, "Being a Negro would be *niiiiiice,*" drawing out the word to pack in a lot of meaning, a lot of cool, and a little swagger. Ron rightly identified that as pride—one of the reasons we would stay Negro. He then went on to speculate about what he called "the reward of struggle," quoting Larry's response: he would "stick to Negro," he said, because "sometimes I just love the challenge." Ezra, predictably, said, "I'd become a West Indian Negro again!" Lowell Johnston said, "I regret nothing."

Riesman's comments on Ron's paper were there too. He thought the "reborn" question was "ingenious," and he challenged Ron's interpretation that some of us might have been proud to be Negro. Riesman purported that we were in denial, lying to ourselves, because "to admit even to oneself a desire to be white would be a kind of betrayal, as well as giving one a sense of loss and futility."

I sat there shaking my head and read on. Riesman asked Ron how he managed to "overcome the self-consciousness of Negroes in being spoken to because they were Negroes"; he interpreted Travis's words about working for the civil rights movement, not as reflecting honest commitment but as belying "a good deal of repressed hostility . . . beautifully rationalized as a desire to help the race"; he found the "closeness of these Negro families . . . so atypical for the general run of Negro families"; he expressed surprise at "how far ahead we look[ed]" and how "un-neurotic" we were; and he wondered whether "the Negroes, though they do well academically, are . . . really intellectual." Riesman speculated that Jack was "testing [Ron's] tolerance" because "such testing is exceedingly common in the insecure position of the Negro." Finally, he suggested that he understood prejudice better than we did when he said that "the belief of some of the freshmen that white Americans are really basically prejudiced is a kind of way of saving themselves from disappointment."

I'm not by nature an angry man. I had to keep in mind that this "study" was instigated by my best friend at Harvard, Jack Butler, a smart and race-conscious guy. And apparently we had all cooperated with it and were not offended by it, or at least not offended enough to refuse to participate. I don't recall feeling one way or the other about answering Ron's questions and all of us had welcomed Ron to our rooms and spent our precious time answering the questions. And hey, we liked Ron—he was one of the integrators of the Black Table—and we probably empathized with him, because we all had papers and projects to do. But I was outraged by Riesman's degrading view of us. Wasn't he one of the infamous lefties of academia? It is not my habit to use the word "racist" capriciously, but this man seemed like one to me.

Indignation, like misery, loves company. My classmate John Woodford had a pretty clear memory of the Blau study, as well as an incisive mind about such things. Once I'd calmed down enough to press the right phone number, I called him. Without exactly forgiving Riesman, he broadened my thinking, saying that I needed to look more closely, not only at the paper and Riesman's response but also at the assumptions and theories of the day—there, he said, I would "see these extremely racist and racialist assumptions about what Black people were about, what their experiences might make them do." John agreed with me that Riesman was, for the time, a very progressive thinker. But, John said, "you can just see the assumptions behind these theories. They lock people into their categories of judging and assessing people, and it's like a mental impairment if they don't shake loose."

To get a better picture of that "mental impairment," I consulted Ron's sources. Predictably, he cites Gunnar Myrdal's *An American Dilemma,* the monumental study of Blacks in the United States. Begun in 1938 and published in 1944, it is often named as among the most important sociological books of the century. As influential and famous as Myrdal's book has become, I found out that reading it is a ponderous project. Like the Bible, it's a big book that everyone knows something about but few have read cover to cover. Both the Bible and *An American Dilemma* also have created an orthodoxy so famous that no one has to have read the original to subscribe to the creed. The Myrdal orthodoxy is that the United States is in a moral "dilemma" because of the contradiction between its belief in equality and its systematic oppression of the Negro, and because of the Negro world of woe produced by its legacy of slavery and ongoing oppression. Who could argue with that?

Well, Ralph Ellison could, and he did so brilliantly. Ellison was relieved to find that Myrdal rejected genetic inferiority, and he agreed that slavery and oppression had certainly influenced Negro culture, society, and psychology. But Ellison raised the question: "Is wretchedness *all* that has resulted? . . . Can a people . . . live and develop for over three hundred years simply by *reacting*? Are American Negroes simply the creation of white men, or have they at least helped to create themselves out of what they found around them?" To Myrdal's recommendation that Negroes do everything possible to "become assimilated into American culture, to acquire the traits held in esteem by the dominant white Americans," Ellison shot back, "Aside from implying that Negro culture is not also American, [this] assumes that Negroes should desire nothing better than what whites consider highest. But . . . lynching and Hollywood, faddism and radio advertising are products of the 'higher' culture, and the Negro might ask, 'Why, if my culture is pathological, must I exchange it for these?'" This is a mighty attempt to unlock minds, but although Ellison wrote his critique in 1944, it was not published until twenty years later. Nobody seems to know exactly why publication was delayed, but in the spirit of my Bible analogy, I could cite "blasphemy" as a probable reason.

The next source that Ron cites in his paper is Abram Kandiner and Lionel Ovesey's 1951 *The Mark of Oppression: A Psychological Study of the American Negro.* That book laid out "The Social Environment of the White Man" first, as the standard against which the Negro would be compared. I was hardly surprised to find that we didn't measure up: our mothers were "often loveless tyrants" and our fathers "frequently . . . either seclusive, taciturn, violent, [and] punitive . . . or submissive to the mother"; our marriages were "multiple and discordant," our families unsettled, and our communities devoid of "genuine religiosity." The authors continue with psychoanalytic case studies of the twenty-five individuals from Harlem whom they submitted to Rorschach tests, dream studies, free association tasks, and various other assessments and analyses. They wound up describing the "basic personality of the Negro" as one of cultural, social, psychological, and even psychiatric deficiency. As Kandiner and Ovesey put it, "The Negro has no possible basis for a healthy self-esteem and every incentive for self-hatred." That's more or less what Riesman was saying in his comments about Ron's paper.

I can't find comfort in the fact that sociologists attribute this pathology to slavery and discrimination, and the occasional offhand reminder that "these features are not universal" sounds hollow to me. No wonder Ron expected to find that we were suffering from "continual conflict," even "violent discord": that was the liberal, scholarly, enlightened view of the day.

After I'd read the paper in its entirety, I could see that Ron didn't always know quite what to make of our responses to his questions, since they seldom fit the canon, so he often merely reported what we said. At other points in his conclusion, Ron flatly rejected the prevailing wisdom, insisting that we were very different one from another, and that we "do not appear to fit the usual stereotypes of the American Negro, even those presented by sociologists."

By contrast, Riesman—the scholar, the professional—looked at Ron's inconclusive raw material and contorted his findings to match his own assumptions. Ron took the fact that we all wanted to keep being Black at more or less face value, while Riesman took it as evidence of a pathological denial. Ron described our personalities, while Riesman marveled at how "un-neurotic" we seemed. Ron talked about various ones of us as "an original thinker," "a sharp thinker," and "polished, educated, and self-assured," while Riesman wondered whether any of us were really intellectuals. I would wind up as a social science major, and Riesman's assumptions and worldview were baked into the "knowledge" from which my professors looked at me and graded my papers. Of course, that was the view toward all of us, but particularly, I suspect, toward those of us from humbler backgrounds. It is as if those scholars were living in a different universe—or as W. E. B. Du Bois had put it a half-century earlier, it was as if we Negroes were "shut out from their world by a vast veil."

I admit to not knowing much about Du Bois before I started my journey of reconnection to my Harvard past. I might not still had he not been a famous Harvardian. Sometime years ago, I had read bits and pieces of his 1903 *The Souls of Black Folk,* and probably had been fooled by the old-fashioned phrases and classical references into thinking it a relic of the past. But now I was awakened to how strikingly fresh and pertinent it was. Rereading Du Bois, I found myself warned in the very first chapter about the questions of whites. Even the most carefully worded questions, as well as those unasked but alluded to, sit out there in the air, Du Bois said, "between me and the other world." They "flutter around" the fundamental question, which is: "How does it feel to be a problem?" Du Bois described "a peculiar sensation, this double-consciousness, this sense of always looking at one's self through the eyes of others, of measuring one's soul by the tape of a world that looks on in amused contempt and pity." That's exactly what I felt reading Ron's paper, and especially Riesman's comments and the conclusions of the various sociologists—as if I were on the other side of the "veil," seeing but unseen, answering questions only to have my answers garbled and contorted by being interpreted through the veil.

We all got through that first year at Harvard. Nobody flunked out, and nobody was beaten up or expelled. We had friends and participated in sports. Wesley knew over three hundred of our classmates by name. Hobie found success and a touch of fame playing freshman football. Ezra did the same as center forward on the freshman soccer team, and so did Lowell Johnston as captain of the freshman crew. We learned things in our classes and about ourselves. Gerry did enough volunteer work in a local hospital emergency room to know that his major should be government, not medicine. George, after bombing his first chemistry exam, buckled down and bounced back with an A for the yearlong course. Jack also struggled with chemistry, but he loved economics and made plans to change his major. Larry learned to swim, and Kent Wilson surprised himself by making the dean's list. John and Travis picketed for civil rights. Freddy probably played too much bridge, but not so much that he hadn't squeaked through his classes. We all made it through our freshman year, we would all be back in September, and some of us, me included, hadn't yet turned eighteen.

I don't remember my last day on campus freshman year, but I like to imagine that I dumped that toilet cleaning canister in its closet and slammed the door.

# 5 *House Negroes: Fall 1960, Spring and Summer 1961*

*In mid-September of 1960, Jack Butler and I were hauling a first load of* gear up four switchback flights of stairs to the top floor of Eliot House. We flattened ourselves against the wall to let a couple of guys struggle by with a beat-up leather easy chair, and other guys did the same for us as we brought up our stuff and they jogged back down to fetch more of theirs. Finally, at the top floor, we took our first tentative steps into the spacious suite where we would live, along with five other guys, for the next three years—a warren of individual bedrooms to the right and left, tucked up under the eaves, bathrooms squeezed between them, and a couple of much larger common rooms with tall windows at the far wall and fireplaces opposite. A few bits of mismatched furniture had already arrived; eventually we would make the place homey in male dormitory style. Jack and I each claimed a bedroom to the left by dumping our cargo on the narrow beds, took quick peeks into the other rooms, and then went back down, dodging and weaving and nodding our greetings to the upward-bound boys.

Before tackling another trip up, we wandered out onto the broad terrace that faced the Eliot House courtyard, where in a few short years we would be handed our diplomas. We shared stories about our summers. I'd worked in the sporting goods department of Gertz Department Store in Queens until September and then taken a few days to relax and watch the Rome Olympics. Had Jack seen Cassius Clay win the gold? I asked, goofing around with a couple of punches and a flat-footed version of what would one day be called the Ali Shuffle. Jack had spent the summer with his father in Detroit, and he was more interested in talking about the stories of independence coming out of Africa—what did I think of all that was happening in Somaliland, Niger, Gabon, and Senegal? As I stammered a reply, we were politely interrupted by a small trim gentleman who stepped up with an outstretched hand: "Mr. Garrett, Mr. Butler, welcome to Eliot House. I'm Master Finley." He shook our hands, smiled, made a little bow, and ducked away to greet other boys. Jack and I exchanged a glance in wonderment that he knew our names, and then picked up our chat as we tackled another load.

If my first arrival at Harvard had been unlikely, my arrival in Eliot—the house famous for being "more Harvard than Harvard," for attracting the preppiest of the preppy, the wealthiest pedigreed boys—was just about preposterous. How did I, the Negro who grew up in the projects, wind up in a suite with David Rockefeller Jr., scion of the wealthiest family in the country? Not exactly through coincidence—the house system was designed to do exactly that kind of mixing, though it's hard to imagine a more extreme example than David and me.

President Lowell, the same president who had to be forced to allow Negroes in the dormitories and who had finagled a quota on Jews, had designed the house system to undermine social class segregation in college housing. When he assumed the Harvard presidency in 1903, rich boys lived in private dormitories nicknamed the Gold Coast. Designed and built in luxurious style, these dorms had steam heat, private baths, sitting rooms, and all the comforts and ornaments that money could buy—some lived up to the nickname with actual gilt! Everyone else lived elsewhere on campus in spartan rooms with no central heating and undependable, if any, hot water, or they commuted from home or from rented rooms in private homes around campus. President Lowell changed this by requiring all freshmen to live together in the Yard and upperclassmen to join the smaller community of a house.

Each house comprised a building or cluster of buildings with its own dormitory rooms, dining room, common rooms, library, and other amenities, which varied. Adams House, for instance, had a swimming pool; several houses had squash courts, a few had darkrooms, others had pool tables, and most had music rooms. Thus, a house would be the "center of social, athletic, and extra-curricular life," hosting "dances, smokers, teas, concerts, lectures, forums, debates, and teams." Athletic teams were central to house life, providing "genuine amateur athletics at its best"; each house had uniforms and equipment enough to outfit teams for football, baseball, squash, lacrosse, and just about any other sport you could name.

Eliot House at the time was farthest from Harvard Yard. Approached from that direction, the buildings seemed to have their backs turned to the rest of campus; the simple main entrance sat humbly on the same side as the kitchen delivery doors.

But to anyone approaching Harvard from the south or west, across the Charles River, Eliot House was commanding and quintessentially Harvard. As you crossed Anderson Bridge, on the far bank of the river, you could see the grand Weld Boathouse on the right and, in good weather, sculls skimming gracefully across the water. Beyond the riverbanks rose the clock tower and spire of Eliot House, nested snugly in the triangle created between Boylston Street and Memorial Drive next to the river. The house itself was red brick with white trim and five stories tall; it enclosed a triangular courtyard that was just the right space, as they say, for tossing a football around.

Another thing they say is that a house is not its building but its people. The central person in my day was each house's "master." The master gave guidance—the phrase of the day was "pastoral care"—for the social and academic lives of his three or four hundred boys, and he created and maintained the spirit of the house. The master and his family lived on the premises, and along with a senior tutor and a flock of resident and nonresident tutors, they provided, as Harvard bragged in the information booklet, the "informal, friendly student-teacher relationship which is so valuable for a liberal education."

By the time Jack and I were sweating our gear up to our fifth-floor suite, Eliot House had been under the mastership of John H. Finley Jr. '25 for nineteen years, and Master Finley was in the twenty-seventh of his eventual forty-three years as a professor of classics—and an institution—at Harvard. He was an excellent teacher and mentor, an urbane man of impeccable manners and comportment. He loved Harvard, and even more so, he loved Eliot House, referring to it regularly as "Arcadia," i.e., Utopia. To help his boys get started feeling the same way, he studied their photos and learned their names over the summer. He tended (and intended) to attract prep school boys, and often the most elite among them. His favored activity was the "sherry party," for gracious talk that ran the gamut of intellectual topics and often turned to sports. Finley was proud of his house, and proud of his boys. In a beloved quip that dates from 1951, when Eliot housed Henri Matisse's and James Joyce's grandsons and a descendant of the prophet Muhammed, Finley reportedly boasted, "Where else would you find, in one room, the grandson of Matisse, the grandson of Joyce, and the great-great-great-great-grandson of God?" He had no idea then that in a few short years he could count among his boys Kent Garrett, the great-great-grandson of a slave.

Jack and I hadn't chosen Eliot House so we could rub shoulders with the illustrious. Back in the spring of our freshman year, we simply decided that we hit it off well enough to be roommates, so we scribbled each other's names, along with our first, second, and third choices of house, onto index cards. The other Negroes in our class and our thousand or so classmates filled out their cards too. The choice process was supposed to be based on finding a good "fit"—Winthrop had the reputation, for instance, of being the house for the jocks, and Adams for the social activists, the EPIC kind of guys. I don't remember knowing much about the houses or their masters or reputations, but we knew that Eliot was on the river and that sounded very nice.

All eleven hundred of the boys' cards were collected and the masters and tutors started categorizing, reviewing, considering, sorting, re-sorting, and even sometimes interviewing, until they had finally divvied us all up. Official policy was that each house should end up with a cross-section of student types, but masters also had their own priorities and preferences about what kind of boys they wanted. Master Finley was famous for taking the selection process very seriously, snagging the athletes he needed to land a sports championship as well as the intellectuals he needed to augment the house's reputation for nurturing Rhodes Scholars. I like to imagine Master Finley, with knitted brow, considering whether to accept a fellow master's backroom offer—"I'll trade you this Choate coxswain and one public school grind for Rockefeller and a Negro."

Aside from Jack and me, all of the other guys in our suite were from private prep schools and wealthy families. The surprise was to find that fellow Negro Lowell Johnston was one of them. Lowell had submitted his card in a group with four of his friends: Spencer Borden IV was from Concord, Massachusetts, and went to Milton Academy, rowed for the Harvard varsity crew, and, yes, was heir to the Borden milk empire. I remember him as a tall, gangly blond guy with a proclivity for cursing. Eliot Wadsworth Scull had come to Harvard from St. Paul's School in New Hampshire, one of those schools at the top of the prestige heap. He had a VW Beetle and gave me rides back to New York City on his way home to Philadelphia. At the time, I was amazed at how frugal Eliot was—he wore the same shoes, for instance, until they were long past what I would consider the throwaway stage; as I look back, I think it was that kind of deliberate frugality that the very wealthy can afford to flaunt.

Then of course there was David Rockefeller Jr., who'd gone to another high-prestige prep, Phillips Exeter Academy, made his primary home in a grand five-floor house on the Upper East Side of Manhattan, and had a terrific singing voice. Rounding out the group was Ellwood Comly "Lee" Parry III from the William Penn Charter School in Philadelphia. Lee would be asked to take a year off after being caught shoplifting a pair of socks from the Harvard Coop; whether the incident stemmed from a prank or was the sign of a problem, probably no one will ever really know. In any case, Lee came back to Harvard, but not to Eliot House, graduated, and went on to a notable career as an art historian. The vacancy Lee left in the suite would be taken in our senior year by John Mason Morfit from Rye, New York, who'd been to Choate and to St. Edmunds in England and was the son of the TV personality Garry Moore.

So it was all those preppies and the two of us: Jack from his single-parent home in Pittsburgh and me from the projects in Brooklyn. President Lowell would have been pleased, though more for the other men's sake than for Jack's or mine. One of his reasons for promoting such "diversity" was his opinion, as he put it, that "it is important that the future railroad or bank president should spend the most impressionable years of his life . . . in becoming intimate with strong men of the most different kinds." I'm not sure if we were the exact sort of "different" kind Lowell had in mind, but there we were, working-class Negroes, ready to help our roommates learn how to be better aristocrats. Even today I like to think that I made David Rockefeller a better banker. More important, the social gap between those guys and Jack and me tended to throw the two of us together even more often and more firmly. Our friendship would influence my thinking and, in some ways, the rest of my life.

Whether Eliot House actually gave any of us "the priceless gift of character" is a mystery to me, but as for cultivating a sense that you belonged to something, a social unit with some kind of spirit, well, when you meet a fellow alum, the first question is usually "What house were you in?" I recently met a young grad and asked her that question: her reply was "Adams—in other words, the best one." Another time recently, I was thrilled to hear that a friend's son had chosen my dear old Eliot. Yes, I think that a lot of us do come away with a certain nostalgic allegiance to our house.

And it all started at dinner that first day as Eliot-ites, when we heard Master Finley's cultured voice, greeting us as he always greeted the new housemen: "Harvard is the best place in the world, and Eliot House is the best place at Harvard—so let's all be happy." And I was happy. I had a new, more comfortable major in social relations (or "Soc Rel," which we pronounced "sock-

RELL"). Plus, I was out from under the Dorm Crew. No fool to the system this year, I had hiked my butt over to the Harvard Student Agency right away and landed a great job. Starting that fall and continuing through senior year, I worked in the Cambridge offices of EDC, the Educational Development Center. In the first years I worked there, EDC was busy developing science curricula for elementary and secondary schools that would ramp up science teaching and catch up with the Commies in Russia; in my later years there, EDC would begin developing curricula for African schools and the controversial social studies curriculum, *Man: A Course of Study*. I didn't care much about what they did there at that point. What mattered was that instead of cleaning toilets in my dungarees, I had a clean-clothes job: a couple of days a week after classes, I walked over to the pleasant EDC offices and mimeographed stuff, went for coffee, and was treated with respect.

Jack was feeling good about the coming year too. He had changed his major from pre-med to economics, despite his mother's strenuous objections. And like me, he had a job that he liked, working with a professor on some kind of computer project. Jack spent his work hours punching programming code onto manila cards; he'd come back to our room either elated that his stack of cards went flipping through the machine successfully or dejected that there were errors, the cards had been spat out, and he'd have to do it all over again. Despite that, he developed a love for computers that lasted. Jack and I had work that we liked and that not only met our obligation to the bursar but also gave us a little spending money, we had found agreeable courses of study, and we had a plum suite with a view of the river.

The other Negroes, too, were getting settled into their new upperclassman lives in the houses. Adams House was at the time noted for its drama and music and for celebrating its place at the bottom of the athletic pack; oddly enough, Adams got the serious biology student from Muskogee, George Jones, plus the dynamic duo of Hobie Armstrong, football and track star, rooming with Harlem wiseguy Freddy Easter. Dunster House was at the time just beginning to recover from a reputation as a party house; the race activist Travis Williams ended up there. The house of the Barbadian Anglophile Ezra Griffith was a perfect fit: he went to Lowell House, with its Anglophile master Elliott Perkins '23.

An extensive, well-equipped house intramural sports system coordinated dozens of varsity and JV sports teams. If you didn't make the varsity or didn't have the time, there was always the house team, and almost everyone played on one or the other. Lowell Johnston, for instance, had captained the freshman crew; they rowed year-round, and soon he found himself "spending two to three hours a day, at least, with crew, starting with walking down to the boathouse and then working out. I would get to the library at night and fall asleep, because I was always so tired by the workouts." So Lowell turned to rowing for Eliot House instead of the varsity team, much to our benefit.

Interhouse sports could be cutthroat, but more often it was just fun . . . or at least mostly fun. Hobie played varsity football in the fall and was on the varsity track squad in the spring, but always seemed to be up for another challenge. One time he boxed for Adams House, with Freddy as his corner man. The reigning campus champ was Hobie's good friend and teammate Rick Rice, an enormous tackle; Hobie figured he'd have a chance, though, based on the times the two had fooled around playing "hot hands" and arm-wrestling. In the semifinals, however, against some guy whose name nobody can remember, Hobie "was dancing around," Freddy recalled, "and I thought he was winning, because he was quick and his hands were lightning fast. He was peppering the other guy, but he ran out of gas." Hobie recalled that moment differently: according to his recollection, he was seized with a nasty leg cramp. Whatever the cause, at the end of the second round, Freddy said, "Hobie just dropped his hands and stood at the rope looking out of the ring. The other guy didn't quite know whether this was a trick, and he got Hobie a couple of shots before the bell rang. Hobie came back to the corner and said, 'Take these fucking gloves off me.' The ref came over and said, 'There's another round,' and Hobie said, 'Not in this match there ain't.'" In the finals, Rick Rice wound up knocking out the guy who beat Hobie, who later told me in an email that he thought he "should get some credit for softening him up for Rick."

For the nonsporting types (and many of the sportsmen too), there were clubs for pursuing a dizzying array of interests: the usual options to try out a little acting, music, or writing (your choice of nine different publications, including the famous *Lampoon*), community service (prison tutoring or blood drives, for instance), debating, and student government. Then there were clubs for just about every intellectual interest, and hobby groups for everything from ham radio to mountaineering. But one activity was firmly off-limits for us: the "Final Clubs." The term "Final Club" dated back to the nineteenth century, when a Harvard College student would join a "freshman club," then a "waiting club," and eventually, in his junior or senior year, a "final club." By the time we were there, only Final Clubs had survived, and they were really just super-exclusive social clubs. They held a near-mythic status on campus (and beyond) for their arcane traditions, extreme selectivity—members of the Final Clubs were virtually all from the most socially prominent families and graduates of the highest tier of the New England prep schools—and smug secrecy.

Each Final Club owned a building near campus, tricked out with a library, game rooms, trophy rooms, and always a well-stocked bar; originally the clubs served all meals to their members, but in my day they offered just lunch and a weekly dinner. All of this took a lot of money, which came from steep membership dues and alumni support, which is one reason why poor or middle-class students, or even upper-middle-class students, weren't seriously considered for membership. The fall of sophomore year was the "punch" season: potential new Final Club members were invited to the first of a series of soirees; then a decreasing number of invitations were issued to increasingly tony and expensive events; and finally, the lucky few still standing were invited to join.

Does it go without saying that there were exactly zero Negroes in the Final Clubs?

Among our suitemates, Rockefeller and Scull made the Final Club called "Fly," which had the reputation of being for rich preppies. Undoubtedly, some of our other white suitemates were "punched" too. Lowell Johnston recalled that Rockefeller asked him whether he was interested in being considered for Fly. It's likely that neither of them knew it at the time, but being invited to join would have made Lowell the first Negro in a Final Club; as it turned out, the first came along some eight years later. Lowell declined anyway. He liked his friends, but he had neither the money nor the desire to travel any further into that world. As he told me years later, "I didn't see them as being people I would work with for the rest of my life. I knew that I was going to be doing something entirely different and they really didn't get me." Even after we were gone, a *Crimson* writer could say with confidence that "the tacit ban on Jews has been relaxed in most clubs, though the ban on Negroes is still in effect." Of course, the Final Clubs' membership was blatantly, if not officially, discriminatory. The fact that Harvard turned a blind eye to it would only occur to us a few years later.

Our lives were certainly rich in opportunities for industry and diversion, so what more could we want? Girls. One of Master Finley's famous statements was that his goal with his boys was "to reduce the time they spent thinking about women from 80 percent to 60 percent." I would have quibbled with his figures: as far as I could see, if he was lucky, on a good day he might bring it down to 90 percent.

What turned out to be the greatest addition to our romantic prospects was getting tuned in to the larger Boston Black community. For one thing, we were all granted a certain uncomfortable stardom among the local Black bourgeoisie with marriageage daughters. John would remind me of that whole scene: "You could almost make a comedy movie of it because there were these people in the local Black bourgeoisie, Ivy League–worshiping types, and they would try to introduce you to girls. There was this woman, I can't remember her name, but she would get girls at her house for a matching up." Apparently, this was typical of Boston's Black Brahmin postwar society, which at the time I knew nothing about. A daughter would come out as a debutante and be reserved for only the best of the best, including the few Black Harvard men. But we were not looking for sedate chaperoned dates or formal teas . . . and we certainly weren't looking for wives.

No, the action was not in "high society" but in the ordinary Black Boston community. The Black population of the city nearly tripled between 1940 and 1960. Segregation in Boston had long been strict—some said it was the worst in the North—and its Black community had a long history of creating its own institutions and culture: starting in the eighteenth century with Black abolitionist groups, it would come to include active chapters of the NAACP and the Urban League, newspapers and theater, literary groups and women's clubs, and finance agencies and self-help organizations. We were entering a vibrant Black world.

Ezra Griffith had found a second home there already by freshman year. Boston was a prime destination for immigrants from the West Indies, particularly from Jamaica and Barbados. Ezra found a Caribbean Episcopal church with a strong Barbadian presence in Boston. He was invited to Sunday dinners, dances, and other social events where he "ate West Indian food and was treated royally." It was tremendously important to him; in his words, "I had a natural culture-bound group on whom I could rely for comfort and food and music I liked. And a religious dimension too, because I was always religious and churchgoing." It was through these associations that Ezra also began a lifelong passion for Afro-Cuban drumming, playing in clubs around Boston and gaining no small amount of acclaim.

As sophomores, out in the houses, we started meeting the older Negroes in the Harvard classes ahead of us; we looked up to guys like Arthur Hoyte '60, Terry Bannister '61, and especially Howard "Bobo" Gray '62, who grew up in Roxbury, the Black part of Boston, and really knew his way around. These guys hung with a group of Black students from Boston University, Northeastern, Emerson, and Tufts, some of whom had their own apartments. Once a guy was in the loop, no formal invitations were needed; they found out about the parties through the grapevine, and the Negro upperclassmen in the houses would let us tag along, especially if we chipped in with gas and liquor money. The legal drinking age in Massachusetts was twenty-one, but Fred remembered that "in Cambridge, if you went to Harvard, you were old enough to drink. No place ever turned down any Harvard student for any alcohol, period." We could take public transportation to Roxbury, but the trains and buses quit at one in the morning, just when most parties were really getting good. So a car really was the thing, and a few guys had one.

We would pile in and set off, and as we rolled up the dark street, we could hear the pulsating bass beat blocks away. Inside, through dim lights and a haze of cigarette smoke, wall-to-wall Negroes were slow-dancing to doo-wop on the record player. So good, so fine—I had grown up on doo-wop music. Evenings in Queens, I'd be there on street corners with four or five other boys trying to sing and make some ensemble moves. We knew all the words and imagined our fifteen-year-old selves as Frankie Lyman and the Teenagers singing their hit "Why Do Fools Fall in Love?," or the Flamingos with "I Only Have Eyes for You," or the Five Satins with "In the Still of the Night." And now here I was at a party with men and women and alcohol and music I loved.

Stay cool, say "yo" to a few guys, ramble over to the bar area to set down our bottle and pour some drinks. They knew it and we knew it: the crew from Harvard was in the house. There was a "Harvard advantage" at these parties, but you still had to be able to dance and have some kind of engaging rap. I could rap and I could dance. No jacket and tie, no managing our Negro-ness, no punch and cookies, no stares, no foxtrotting, no white people. Equally liberating for me was that the young people there were college students, kids my age with intellectual interests and high aspirations; besides a dance and a drink, you could get good conversation. Even Jack Butler, who had hardly dated at all in high school, got into the Boston scene.

If a Black guy was into dating white girls, there were more options close at hand, but things were much more complicated for him. A Harvard Negro who came after us would put it succinctly: "Dating white girls solved one problem but created others." Taking a chance and approaching a white Radcliffe girl in class was just that—taking a chance. Some did it, but not me. Freddy didn't either. As he told me, "The Cliffies were not interested in anybody as dark as me, period."

John Woodford had not only dated a white Radcliffe girl but was on the slippery slope to falling in love. He had met Eliza Duffy in his section of freshman seminar, and they'd taken some bike rides and had long talks about life and books. John and Eliza corresponded over the summer, and John joined Adams House for sophomore year. That fall he and Eliza went to movies together, met for coffee, and talked, but at least to others, it looked like friendship more than romance. Academically, instead of finding himself in a more agreeable place, as Jack and I had done with our changed majors, John was still up in the air. He was pre-med, planning to be a doctor like his father, but he hadn't been set afire by his first-year courses. Even in freshman seminar, he would tell me, he "didn't think critically about much. Ideas either made sense to me and seemed to be important or interesting or they didn't. And a lot of what they were talking about was very anthropological and existential, and I just didn't take to it." He also wasn't intellectually stimulated by his science courses, which he found mathematically demanding. What he loved about Harvard, in his words, was "hanging around with different groups of guys from different parts of the country and sitting around yakking through the night." By the end of the fall semester of sophomore year, John had decided to take a semester off. He was experiencing some academic malaise, of course, but he would also say later that taking time off "let me devote more time to my 'chase.'" His chase of Eliza, he meant.

Taking a semester or a year off was pretty common—one source says that in our day something like 10 percent of students did it, either entirely by choice, as John did, or with the polite but firm suggestion of a dean. At the end of freshman year, Freddy had already received such a suggestion. He is the first to say that he wasted time that first year and wound up with, as he recalled, three Cs and a D. "The dean called me in and said, 'You gotta do better than this.'" Fred promised that he would: "I said, 'I know I can'—and I did know I could—so they let me come back for sophomore year." So far in that fall of sophomore year he hadn't shown a strong turnaround. Freddy enjoyed dating, parties, bull sessions, sports—he earned the nickname "Freddy the Fourth" for his perpetual willingness to join a bridge game at any time, and studying was taking a backseat to pretty much everything else.

Up in the common room in our Eliot House suite, it wasn't just Freddy who was wasting time. I did my share of yakking, and I played bridge now and then. Unlike Fred, I wasn't much of a games enthusiast, but I watched with confused fascination when the guys played Risk—The Game of Global Domination. A typical foursome consisted of Larry, Jack, Terry Bannister, and Al Jefferson, a Black guy nobody knew very well. He was always around our suite, though, sometimes for days at a time; he'd sleep on our beat-up sofa, and then one day he'd be gone. A tall, light-skinned guy and a nice dresser, Al was always up for a good yak session, but also hard to pin down. Lowell Johnston remembered Al too; at the time, we assumed that he was one of the older, wiser Negro grad students. Was he in law, we asked, or med school? And then one day Al just disappeared. Maybe he knew we were on the brink of realizing that he wasn't a student at all, although that wouldn't have bothered us much, since another Black guy was always welcome.

Many evenings, especially the long winter ones, somebody would grab the flimsy cardboard box and flip off the rubber bands with a flourish, in silent challenge to compete for control of the world. The Risk game board would be slapped onto our scuffed-up old coffee table, the players would divide up a bunch of little colored cubes and deal out some cards, and then they'd sit hunched over the game until one of them had conquered the globe. I could see that was the point of the game, and I knew that the cubes represented armies, but I just couldn't seem to care enough to learn the exact rules. Guys would say things like, "I'm attacking Egypt from southern Europe," or "Kamchatka from Irkutsk," and the game would go on for hours. From time to time, two guys would leave the room for negotiations, making alliances or calling truces. I'd watch for a while as some guy's armies started to build up and spread over a lot of the board and another guy would be down to just a few lonely little cubes; I'd go out and have a shower or do some reading, and when I came back, the whole situation might have reversed itself, with some other guy's armies all backed up into Australia. Each competitor seemed to have his own preferred strategy. Jack would always try to dominate Africa first and put lots of cubes on its countries in shades of rich red-brown—Congo, North Africa, Madagascar. Jack was becoming fascinated with Africa, and not only while playing Risk.

Starting in 1959, a Harvard admissions man, David D. Henry, made yearly trips to Nigeria as part of a consortium of Boston-area colleges to recruit promising boys to get American degrees and then go back to help build an independent nation. Nigeria was emerging from 160 years of colonial rule by the British Empire, and in the fall of 1960, Nnamdi Azikiwe would be named governor general. Azikiwe's son, Chukwuma, most often called Chuma, was one of about two dozen Nigerian boys who came to the United States to study at Boston-area colleges, and he joined our class as a sophomore. Like others in our class, I remembered Chuma as friendly, outgoing, and fun, although he also had a certain sense of entitlement that must be tough to shed when you are the eldest son of a head of state. Chuma was a good athlete; he played soccer with the varsity, but was even more skilled as a jumper—he competed in the hop-step-jump and the long jump. He was also likable, easy to talk to, and, like us, always on the lookout for parties and girls.

John Woodford remembered going to the Nigerian independence party in Boston with Chuma. "I remember first meeting him," he told me, "and how ignorant we were. We even asked him, 'What language do you speak in Nigeria?' We barely even knew what Nigeria was." I was also pretty clueless about Africa, and given the temper of the times and the nature of the US history and geography curricula, I can safely say that I was far from the only one. But Africa was already on Jack's radar; he would later say that it was at Harvard that he got his "first real contact with Africans." Jack was the first of us—certainly the first guy I knew personally and almost the first I'd encountered in any way whatsoever—to start thinking that we eighteen "Negroes," from wildly diverse backgrounds and thrown together in that crazy white man's place, were African.

The biggest news on campus that winter, though, wasn't Africa but the victory of Harvard's very own John F. Kennedy in the presidential election. Subfreezing temperatures didn't keep thousands from traipsing around campus early one morning, stamping and shivering, hoping for a glimpse of Harvard's very own president-elect of the United States. Kennedy was in town for a meeting of the Board of Overseers, and the whole city was on alert. The *Boston Globe* had printed a detailed schedule, and citizens, students, and the press had staked out all potential viewing points; every time the man appeared for even a brief moment, the crowd erupted in cheers, squeals, and flashbulbs.

Three reporters from WHRB, the Harvard radio station, were waiting at the entrance to the new Loeb Drama Center, Kennedy's last stop, because President Pusey had gotten JFK to agree to a brief interview afterward. But at the last minute, Kennedy realized that he was already way behind schedule, apologized, and left out a side door. The young reporters made chase, two of them slowed significantly by a fifty-pound tape recorder. The lucky first guy caught up with Kennedy, started to ask a question, and before he knew it was in the car with JFK. "I'm glad to see that there is still a good deal of vitality here," Kennedy said to the stunned young reporter, referring to the hundreds of students who had mobbed him everywhere on campus. It reminded him of the "riots" of his day, he said, adding, "I'm delighted to be the object of such a riot."

Ever since November's election, Harvard had been in the news, usually when some college official carried on about how Kennedy was "raiding" the Harvard faculty for his new administration, the note of alarm rarely disguising an overweening pride. Americans would remember those days as filled with a sense of youthful hope and energy, when the "torch was passed to a new generation." Negroes, at least some of us, had begun to believe that they might be a recognized part of that new generation, and whites were confident that, with patience on all sides, and discounting a few horrible southern bigots, integration would proceed—if not always in an orderly fashion, at least always toward a better day. Just six weeks into his presidency, Kennedy signed Executive Order 10925; stating that it was the "plain and positive obligation of the United States Government to promote and ensure equal opportunity for all qualified persons, without regard to race, creed, color, or national origin," EO 10925 barred discrimination on all government contract work and established the President's Committee on Equal Employment Opportunity to see that it happened.

Harvard was out in front of that curve, having just appointed a young Negro named Archie Epps to the Department of Middle Eastern Studies. Epps taught courses while living the life of a junior scholar in the Divinity School at Harvard. He was even then a presence on campus—a star singer in the Glee Club, he was known for being formal, cautious in word and deed, and proper and diligent, as well as for his ever-present boutonniere. In just a few years, Epps would get his start in a long career in the Harvard administration, beginning as an assistant dean—what was

*Archie Epps, early 1970s*
© THE HARVARD CRIMSON, INC.

quaintly called a "baby dean" at the time—in apprenticeship to Dean John U. Monro.

Archie C. Epps III grew up in Lake Charles, Louisiana, earned a bachelor's degree at Talladega in Alabama, and came to Harvard to continue his studies in theology and education. He was working on a doctorate when he got his start in administration, and he never looked back. Epps became an institution at Harvard. One of the first Black senior administrators—and for a long time the only one—he would play the difficult role of mediator in both small and big struggles over racial issues that would arise in the coming decades, including one whose seeds were being sown right up under the eaves in our Eliot House suite. Jack Butler had begun to talk about starting a Black student group.

# 6 | *So-Called Negroes: Fall 1961*

*"There is no more apartheid in South Africa than there is in the United* States." The audience hissed. Malcolm X paused, turned, and smiled his forbearance at the moderator to his right, who had warned him about the Harvard tradition of hissing for "everything from a bad joke to an additional assignment." No matter what the hissers might have meant, there were those in the audience that night who found little to applaud in the words of this sober-looking man who glared toward his listeners as he spoke with disturbing force about dark things.

Sanders Theater, that same place where less than two years earlier, as a freshman, I had sat apprehensively thinking about the next four years, was packed far beyond capacity. The crowd was estimated at 1,600 by the FBI investigator who was there. All three of the men on the dais that night—and probably many more in the audience—had FBI files. The agent estimated the crowd to be about 20 percent Negro, most of them "judged to belong to the NOI [Nation of Islam], based on the headdress worn by females and golden emblem worn in the lapel of men's suitcoats." If the FBI was correct, that would mean that over 300 Negroes were in Sanders Theater that night.

The forum moderator, Roger D. Fisher '52, had done his homework: before the debate got under way, he had asked one of the Nation of Islam entourage about using the word "Negro" in his introduction. To say "one Negro and one Black" to describe Malcolm X and the other guest, Harvard alum Walter Carrington (AB

1952, JD 1955), sounded odd, he thought, and "it would have been provocative . . . to say that we had two 'Blacks.'" Malcolm X's lieutenant was adamant: "Don't you dare call Malcolm a Negro. The word reminds us of 'nigger.'" Malcolm X broke into the conversation and said that although "Negro" was not a word he liked, it was at times useful; he told Fisher to go ahead and use it.

*Malcolm X at Harvard, March 24, 1961*
© THE HARVARD CRIMSON, INC.

The third man onstage, Walter Carrington, was commissioner of the Massachusetts Commission Against Discrimination. Just thirty years old, Carrington was the youngest person to hold that post at that time, and also the youngest to serve on the board of directors of the NAACP. He would soon leave Boston for a Peace Corps posting to Senegal; after his posting, he would stay on the continent for ten years as the Peace Corps director for Africa. Carrington's subsequent career would include directing the African American Institute and serving as ambassador to Senegal and to Nigeria. Carrington was on the panel that evening to argue in favor of the nonviolent, integrationist, legalistic approaches of organizations like his own: the NAACP and the Congress of Racial Equality (CORE).

Fisher, Malcolm X, and Carrington sat framed against Memorial Hall's trio of VE-RI-TAS shields rendered in stained glass. A phalanx of unsmiling members of Fruit of Islam (FOI), the all-male military wing of the Nation of Islam, stood stiffly down in front of the stage in black suits with white epaulets, black bow ties, shiny black oxfords, and caps emblazoned with the FOI insignia. Fisher introduced Malcolm X and slid the microphone across the table.

"We thank you for inviting us here to the Harvard Law School Forum to present our views on this timely topic, 'The American Negro: Problems and Solutions,'" began Malcolm X. "However, to understand our views, the views of the Muslims, you must first realize that we are a religious group, and you must also know something about our religion, the religion of Islam." For the first few minutes, Malcolm addressed nothing explicitly to the "timely topic," instead going through the windup: the significance of Allah, the prophets, divine obedience, the Honorable Elijah Muhammad, God's purpose. Then came the blazing fastball: "The only solution to America's serious race problems is complete separation of the two races."

Drawing out his argument with references to history and theology, Malcolm described an Old World in which "practically the entire earth has been deceived, conquered, colonized, ruled, enslaved, oppressed, and exploited by the Caucasian race," a world he likened to a "wicked old house" that would soon collapse. He compared Elijah Muhammad to Moses and to Jesus, and he argued for separate states for the twenty million of us "so-called Negroes," who were no longer able to wait for "Caucasians to be re-educated and freed of their racial prejudices." He scoffed at integration as a mere token: "A cup of tea in a white restaurant is not sufficient compensation for 310 years of free slave labor." He called Thurgood Marshall—who would be the first Black appointed to the Supreme Court six years later—a "20th century Uncle Tom" and criticized Christianity for "teaching us to call ourselves 'Negroes' and telling us we were no longer African."

In the final minutes of his speech, Malcolm brought his argument home to this audience of teachers and learners. "No man with equal education will serve you," he cautioned. "As your colleges and universities turn out an ever-increasing number of so-called Negro graduates with education equal to yours, they will automatically increase their demands for equality in everything else. This equal education will increase their spirit of equality and make them feel that they should have everything that you have . . . In fact, the same Negro students you are turning out today will soon be demanding the same things you now hear being demanded by Mr. Muhammed and the Black Muslims."

Way up in the balcony seats, two of those so-called Negro students, Jack Butler and Lowell Johnston, looked at each other, and a bolt of excitement shot between them. They turned again to face the speaker as he concluded with the warning that, without repentance, "all of you who are sitting here, your government, and your entire race will be destroyed and removed from this earth by Almighty God, Allah." The "you" to whom he had addressed his entire speech was the other 80 percent of the audience—the white people in attendance.

After a short burst of uncertain applause, Fisher introduced Carrington. He said that the NOI was "the greatest boon to the Ku Klux Klan since the invention of the bedsheet." He said that even if the "Black Moslems" really did have 100,000 members, as they claimed, that was still an insignificant proportion of the Negro population of the country. The other 9,900,000, he said, wanted integration and were not about to sit and wait for this Armageddon the NOI talked about, which might be years away. What had the NOI actually done for the Negro, he asked, and what was actually taught in the mosques and on the streets? Carrington's speech was interrupted several times by applause—the *Crimson* reported that "they applauded with increasing enthusiasm as . . . Carrington defended the NAACP position." According to the FBI and the *Crimson,* the Muslims in the audience sat silent, only applauding when they could see that Malcolm X did.

A brief but lively back-and-forth followed, during which Malcolm X often leaned forward and sometimes pointed a finger at the audience, while Carrington tended to lean back and smile.

The *Crimson* reported that Malcolm X "became more passionate" and told the audience, "You people wouldn't be here at Harvard if your forefathers hadn't said 'Liberty or Death'—we say the same thing."

Then the moderator declared the session over and gave perfunctory thanks to the participants. As the audience began to jostle toward the doors, a tall young Black man with a trimmed beard strode to the podium and got Malcolm X's attention. The two men shook hands and passed a few words; Malcolm smiled broadly and talked to the young man before turning to join his entourage and exit the hall.

The tall young man was Bill Strickland, at the time a regular around our Eliot suite, and one of the older guys who'd befriended me and Jack and the others.

Bill entered Harvard in 1954 as a member of the class of '58, but he left to serve in the Marines and came back after four years to take up his studies where he had left off. When I got in touch with him again in 2010, Bill was living in Ibiza, Spain, having mostly retired from his lifelong career as an academic and activist, though he still advised doctoral students and was a consultant with the W. E. B. Du Bois Center at the University of Massachusetts. He told me that there was "a tradition of older Black Harvard boys who welcomed us and explained what Harvard was all about." And he was the one who passed that tradition on to us.

Bill grew up in the Roxbury section of Boston and was just a kid in the early 1940s when the young man then known as Malcolm Little was living nearby with his older half sister. Having grown up in the Midwest, Malcolm was dazzled when he arrived in the city: "I didn't know the world contained as many Negroes as I saw thronging downtown Roxbury at night, especially on Saturdays." One of those Negroes was Bill Strickland's cousin, Leslie Edman, and the two became friends and fellow members of a sports club called the Panthers, who, as Bill remembered, "wore these shiny black jackets embossed with the orange emblem of a black panther" that impressed Bill to no end. Edman also was friends with Louis Eugene Walcott, who would become a powerful member of the NOI, first as Louis X and later as Louis Farrakhan. As a little boy, Bill hero-worshiped these cool older guys, but it wasn't until that night in 1961 in Memorial Hall that he met Malcolm again. As he told me, "I walked up to the podium and just said my cousin's name. And then we were tight until Malcolm was killed."

Spencer Jourdain was another of our mentors who was at Sanders Theater that March night; he took the *Crimson* to task a few days later with a letter to the editor. The *Harvard Crimson* had called Malcolm X's speech "long and repetitive" and suggested that the audience had been much more responsive to Carrington's. Spencer seemed to catch a whiff of disdain for Malcolm X, and he was not about to let it go unchallenged. He began by saying that the forum "raised many eyebrows, but in the raising caused an equal number of eyes to be stretched open to a set of very hard facts about the racial situation in the United States." In his thoughtful measured words, Jourdain explained that he doubted that the NOI "will be the vehicle of the Negroes' attainment of social equality," but he defended the Muslims' forceful and accurate descriptions of race relations.

For Lowell Johnston and Jack Butler, the evening was momentous. Lowell told me when we talked in 2017, "I'd never heard a Black man speak the way he was speaking. It was an *event!* I still keep pictures of it in my mind. Malcolm X was charismatic, electrifying, very persuasive." Lowell hardly slept that night, he remembered, just thinking about what he had heard, and he considered that Harvard Law School Forum "one of the signal events of my life." Unlike the *Crimson* reporter, Lowell felt that the audience, both Black and white, was impressed and moved. Louis X would agree; in his words, "the white audience was enamored with this black man who could answer their questions with ease."

Roger Fisher, the moderator, would write about that night thirty years later. Over dinner at the faculty club earlier that evening, Fisher had talked with Malcolm X, asking about his life, raising the sticky issue of whether to use the word "Negro," and warning him about the Harvard "hissing" phenomenon. Although Fisher remembered that Malcolm's grasp of history had some "remarkable" gaps, what made a lasting impression was the man's openness and sincerity. Fisher described him as "filled with energy, purpose and conviction. Apparently a man of complete integrity. Committed to righting years of injustice. Out to change the world, and doing it."

The general public's first look at the NOI had come on TV in the summer of 1959, right at the time when we Harvard Negroes were preparing for our freshman Arrival Day. That July, New York's public television station aired a documentary series about Black nationalism, produced by Alan Lomax and Mike Wallace and titled *The Hate That Hate Produced.* According to the historian and Malcolm X biographer Manning Marable, Lomax had gathered the film footage and conducted the interviews, and Wallace "edited and narrated the series for maximum shock value." Wallace repeatedly referred to the NOI's philosophy as "racism," and he emphasized Elijah Muhammad's and Malcolm X's brushes with the law. The airing of the documentary "sparked a firestorm": pretty much everyone was aghast, outraged, disgusted, or scared. Immediately, however, Wallace heard from several prominent Blacks, including the baseball great Jackie Robinson and the NAACP's Roy Wilkins, who stepped up to decry the sensationalism of the broadcast, saying that it had "overstated" the threat and the hatred. These voices, however, were drowned out by excoriations of the Nation of Islam, including predictable charges of connections with communism.

During the next few years, Malcolm X and the NOI set out to improve their image. Malcolm started the newspaper *Muhammad Speaks* in 1960, and for the next few years he traveled almost unceasingly, speaking in forums and debates, at rallies, and on the radio. As Marable puts it, the Nation of Islam wanted to "confront its critics. And there was no better venue for such confrontations than American universities."

In 1994, Bill Strickland would write that, before Malcolm X, Americans were complacent, naively believing that "race was an about-to-be-conquered problem." "Most of us," Strickland said,

"Black and white alike, basked in the aura of American goodness." And then Malcolm X "exploded like a wanton shell burst and changed forever the way that 'Negroes' and America thought about themselves and one another." This is how Malcolm's speech at the forum had affected Lowell Johnston and Jack Butler, but the sound waves of the explosion had not reached my ears.

I've thought a lot about why I didn't go to the debate that night in Sanders Theater. Of course, it's possible that I had a paper due or a heavy date. Travis Williams would later recall that, in the mid-1960s, Black students were afraid to listen to Malcolm X, that "most of us fled his naked language." Some fifty-five years later, I read the speech that Malcolm X gave that night, trying to imagine what I would have thought had I gone to the debate. Travis might have been right; there was some very "naked language" there, and I might well have been put off by it. Lowell and Jack were angry young men, much more aware of racial politics than I was. Each of them also had experienced a personal tragedy that would fuel that anger—both had lost their fathers, both pretty recently, and while Jack was angry *at* his father for leaving the family, Lowell was angry *about* the role of racism in his father's suicide. I hadn't lost my father, and he and my mother shielded me from many of the realities of racism. My dad simply refused to let racism rain on his parade. As he told me over and over, anger was no solution to problems. His parents, my father explained, "told us about racism and how to get around it—you don't do certain things or go into certain places. But we were looking at it from the standpoint of things are going to be better, and that didn't give us a real serious anger." That's the way my parents had been with me too, and maybe I wasn't ready to lose that freedom from anger.

Quite likely, given my increasing skepticism about organized religion, I would have rejected Malcolm's insistence that Elijah Muhammad had been sent here by God, and I probably would have had mixed feelings about his insistence that "complete separation is the only solution." Up to that point, my life had effectively been segregated and now, here at Harvard, the integration process seemed to be going along pretty well. The idea of us all going off somewhere and starting a new society would have sounded pretty far-fetched to me at the time.

In the end, though, it hardly mattered that I didn't go—because starting the next day and forever after, it seemed like every conversation with Jack would somehow come around to Malcolm X, or Negro responsibilities, or "the movement." We spent most of our free time together then, and I made a good sounding board for Jack. Over burgers at Cronin's, it might be, "We can't sit around and wait for the NAACP; that was our parents' generation, and we aren't going to be like them." In Lamont Library, it was, "Okay, we are getting an education here and that's great, but if we don't act, and act together, we aren't going to change anything." Up at our suite, bull sessions were still about girls much of the time, of course, but now Jack tossed out a fierce rebuke: "I used to date white girls, but no more. It's a matter of principle, and if I dated a white girl, I would be a traitor to my own feelings. I mean, maybe you're just being rebellious against conventionality, but you get a false sense of equality." In more private conversations, Jack told me that he was disappointed that so many Negroes at Harvard just didn't take this whole matter more seriously, or that they were more concerned about their own affairs than about helping the cause. I'm not sure why he kept hanging around with me, except that maybe he could see that he was getting somewhere with me.

I was certainly awakening to "the cause," as he often called it, and there was so much more going on in the world that spring, events that would shape our early adulthood and beyond. The Peace Corps was created, the Soviets put a man into "outer space," the Freedom Riders were organizing their first trips south, Vice President Lyndon Johnson went to Saigon and came back talking about the "domino theory," and the United States lost a mini-war in Cuba's Bay of Pigs. It strikes me now as comic that what actually brought thousands of Harvard students out of their comfortable houses and away from their important studies to protest, speak out, wave flags, and make noise was just a piece of paper.

Sometime in April, a Radcliffe girl caught wind of the fact that the diplomas to be ceremoniously given out in June at what Harvard called "The Happy Observance of Commencement" had already been printed, and that they were written in English. The previous 324 classes had all received theirs in Latin, the official language of scholarship. Someone in power, at some meeting, or in a moment of decisiveness, had decreed that since Latin no longer held that distinction, it was no longer appropriate for Harvard's diplomas. Commence the riots!

Before cities across the country burned in the riots of the late 1960s, the word "riot" often simply referred to general college mayhem. Especially in the Ivy League, a riot was considered a harmless—if usually annoying and often destructive—way for young people to let off some steam. Sometimes Harvard students sought redress for real or perceived injustices, but far more often a riot was nothing more than a combustible mixture of youthful exuberance, boredom, beer, spring weather, libido, hazing rituals, fighting, sports, and crowd mentality.

The Diploma Riots at the end of April 1961 involved as many as four thousand rioters—or "revelers," as they might better be called. The events included a speech in Latin by a toga-clad, torch-bearing senior and a march to the president's house accompanied by chants of "Latin si, Pusey no!" to which Pusey responded in rhyme: "What's pat in Latin / Or chic in Greek / I always distinguish / More clearly in English." He said, no, nothing would be done. That sent several thousand young people storming around the campus and out into Cambridge streets—stopping traffic, throwing things, chanting and yelling, and at the same time feeling self-righteous and entitled to their free-for-alls. Subsequent breaking news that the diplomas would be smaller in size and printed with less expensive techniques on less luxurious paper—someone described them as looking like a "YWCA certificate"—would be greeted with even larger and noisier crowds. The mayhem continued to the point of tear gas and arrests. Soon, the whole thing died down, and henceforth diplomas have been in English.

I don't remember the riots at all; I didn't care what my diploma looked like, as long as I got it. I kept working, studying, keeping my head above water.

Bobby Gibbs, on the other hand, committed the Harvard version of flunking out at the end of sophomore year. Harvard didn't call it flunking out, and for a very good reason: students whose academic performance was poor were usually only required to take a year off, or sometimes to take summer courses, after which they could come back. Bobby had done well freshman year but floundered academically as a sophomore, when he changed his major from chemistry, first to Far Eastern literature, and then to economics. The courses were challenging, but more important, he was distracted. Bobby had requested Winthrop House because of its reputation for putting on so many theatrical events. He surprised me (as he did many times in our chats) by telling me that he played the cello. He remembered playing in the orchestra for the Winthrop House production of *On the Town* that April, for instance. He told me, "I thought I saw my day on Broadway coming up. You know, you get that theater buzz!"

The buzz, too, was the gay scene around the Loeb Drama Center, and also in a seedy downtown section of Boston nicknamed the "Combat Zone." There was a vibrant gay life in Boston at the time; as one writer put it, "Sure, it was risky and certainly underground. But for those who went to bars, nightclubs and restaurants that attracted a gay clientele, Boston gay nightlife was rich, varied and even glamorous." The Cliffie Mary Vogel recalled Bobby coming back from one of his nights out and teaching everyone at a Winthrop House party how to do a new dance called the Twist. Good times, fun days, but Bobby was overdoing it; as he put it, "I was a mess. I had as much good time as I possibly could. Of course, you can't do all that and do your homework." He cut all his sophomore final exams and was invited to take a year off.

By the end of sophomore year, Fred Easter, too, had worn out his welcome academically. He'd been allowed to come back after a poor showing freshman year only because he promised he could and would do better. But in the end, he played bridge, enjoyed himself, and on exam day concocted answers using what he knew mortared up with bullshit. When his final grade in history was posted as failing, he went to talk to the instructor about what he assumed was simply a mistake. The professor glared, fished Fred's blue book out of the pile, pointed to several passages underlined in angry red pencil, and said, "Here, see this? See that? Nobody who says *that* can pass my course."

So Fred got the bad news: "You've got to go home and decide whether you really want to do this or not." His chat with the dean was easier than the one he was about to face at home; in those days, the college wrote to or called parents to advise them of such matters, so by the time he got home, his mom knew. "It was one of the few times I saw my mother cry," he said. "I can remember coming upon her sitting in the living room crying and I said to her, 'Don't worry, Mom. I'm going to go back, I'm going to finish, it's only a year off.' And it was like she wasn't going to take her next breath until I did that. I felt like shit."

The rest of us had made it through another year; my grades, by the standards of those days before grade inflation, were solidly passing if not stellar. I was pulling Bs and Cs in subjects like anthropology and history, though some of the science courses gave me trouble and I had a nasty D in one of them. But I liked my humanities courses; I was finally pursuing something that felt like "knowledge for its own sake." So, although I wasn't about to make my mother cry, as Freddy did, I had to break the news that I didn't think I was still on the path to medical school. My mom suffered from a bad case of "my son the doctor syndrome," and "social relations" as a major meant as little to my parents as it had to me two years earlier. At the time when I was making college plans, my folks and I had few ideas about what college would be like, and even fewer about what it was for exactly. The only jobs we knew that required college were teacher, lawyer, doctor, and maybe preacher, and without a lot of thought, doctor came up as the one for me. Whatever they thought of my prospects, my parents accepted the change of major and were just happy that I was in college and also happy, I think, that I was happy there.

The only trace of the Diploma Riots at Commencement that

spring was a hand-lettered sign someone carried in the raucous and rain-soaked Alumni Parade. The next day the sun came out on the Yard, men donned top hats and cutaway coats, and the ceremonies went forward. *Life* magazine covered the festivities and printed a six-page spread in a late June issue that also carried an article about college cheating and featured Princess Grace Kelly on the cover. Another year down, another summer coming up.

*Kent at home in Queens, summer 1961*

My hot attic bedroom in Queens was still home, though it was no Eliot House. I'd only been home a few days, enjoying the schedule-free days and my mother's cooking, when my dad came upstairs with news—one of his floor-waxing customers had set me up with a summer job. I wasn't sure what to think until he said the job would be at Jones Beach—that certainly sounded interesting! Like so many other things in life, the job wasn't quite what I expected. It's not as if I pictured myself as a lifeguard, walking among the girls in their new-style bikinis. Neither, however, did I picture myself as a nerd walking the boardwalks with a clipboard and a pocket protector, which is how it turned out. I wound up working for the New York State Office of Parks Department, sticking a thermometer into piles of potato salad and mounds of ground beef at boardwalk concession stands to ensure that they were chilled enough to prevent food poisoning. The pleasure of that chore was broken up by such occasional fascinating tasks as counting the cars in the various parking lots.

I was free of the Jones Beach job after Labor Day and then, almost before I had a chance to relax, it was moving-in day and Jack and I were cruising into Cambridge to reprise the previous September. This time we were so much more casual about it, hauling our gear up the stairs in Eliot House, greeting old friends, and welcoming the new Eliot boys. Jack looked different in a way that I'd only much later realize was significant: his hair seemed to be too big, like he hadn't had time to have it buzzed off before school started, and he also came to moving-in day in what looked like army duds. But as guys for whom fashion was at best an afterthought, we got back in the swing of our friendship and back into our jackets and ties. There were things to do and people to meet —sophomores and other boys who had the luck to wind up in "the best place in the world."

Up in our now-familiar Eliot digs, we met a new suitemate, Mason Morfit. Not a sophomore but a member of the class of 1962, Mason had taken a year off to travel around and find himself. After a brief period of unsatisfying experiences as a Jack Kerouac wannabe, he found a job as producer of a radio variety show in St. Louis. I don't remember when I discovered that Mason's father was the entertainer Garry Moore, née Thomas Garrison Morfit, who at the time was the star of a popular prime-time network television variety show. Mason returned to Harvard, was invited to join Eliot House, and then was told that he would be living in the "UN Suite"—apparently some dean's way of edging into the announcement that he would be joining a group of three whites and three Negroes. What makes that combination international, I can't imagine, since everyone in the suite was American-born.

Eliot House also got a new Negro that fall. Napoleon Bonaparte Williams was an assured and strong young man in the class behind us who didn't need much assistance from us older guys. A native of Memphis, Napoleon had been a mathematics prodigy in high school, and in Eliot he was one of the few people who socialized (i.e., talked math) with his classmate Ted Kaczynski, who would one day be known by the moniker "the Unabomber." Growing up in Memphis, Napoleon might have suffered the indignities of racism more than any of us. While on a city bus, a mob of whites attacked him and broke a bottle over his head. Many times when Napoleon and his friends walked home from school, local police cars would roll up and white policemen would jump out with rifles, laughing as they taunted them: "I wasn't gonna shoot you, we just like to see niggers run." Napoleon had an eager mind, and before the end of his freshman year, he had started going to the Nation of Islam Mosque No. 11 in Roxbury, at the time headed by Louis X. Napoleon had been fascinated by C. Eric Lincoln's new book, *The Black Muslims in America,* particularly because he couldn't bring himself to commit unconditionally to nonviolence—yet even in Lincoln's overall negative appraisal of the NOI, Napoleon recognized that "they were saying some things that resonated with me, like 'Be proud and stand up and defend your rights.'" Napoleon was also drawn to the discipline and deep conviction he saw at the mosque, which he visited, he recalled later, "to make sure I would know these people, understand them, and be supportive of the things I believed in and not be supportive of others."

As always, the campus was alive with lectures and talks and panels that delved into all manner of hot topics, including race and the civil rights movement. One Harvard Law School grad, then practicing in Mississippi, told a small audience that fall of 1961 that voting rights constituted the most important frontier in civil rights and predicted "less violent resistance against this trend than against school integration." One wonders what he meant, given the violence inflicted on the Freedom Riders, whose activism had been going on for months by then. In addition that fall, another Law School Forum tackled the topic of "Liberalism in Dixie"; the magazine of the Catholic organizations on campus published a piece on discrimination in Boston; CORE's James Farmer spoke of the "new Negro" and warned of collusion between the NOI and the American Nazi Party; and the Young Democrats and the Liberal Union joined forces to raise money for the voting rights campaigns in the South. Even the Young Republicans got on board and set up a committee for "the advance of equal opportunity."

The fall's course offerings reflected a growing attention to race too, including a graduate seminar given by the renowned psychologist Dr. Gordon Allport, who'd been teaching at Harvard for over thirty years and whose book *On the Nature of Prejudice* was and is a classic on the topic. Bill Strickland, though still an undergraduate, was accepted for the seminar, and he joined some famous grad students, including C. Eric Lincoln and Atlanta's Whitney Young, who was in Boston for a few months before he took on the leadership of the National Urban League and began shaping it into a potent force in the civil rights movement. Strickland later wrote of this time that "the race question was all around me, motivating me to write my thesis on the Nation [of Islam]." As part of his responsibilities, Strickland also led discussion groups in Dunster House and Eliot House. More and more, he was becoming a trusted source of new and interesting ideas about race, especially for Jack Butler.

So it's not surprising that on a Sunday evening in late October, Jack headed over the river to Boston's Jordan Hall, the grand concert venue of the New England Conservatory of Music, which was hosting the weekly Ford Hall Forum that night. Started in 1908, the forum remains the oldest continuous free public lecture series in the country to this day, and it has never shrunk from contentious topics. Just that month, for instance, it had already featured future attorney general and key Watergate figure Elliot Richardson, speaking on "Corruption in Massachusetts"; the journalist and peace activist Norman Cousins enumerating the risks of the nuclear arms race; and Vance Packard, author of *The Hidden Persuaders*. The theme for October 29 was political extremism: C. Eric Lincoln would speak on the topic of the Black Muslims and Arnold Foster on the archconservative group of the day, the John Birch Society. Jack was not going to miss it.

His companion that night was a sophomore who had joined our social circle that year, a white guy from Detroit named John Hartman. He and Jack had Detroit in common, and they shared a passion for all ideas related to the civil rights movement. John had taken a freshman seminar on the topic of housing segregation (another of Gordon Allport's courses), and he had traveled over the summer to North Carolina, where he'd met the activist Robert F. Williams, who preached about Negro self-defense and would soon write his landmark book, *Negroes with Guns*. John had been in the audience when Malcolm X debated Walter Carrington back in March, and like Napoleon, Jack, and Lowell, he was energized by the power of Malcolm X to speak so plainly and forcefully about the truth of race relations in the United States.

When Jack and John arrived at Jordan Hall, they joined a long queue inching toward the main entry. Some eight hundred mostly white people would be in the audience. At around 7:45, the moderator, Dean Clarence Q. Berger of Brandeis, made a few announcements and introduced Foster, a representative of the B'nai B'rith Anti-Defamation League, who described the John Birch Society as similar in many of its aims to the Soviet Communists; both entities sought "to destroy, among other things, NATO, the United Nations and the vital American system of economic and military aid to underdeveloped countries." At a few minutes before 9:00, the moderator introduced Lincoln, who would speak on the Black Muslims. Lincoln had barely begun speaking when Berger interrupted him and announced, "There is no danger, but we have been asked to leave." The crowd began to file out of the building as the police started searching for the bomb to which a caller had alerted them. No bomb was found, and about half of the attendees reassembled at the nearby YMCA, where Lincoln continued his presentation. The caller was never identified, nor did he indicate why he'd made the threat or what, if any, organization he represented, and in its account of the incident the *Boston Globe* made no speculations about these questions.

The *Crimson* intimated, however, that it was the Black Muslims who had made the threat. Jack and John Hartman together countered this accusation in a letter to the editor that was published in the November 3 issue. They made their points effectively, demonstrating how the *Crimson*'s quotations from Lincoln's speech subtly insinuated that someone from the NOI temple in Boston was the likely source of the bomb threat. "We feel that this implication," they continued, "may not be so much a malicious attempt to malign an Afro-American protest movement as a poorly conceived article stemming from gross ignorance about the movement." Furthermore, they asked, given that Malcolm X had gone public with his evaluation of Lincoln's book as a "fair representation" of the movement, why would a Muslim want to stop him from speaking? The *Crimson,* they concluded, had, "through lack of understanding . . . put an Afro-American protest movement in a grossly unfair light." They then quoted an article in *Comment* written by James Laue, then a grad student and integration activist: "If the Muslims' goals were better understood and more clearly presented to the public, the defensiveness which often turns reform movements bitter would have no raison d'etre. There are already signs that the Muslims are anxious to be understood by a larger segment of society." That "larger segment" included the Harvard community.

That fall, in fact, one of my classmates and a fellow resident of Eliot House, Stephen Leff, was about to help along that understanding. As WHRB's director of public affairs, he was working on a radio documentary on civil rights that he would remember as "one of the high points of my time at Harvard." He used as the documentary's title a Louis X song, "A White Man's Heaven Is a Black Man's Hell," recorded in the late 1950s and released as a 45-rpm single with Louis X on the violin and as lead singer, backed up by several other Muslim men. In his former life as Gene Walcott, Louis X had been a first-rate entertainer. Handsome and gifted, he was "the musical pride of the West Indian immigrant community." Bill Strickland described him as "Boston and New England's own version of Harry Belafonte, playing the violin and performing calypso music under his stage name: The Charmer." When he turned to the NOI, he brought along his stage presence, his charm, and his musical talents.

Thus far, Leff had interviewed other civil rights leaders, including Whitney Young and the field secretary for the Student Nonviolent Coordinating Committee (SNCC), Bob Moses, who had told of the violence that voter registration activists had faced in Mississippi. Leff thought that it was no surprise that Negroes might be angry, militant, even on the verge of violence. What he needed now for his documentary, he thought, was an interview with Malcolm X. So he went to his friend Bill Strickland, who said that he would see what he could do. Before long, Leff found himself having tea with Louis X in Roxbury. They parted without having settled on a specific date, but it looked like Malcolm X was going to do it.

Days passed, and Leff kept working on the radio piece, until the phone rang. The caller was brusque: Malcolm X would be there to record an interview that afternoon, Wednesday, December 13. "Of course," Leff remembered, "we dropped whatever we were doing to be ready and arranged to have several people come to Studio B." Malcolm gave the interview, reiterating the key themes of the NOI and pulling no punches with regard to its condemnation of the white man and of the integrationist civil rights movement. He wound up and then, off microphone, turned to the group and said, smiling, "I guess I really sounded like a racist, didn't I?" The *Crimson* reporter who'd come to cover the event said that Malcolm "did not sound like a racist, but rather a deeply religious man, morally indignant over the treatment Negroes have received at the hands of white American Society." Like so many before them, the guys there were taken aback by his message, but won over by his magnetic presence.

The *Crimson* article quoted Jack Butler's comment on the radio broadcast: "Although few young Negroes can subscribe to the Muslim eschatology, they appreciate the articulate, forceful, and accurate Muslim description of the plight of the American Negro." Jack also indicated that he was about to start up a magazine for Harvard Negroes. Jack went to Strickland to see if there was any way to get Malcolm to come to Eliot House, and Strickland made it happen. Malcolm X took a meal at Eliot House with a rapt group of students. I was there. I didn't miss him this time.

Jack claimed a table that evening in a small room next to the main Eliot dining hall; the ethic at Harvard was that men sat wherever they chose, and it was an unwritten rule to welcome any and all tablemates. Jack and I and several other Negroes took our places, as did our white suitemate, Mason Morfit. I suppose we ate, but I can't even be sure of that. What I am sure of is that Malcolm X, speaking to us young boys, us "so-called Negro students" whom he had predicted would soon be making demands on Harvard and all of white society, was relaxed and warm, emphasizing things like self-respect and self-sufficiency with intelligence and conviction. He was also patient with our naïveté—even the "white devil" Mason remembered that "Malcolm was nice to me. I asked him a couple of dumb questions and he gave polite answers." We had the unparalleled thrill of seeing Malcolm X the man up close, still controversial and preaching separation, but with less hot rhetoric and more wit and even a kind of sweetness.

At one point, however, things heated up. Malcolm X, as he had done many times in the past, criticized Martin Luther King, not only as a leader but as a man. I've always believed that Malcolm made some comment about what Ralph Abernathy would many years later refer to as King's "womanizing," but that could be a trick of my memory. In any case, the one professor at the table was so outraged that he spat back that he had connections and could get Dr. King on the phone right now, and would Malcolm care to make his accusations to the man's face? Malcolm defused the situation with grace—this was, for heaven's sake, a man who had faced down the police and countless aggressive journalists—by assuring the professor that that was indeed the right thing to do, and that he would speak to King as soon as he had the chance to meet him, which he was very eager to do. We sat there on the sacred ground of Eliot House and watched a white professor taken down with quiet but steely authority by a Black man.

And then he was gone, I was Kent Garrett Jr. again, and I suppose I started breathing again. Maybe it was better that I hadn't gone to the March debate; I hadn't been ready then. But now, like many others before and after me, I was inspired not only by Malcolm's message but also by his sincerity and charisma, as well as energized by the pride, even arrogance, that was so tempered with humility. Was I transformed into a militant, enlightened race activist? No, but something shifted inside my young mind and soul.

A few days later, it was time to go home for the holidays. The end of a semester usually found me with a head cold and a self-indulgent case of exhaustion that would make me especially worthy of my mother's ministrations. Undaunted by the sleety mix coming down intermittently all morning, my dad drove up in the Pontiac and parked on Mass. Avenue right on time to take me back to Queens. I chucked a pillowcase full of dirty clothes in the back and slumped onto the front seat, looking forward to a nice long car-nap. I'd barely drifted off when Dad, now out of city traffic and securely on the Mass Pike, set about filling me in on the latest news of the family, this time about my younger cousins Vernard and Marcus, the sons of my mother's sister Aunt Mag, and her husband, Uncle Haskell. Uncle Hass had died a few years before, and my dad stepped in to help Aunt Mag with the boys. Ten-year-old Vernard, he told me, was a good boy who listened when Dad told him what was right and good, but his little brother, Marcus, was proving a trial to everyone.

They lived over on 135th Avenue, maybe a half-mile from us in Queens, and Dad went on and on about how he had asked Aunt Mag about bringing the boys over to Calvary Baptist—you know, to get them in with a good group of people who would watch over them. Aunt Mag had said, "Well, now, I don't know, maybe you should let them stay and do whatever they want to do," and Dad couldn't really argue with that, but he was going to keep on trying because those boys "need some guidance . . . like that boy from my Sunday School class whose father was killed in World War II and his mother remarried and . . ." (on through Massachusetts) . . . "you know I am good with directing people, I talk to young people all the time . . ." (the Connecticut border) . . . "so he wanted to get some sneakers, and she didn't want to buy the sneakers because she said that nobody wears sneakers but bums, ya see" . . . (the New York border) . . . "she said he is a different young man and what did you say to him, and I said well, now, that's confidential between us . . . he took that job as a runner up at DuPont."

More stories followed, and I dozed on and off during a few periods of silence, and then we were back in New York City, which lifted my spirits a little and brought up other things to talk about, like the grim season the Knicks were having, especially up against the Philadelphia Warriors with the amazing Wilt Chamberlain, how things were with my sometime girlfriend and next-door neighbor, Ellen, and her family, what we thought of this year's great-looking new Pontiac models, and why anybody would want one of those little Beetle cars.

I talked about my dinner with Malcolm X and passed off a few of Jack's and Bill Strickland's good lines as opinions I'd been mulling over thoughtfully for some time. Full of myself at nineteen, and with two years of Soc Rel under my belt, I showed off some of my new vocabulary, words like "socioeconomic" and "group consciousness." My father listened and drove, shifting his gaze left and right in the stop-and-go traffic as we neared our crossing of the East River on the brand-new Throgs Neck Bridge. He was concentrating on driving, I figured, and I could fit in another little snooze. But once we were safely on the other side of the bridge and in Queens, he started talking again.

*Kent's grandfather*
*John E. Garrett, 1964*

"Your granddaddy," he said, "he always told us to think for ourselves. And always listen, listen, listen, and don't say too much, and think before you speak." I knew this, he'd told me this so many times before. Maybe he expected me to say something, but hey, I was listening, listening, listening, and expecting a cascade of warnings about this Malcolm-X-Black-Muslim-Islam-Nation nonsense.

"But your granddaddy also taught us how we need to have support," Dad said. "He would scratch out a circle with his foot in the dirt outside our house down there in South Carolina, you know, on the farm—a circle about a foot, a foot and a half around. And he'd tell one of us to go stand in it, and you'd stand in that circle, and he says, 'Now, what if the wind would blow, what are you gonna do? You know you gonna fall over.' And Granddaddy would be the wind and push us around a little, and for sure we'd fall. Then he'd tell one of us to draw out a big circle, five or six feet, and he'd tell all seven of us brothers to go stand in that, and all seven of us would go stand in there. And he'd say, 'Now, you see, whatever happens, if the wind was blowing or there was anything coming'—and he'd come around pushing at one and then the other, and we'd grab on to each other and laugh—and he'd say, 'Now, look at the support you got.'"

# 7 *The Lost Negroes*

*Early in 2011, I learned that Jack Butler was in New York City for another* round of cancer treatments. Before I had a chance to visit or even call, he'd had major surgery. At ten years and counting, he was a champion survivor, and the support he got from the multiple myeloma community was encouraging, especially because they kept members supplied with hopes for various new advances in treatment. I let myself believe that this surgery would be one of those new therapies, and that I'd find him a little beaten up by the ordeal but on the road to recovery and release. We would reminisce some more, I might even do a brief interview on tape. But the nurse's face when I asked for his room number said that was not going to happen.

Jack's wife, Roni, and I embraced in the hallway. We did that little upbeat conversational dance that people do, she talking about Jack's spirit and sense of humor through this ordeal, thanking me for caring, and asking about my family, while I listened and made a few clumsy comments. Roni motioned me away from the door and explained that during the surgery the doctors had decided that it was best to just sort of patch him up and keep him comfortable. Jack had been hospitalized after calling Roni in distress only about a week or so before, and there at Vassar Brothers Medical Center in Poughkeepsie, surgeons found that the cancer had metastasized throughout his body and destroyed his stomach and intestines. Further care would be palliative.

I was relieved to see that Jack didn't look horribly thin or weak, just very tired. He gathered enough strength to project an attitude of "Goddamn, of all the awful luck." A gregarious guy with lots of friends, he must have had to put on that face many times. And he did it for me as he asked about my work and this book and said almost nothing about himself. Against the stark white of the bleached bedclothes, Jack looked blacker than he usually did, and somehow that felt very right. He died about three weeks later.

My reaction during this sad time was maybe a little callous, but I realized I'd better pick up the pace on this project before more guys were lost—or before I was, for that matter. I drove out to Freddy's. Seeing Fred would be a pleasure and a diversion, and the long drive would give me time to indulge my melancholy. Fred had moved from Minneapolis about an hour south, to the small town of Northfield. During the last few dark and lonely hours of the drive, I couldn't see much more than road and billboards, but I smelled that I was crossing dairy country and farmland. I breathed the night air off newly manured fields—not exactly everyone's idea of perfume, but it was sweet to me from my dairy farming days.

The next morning, Fred drove up to the door of my grim little motel in a brownish Hyundai that looked very well broken in. The passenger-side door shrieked as I opened it. "Just throw that in the back," Fred said when I picked up a metal cane from the front seat. It was a clear day, but as soon as we pulled out of the driveway, the windshield wipers started flapping; Fred muttered and switched them off, but when he did, all the door locks popped down and then right back up again. "Having a few electrical problems," Fred explained. "What do you want at a quarter of a million miles? But it's good enough for getting around town." I hoped so.

The little car was doing pretty well despite its age and quirks. Fred, on the other hand, was not. He'd gained weight, and what was this with the cane? He said that he was recovering from two falls that he'd taken in the winter. First he slipped on an icy pavement and broke some ribs; then, while the ribs were healing, he fell again and broke his right forearm. I had seen Freddy less than two years before, when his health was on the upswing—he was successfully losing weight and had his diabetes under control. He took me to his gym that time, and we had some good laughs as his personal trainer put him to work. Now, after the falls, he was just beginning to be able to grip things securely with his right hand. Inactivity had caused weight gain, and that in turn was aggravating his diabetes. During the two-day visit, we often returned to the topic of his health issues and fears, and given Jack's death and Fred's setbacks, I knocked wood for my own well-being.

Fred had lived in Northfield when he worked at Carleton College—from 1968 to 1976—and had dramatically increased the college's minority enrollment, an accomplishment that he considered his most significant life's work. He'd had good days there and held affection for the small town. It sits astride the Cannon River, with old grist mill buildings on the north side, and I swore I could smell grain in the air—Fred said yes, there was a cereal factory just beyond the old mills. On the other side of the river, we drove around a central square bordered by sturdy red and tan brick buildings that probably once sold dry goods, cigars, and nails and now housed cafés and gift shops.

We pulled up to the back of the house where Fred was living on a tree-lined street of modest older houses, and a young woman leaned out of an upstairs window and yelled hello. She was his roommate, he told me, a Carleton student. The bungalow-style house belonged to his first wife, who now lived in another city. For a few years she had rented it out to students at St. Olaf College in Northfield. In its day, the house must have been a showplace, full of beautiful Craftsman-style woodwork, but the student rentals had taken their toll—lots of things needed fixing. Fred shifted stacks of papers and books around so that we could sit and talk at the dining room table.

As he talked again about his health he revealed, as I had suspected, that he had fallen not only on the cold hard ground but also on cold hard economic times. He was living on Social Security alone, had no pension, and owed back taxes, such that they were garnishing his Social Security check, plus the bank was charging him a fee for the service. Fred had been president of The City,

Inc., a nonprofit, when I'd last seen him two years earlier, but it had closed. And he hadn't prepared well for retirement. He blamed himself, saying wistfully, "I wish I had realized as a young man that I would not always be young." Even when he was young, I reminded him, he had told Ron Blau that success was "doing what I want to be doing." He had to agree, adding, "I have worked for money doing things I would have done for nothing."

I drove back east with worries about Fred; inevitably, as my classmates aged and died, I found myself dwelling on the fact that something like a fall could tip that first domino that led to the end. But Fred and I had already been luckier than four other Black classmates whose lives had been far too short and fraught with troubles.

Travis Williams of North Carolina, whom Ron Blau had called "the most courageous rebel," who picketed Woolworth's and studied Williams's *Negroes with Guns* and said that he "valued freedom above all other possessions," had died at age twenty-seven. In the spring of 1968, Travis's friend Lance Morrow was out of town preparing for his wedding when he got a call from St. Vincent's Hospital in New York—Travis had had a stroke. Lance rushed downstate and found his friend looking scared. Travis called John Woodford from the hospital too and managed to summon an uneasy courage, joking, "How do you like this, Woodford? I bet I'm the youngest guy to ever have a stroke!" Shortly after Lance got home from the hospital, he called to check on his friend. His call was transferred to a nurse who briskly stated that Travis had suffered a second stroke and died.

Lance and John Woodford had both told me about Travis's drinking as a possible contributor to his death. When Travis arrived at Harvard, John remembered, he was "straight as an arrow"; he didn't smoke or drink. But something about being in college had given the two of them the idea that they ought to learn to smoke. They started out with "some horrible mentholated brand," and John gave it up pretty quickly. But, he recalled,

"Travis was more addictable. Once he started smoking, he graduated to Camels and Pall Malls and Lucky Strikes. And he got to like to drink."

*Lance Morrow, 1959*

Lance Morrow remembered the drinking too. "We were drinking buddies," he wrote me. "We had a hell of a good time together, were reckless and heedless." They once went out late at night on the frozen Charles River and "finished a bottle of Jim Beam bourbon and then went back to my suite at Dunster House and got out a .22 rifle I kept there and amused ourselves by firing it into the logs in the fireplace." Another night Lance was awakened by "a shower of window glass" as an empty quart beer bottle smashed through his window. Travis, who, Lance remembered, "had a very good throwing arm," had chucked the bottle up from the street four floors below as he called up, "Hey, Morrow, let's go over to Cronin's." And that's what they did. When they were both working in New York City in the midsixties, they were still putting it away. Lance opined in an email to me, "To be brutal about it, it was alcohol that killed him. He might have had a stroke even if he had not been a heavy drinker and smoker. But I doubt it. It was very serious, very destructive drinking. He was strong as an ox, but eventually it caught up with him."

Travis drank a lot at Harvard, and both John and Lance believed that he had some afflictions that ate at his peace of mind, but Travis had also studied hard (he graduated *cum laude*), made friends, gotten involved with civil rights and student council, laughed and fooled around and learned. Harvard was a good place for him—as Lance summed it up, "It was a very congenial universe to him." And despite his poisonous relationship with alcohol, Travis didn't spiral into a decline, but rather kept working and loving and living it up until the end.

Not so for Charlie Frazier.

*Charles Bernard Frazier, 1959*

Charlie tended to stay apart from the rest of us, and I found as I talked with my classmates that few had many memories of him. He was a tall, light-skinned, handsome guy, with a strong jaw and smooth, even features, who some thought looked like Sam Cooke. He came to Cambridge from Mobile, Alabama, where he graduated from Most Pure Heart of Mary High School. George Jones remembered Charlie from freshman year; they became, in George's phrase, "reasonably close friends." Nonetheless, George felt that he never really knew Charlie, never really understood why he was there at Harvard—as Charlie wasn't entirely sure himself. In his interview with Ron Blau for "Bright Shadows in the Yard" (Charlie was "Herb"), he told Ron that he was glad to be at Harvard, perhaps a little concerned that he was developing "too critical" a mind, but meanwhile "preparing to spend his life doing good for people." Ron noted Charlie's "calm manner" and called him "a retiring person," and that's exactly how I remember him. Charlie told Ron that he was proud of his segregated Catholic high school, where he had all white teachers but where, in Ron's words, "there was no uncomfortable awareness of race." When Ron posed the "reborn" question, Charlie chose Negro, like all of us, and commented that probably his friends would think he was crazy. The staff at his high school tried, he said, to prepare them for the "problems the students would face as Negroes" in the North. I would find out that it hadn't quite worked for Charlie.

As a sophomore, Charlie went to Lowell House and roomed with my Boys High friend and freshman roommate Ezra Griffith. That year, just when Charlie should have been getting settled and comfortable in his new place, he had a brush with danger. As the *Crimson* reported on September 27, 1960, a fire alarm at Lowell House "was turned in at 4:15 p.m., [and] firemen rushed to the fifth floor of M-entry and rescued unconscious student Charles B. Frazier '63. He was [carried] out past a crowd of 200 drawn by the sirens and taken to Stillman [Infirmary], where he was described as 'pretty badly off after incident, but now recovered.'" A firefighter put the blame on a lit cigarette left on a couch. Between the fire itself and the gawking onlookers, this must have been a dreadful day for Charlie.

For years, that was pretty much all I or any of my classmates knew about Charles Frazier, besides the fact that he died in 2001 in Capitol Heights, Maryland, which was reported in one of the class reunion books. At one point, Bobby Gibbs told me that Charlie had been mayor of a small town near Mobile, but nobody in that town had any memory of him, and I couldn't seem to find an obituary anywhere. I remembered, though, that many of those good Black southern schools were tight communities that tended to keep in touch and pull together, and so it was the alumni association at Most Pure Heart of Mary High School that gave me the break that mattered. First, after they sent me a list of Fraziers who were in the school at the time, I sent out four letters in hopes of hearing something. After a few weeks, I started making phone calls to follow up, until I reached Ireola Frazier, who told me that her husband, Walter, was on the case! Walter led me to Charlie's wife, so I wrote to her and waited. Finally, one evening during a dinner party, the phone rang. Typically, we would have let it ring, but for some reason I walked over and glanced at the name—Frazier. It was Lena, Charlie's widow.

She was gracious and happy to talk about Charlie, although the story was a sad one. One of the first things she said was "Harvard broke him. He couldn't take the pressure." He'd never been out of Alabama until he spent one unhappy summer at Phillips Academy to prepare for Harvard. By the time Charlie got to Harvard, however, he and Lena had married and were expecting the first of five children they would have together. Under those circumstances, Charlie must have felt enormous pressure to succeed. Lena said that to relieve the strain, he began drinking heavily, starting a lifelong addiction. The dorm fire, she said, started when he passed out from drinking with a lit cigarette in his hand. Harvard covered up his drunkenness, but suggested that he take the rest of the year off and come back the next fall. But he never did. A functional alcoholic, Charlie maintained a decent life and held down a good job, though separated from Lena and his kids for long periods. After seventeen years, they divorced. He had several strokes, none severe enough to put him down for very long, but enough to drag him down into depression, and in 2001 he shot himself.

We also lost Bill Exum long before his time. I recognized him in the freshman *Register*—a face that was all big smile and big glasses—but nobody seemed to know much about him either. Ron Blau noted in "Bright Shadows" that Bill "had very little contact" with "the other Negro freshmen," but was nonetheless "uncommonly enthusiastic about Harvard." Like me, he concentrated in Soc Rel,

*William Henry Exum, 1959*

but instead of slipping into the bottom quarter of the class, he graduated *cum laude.*

Harvard classes have elaborate reunions every five years, and a class book, called the *Anniversary Report,* is compiled and published concurrently. I was glad to see that someone submitted a few bits of information about Bill Exum for our class's twenty-fifth reunion book, which is where I found out that he died at age forty-four, in 1986. The university newspaper and the *Chicago Tribune* carried brief obituaries that said he predeceased his father, was ill for about three years before his passing, and left a wife and son. I was able to find their names and likely addresses and wrote letters to each of them, but received no answers.

Four years after Bill passed, Lowell Davidson died at the age of forty-eight. Aside from several classmates' vague and disjointed memories, for a long time all I could come up with about Lowell were rumors about his death: he had suffered a terrible lab accident that caused permanent damage . . . he was involved in Timothy Leary's psilocybin research at Harvard and went mad . . . he wound up homeless on the streets, ranting. None of the rumors, it turned out, was entirely baseless.

*Lowell Skinner Davidson, 1959*

Trying to learn Lowell Davidson's life story was the most difficult part of this project. My classmates remembered him from our years at Harvard, but nobody knew much about what happened to him before or after. My internet search hit first on the innovative jazz album that he recorded in 1965; it was still talked about as a classic and praised as "fresh and exciting" all these years later. I bought the album and listened. Not what you'd call "accessible," it was at times lyrical, at times discordant, always suggestive, crazy, and experimental, really far out. One reviewer said that Lowell "exhibits a loose, mercurial approach that will keep listeners guessing," and that was surely the effect it had on me. Although I didn't always hear it as music, it struck me as an extraordinary, almost mystical sound.

On the liner notes, I got a big surprise, and a lead: the other two-thirds of the Lowell Davidson Trio were Gary Peacock on bass and on drums . . . Milford Graves? This had to be the Milford Graves who was in my class at Boys High School in Brooklyn. The tall, light-skinned kid from the projects in South Jamaica who had a little goatee going for him. We rode the buses and subways together each morning. I'd get on at 140th Avenue and New York

Boulevard and save a seat for Milford, who would get on at 108th Avenue. He always had a pair of drumsticks in his hands and a beat in his head. He'd demonstrate by whapping on the seat back ahead of us, and I'd try my hand now and then. There's a particular beat he taught me that I still thump out on tabletops, the steering wheel, and sometimes even on my congas. Milford was an artist and an original thinker, and I couldn't help feeling a sort of psychedelic vibe in what he said and did; it was easy to imagine him being simpatico with Lowell Davidson.

I found Milford teaching at Bennington College in Vermont. He didn't know much about Lowell's early life, though he believed that it had been very different from ours in New York City, which he described as "that real stuff, that real tough street kind of thing—all the bad guys hanging on the corner, a lot of fighting going on, especially on the basketball court, and any time we did anything recreationally it was always to go against the rules." Lowell, he recalled, "was a different kind of guy, he just didn't mix." He was intellectual in a way that most of us in Queens just weren't, even those like Milford and me, who'd been singled out as capable. Milford was attracted to that deeper intellect, and Lowell respected Milford's music: "Hey, this guy is a pretty smart guy and he likes what I'm doing, so I must be doing something right."

Lowell was among thirty-two boys in the class of 1963 who came to Harvard from the renowned Boston Latin School. One of the preeminent public schools in the country, then as now, it was the only public school to serve as a perennial feeder school for Harvard—so much so that, before the 1950s, as many as half of Boston Latin grads went on to Harvard. Lowell had done well academically at Latin and was a star of the track team.

As a Harvard freshman, he was again a staple on the cross-country and track teams, starring first at the Knights of Columbus tourney: "Running anchor on the freshman mile relay team, [he] thrilled the crowd by gaining 45 yards on the Providence leader, and coming within a yard of victory." That year, he roomed with fellow athlete Hobie Armstrong and activist Frank Bardacke. Frank played freshman football and worked out with Hobie in the fall; later in the year he started going down to the track and working out with Lowell. Frank also went to Lowell's family home on Harrishof Street more than once, where he met a racially mixed crowd of young "bohemian music types." Another classmate remembered that Lowell was a "heartthrob that girls would swoon over." Harvey Hacker, who lived next door to Lowell, remembered marveling: "Many, if not most, Harvard freshmen are amazed to realize they were admitted by a colossal blunder of the Admissions Office and have no business being in the same room with the brilliant, accomplished, and confident classmates they meet. In my case, the instrument of this realization was Lowell Davidson." Harvey could still picture "that long frame, sitting sideways on an overstuffed chair reading a novel, while everyone else was studying frantically."

On the form we all filled out for the freshman *Register,* Lowell wrote "psychology" as his intended major, but at some point he switched to biochemistry. Friends remember Lowell as deeply interested in the subject of psychoactive drugs—maybe he had read Aldous Huxley's 1954 *The Doors of Perception,* in which Huxley described his mescaline experiences. The professor-researchers who would fling open those "doors of perception"—Timothy Leary, Huston Smith, and Richard Alpert—were already at Harvard when we arrived, and Andrew Weil, who would first align with and later rat on the others, was a member of our class. By the spring of our sophomore year, the Harvard Psychedelic Project was under way, and the researchers were testing the effects of psilocybin on themselves and their friends, in addition to prison inmates and Harvard grad students. Whether Lowell's interest in psychedelics came before or at Harvard, whether or not his actual use of drugs began then, whether he knew any of the key people, it's undeniable that at the time there was no better place to be than Harvard if you were interested in botanically induced alterations of consciousness.

Lowell seems to have taken a year off after freshman year. He may have spent too much time in that overstuffed chair and been invited to take a year to "find himself." A friend remembered him being absolutely reckless as he sped around on his bicycle, once seriously injuring a kidney in an accident, and so he may have taken a medical leave that year. When he reappeared as a track star, in our junior year and his sophomore year, the *Crimson* noted his "return" to the team with relief.

Lowell made his mark at Harvard not only as an athlete but also as a musician. Classmates remembered often seeing him at a piano—every house had at least one, and many had beautiful music rooms—playing apparently for himself, oblivious to whoever might stop by and listen. It was to music that Lowell would devote the rest of his short life.

After my last visit to Freddy, I was concerned about his health and finances. When I called again later, he told me he was "hanging on" with regard to both. In fact, he told me that he felt a whole lot better than the last time I'd seen him—no more cane, diabetes under control again. And true to form, he was by no means out of passion or out of ideas. Fred was working with a team of activists on a proposal to start nonprofit gardens and food stores for "food deserts," those places where decent groceries at decent prices simply don't exist. The nonprofit's gardens and stores would also provide jobs for people with criminal records. He had his fingers crossed on this one, and even before he was halfway through describing it, I did too.

Before I hung up, we reminisced about Jack. Fred remembered that as freshmen they were in a philosophy course taught by Rogers Albritton. Fred said that he and Jack would study together by "debating stuff. I didn't have a better grasp of it than Jack, but I was full of more shit. I could beat him in a debate, and then at some point, Jack would say, 'Okay, let's switch sides.' Then I would argue what he'd been arguing." Me too, I said, and we went quiet.

Fred had talked to Jack in the hospital a few days before he died. Jack couldn't talk at that point, but Roni said that he could listen and understand, so Fred said a simple "Good-bye and rest in peace."

Freddy and I decided that, although Jack didn't believe in heaven or hell, wherever he is if any of that is true, he's smiling, cajoling, debating, and challenging even the saints and angels to step back for a minute and play the devil's advocate.

# 8 *Rising Sons of Darkness: Spring and Summer 1962*

*Dr. Louis Fieser was halfway down the third blackboard, and I was still* copying from the end of the second, sketching out molecules with little hexagons and Cs and Hs and arrows. Just let him stop to light another cigarette and I'd be caught up . . . and . . . yes! He tapped one out, lit it up between the words of his last sentence, and paused to take a deep drag. I shook out my writing hand while he blew a long stream of smoke up toward the ceiling, and then he was off and running again, *clickety clickety.* I leaned forward, as if getting a little closer might somehow make it all more comprehensible.

Chem 20—a full-year organic chemistry course with lectures and labs and lots of memorizing and problems to work out—was kicking my ass. I'd pulled a B freshman year in Chem 1, so the previous fall I had started out optimistic. But it was hard, and when I went back for the second semester, I knew it would be an uphill climb from what I figured to be about a D+ average so far in the course—could I pull out a C? Fieser told every new group of hopefuls that it was in Chem 20 that he found out who the serious students were; the course was famous for sorting the men from the boys. One of the men was George Jones of Muskogee, who was sitting somewhere across the lecture hall, no doubt keeping up with Fieser and understanding everything. By his own admission a grind, George was in his element in a science class, and he came into our second semester junior year feeling confident enough to spare the time to high-jump for the track team.

George and I were back for round two of what some boys called "Fieser's Folly," but not everyone was. One of the dropouts was Fred Gardner, a spirited kid from New York City whom I'd enjoyed sitting next to the previous fall. Gardner dropped the course after a few minutes of the first class that February, when Fieser casually mentioned that he had invented napalm to help with the "problem" of gasoline running off and evaporating when the military sprayed it on buildings—napalm made it stick. Gardner, a peace and disarmament activist, got up and walked out, never to return. For the rest of his life he would remember this as the moment when he decided to be a writer and not a scientist.

Fieser wound down at last, and I shuffled together my pages of notes, wondering whether I should have taken Fred's route. With Chem 20 and an icy wind behind me, I trudged back to Eliot in the weak winter light with my head down. So many kids had motor scooters to zip around campus and Cambridge—maybe in the spring I could figure out a way to buy a cheap used one? The walk over to Eliot House took me past Thayer Hall South, my old pal from what seemed like a very long time ago.

"Hey, Spook!" I snapped my head up and looked around. "Hey! Negro!" No shy nod of brotherhood from this Black guy, but a full-throated, attention-getting whoop, along with a wide grin that challenged me to look up, look around, be conspicuous. This was the man we would come to call Kilson—just Kilson. At the time Martin Luther Kilson was a new appointee to the Center for International Affairs, but he would eventually pile up a string of "firsts" as a Black professor at Harvard College, and an outspoken one at that.

I discovered that Kilson was alive and kicking in 2010 (and kicking turned out to be an apt figure of speech in his case). So I went up to see him at his home in Lexington, not far from Cambridge. By that time, I had conducted dozens of interviews, in person and on the phone, and they'd been interesting, genial, and easygoing, so I had no reason to believe that this one would be different. It was interesting, all right, but genial? Easygoing? Not exactly.

*Martin Luther Kilson Jr.*
© SARAH PUTNAM

I asked to meet Dr. Kilson in the morning so I could get on the road and be home before dark, but Kilson insisted that he couldn't do it until one o'clock at the earliest. When I pulled up to the house, his wife, Marion, offered tea and apologies—Kilson had gone out to a quick-copy place to have some things printed. His typical schedule, she explained, was to stay up writing until almost dawn, and then sleep until at least noon. Just as Marion got me settled, the screen door squeaked open and Kilson bustled in looking like nothing less than the classic absent-minded professor. He upended a plastic bag, spilled what looked like a ream or two of paper onto the long dining room table, and began shuffling pages around to produce two thick piles, muttering to himself and scratching notations on a couple of the pages. He thrust one pile into my hands without explanation. I realized later that I had a copy of his draft manuscript titled "Black Intellectual as Leftist and Freethinker: Martin Kilson's Intellectual Odyssey."

Marion set a plate in front of the "Leftist and Freethinker," and he ate (slowly) and talked (fast) for the next two hours or so, sometimes getting so excited that he could barely spit out his words and instead spit out his breakfast. Each of the few questions I was able to squeeze in was followed by a long discursive soliloquy, which frequently included phrases like "the absolutely intellectually academically scholarship-wise first-class Black professional personalities." He dropped names and places and dates left and right, often stopping to spell out last names so that I'd get them right. An impressive feat for a man pushing eighty, I thought. Some of the time he talked about me in the third person, as if I weren't in the room, and at other times he looked piercingly at me and sputtered things like "Well, Garrett, that's where you're wrong," or "That, Garrett, is not a useful question to ask." I was starting to feel like I was being scolded by my father.

Kilson came to Harvard to take up doctoral studies in political science in 1953. As far as he could determine, at the time there were about fifteen Black undergrads among the approximately five thousand Harvard and Radcliffe undergrads, and twenty in the combined graduate schools. He told me that in those days "the reach of Jim Crow—of typical everyday American racism—was robust enough . . . to ensure that America's second-class racist marginalization of Black Americans applied to Black students at Harvard." It was just a little over a year after the cross was burned on campus. He said to me, "All of us, as you know, Garrett, those of the first Negroes who came through the door, we experienced those things, and we knew how to bob and weave and bite our lips and grind our bloody teeth and move on."

Nonetheless, there were Negro students who rose to high positions in the 1950s—one as president of the Glee Club, for instance, and another as a member of the *Crimson* editorial board. Kilson was sharply critical of those he labeled "status-pretenders," whose "crass status maneuvering patterns . . . reflected the Booker T. Washington accommodationist mindset"; among his observations was that "more often than not, what appeared to be friendship-ties by Black students to White status-pretender networks were in essence forms of a Black-mascot syndrome—mascot-type deferential relations." In contrast, "a small group of activist-oriented undergraduate and graduate Black Students at Harvard fashioned themselves into a viable activist network," which included Kilson himself and Walter Carrington, who would share the dais with Malcolm X that March evening seven years later. It also included many "leftist White students," including some from other campuses, like Michael Walzer of Brandeis, who would go on to activism that included EPIC.

After Kilson completed his PhD in June 1959, he was awarded a Ford Foundation Foreign Area Study Fellowship and went to West Africa for eighteen months to study nation-state development. If he hadn't done so, Kilson says in his "Odyssey," "*I would have almost certainly joined Robert Moses and his civil rights activist colleagues*" (emphasis in original). He continued by saying that he doubted he'd have been offered positions at Harvard had he taken the activist route. In any case, when he returned to the United States at the end of 1960, he would be appointed a research associate, then a lecturer, then the first Black lecturer, the first Black tenure-track professor, and eventually the first Black tenured professor at Harvard College.*

Kilson said flat out that he didn't remember me at all, so I asked him about some of my classmates. Yes, he remembered Lowell Johnston, he said, and Jack Butler, John Woodford, and someone named Travis. When I mentioned that John Woodford thought perhaps our studies at Harvard had sharpened our critical thinking about race, Kilson went off on an animated riff, the first shot of which was: "That's BS, and you can tell Woodford that Martin Kilson says so." Even rereading the transcript of the interview, I couldn't quite figure out why he thought that idea was BS. Despite the best efforts of a crack transcriptionist, the pages came back studded with "[unintelligible]"; enough of it is readable, though, to reveal the depth and breadth of Dr. Kilson's knowledge of Black history and the keenness of his analyses. I came away with an admiration for the man, but also a sense that in some ways he was a conflicted Black man, torn by the contradictions he felt between being a lifelong resident of the ivory tower and simultane-

* Not the first in the university, but the first at the college. There had been Black instructors and professors in the various grad schools for some time.

ously its bitter critic. I also learned that over the years Kilson had from time to time flung invective-flecked criticism at most of his colleagues, including Randall Kennedy, Henry Louis Gates, and Cornel West. Woodford and I were in good company as objects of his impatience.

When I brought up the idea of our admission as an early form of affirmative action, Kilson had no doubts and much to say: "It's one of those absolutes of history, the dialectical history of the way in which racial dynamics impinge upon American society. An *individual* intervenes in an old established white supremacist institution . . . and takes white people in a new direction. I knew that individual quite well because I spent a year helping to manage that initiative in 1958. His name is John Monro, M-O-N-R-O." Kilson paused to point out that he wasn't talking about US president John Monroe. (What did Kilson take me for? And besides, that was James Monroe.) Dean John Monro, Kilson continued, was "a progressive, upper-middle-class WASP," and one of his early initiatives was to "find a way to expand the presence of Black kids at Harvard College." Did this initiative come out of the goodness of Monro's own heart, or was the college maybe under some pressure? "No, no, no! No pressure," Kilson scolded me. "It came out of—okay, to use the everyday expression, 'goodness of heart,'" he admitted. An "everyday expression" like "goodness of heart" didn't seem to feel right in his mouth, Kilson being a man of many, preferably multisyllabic, words. But he made his point and in turn mine.

Monro had solicited Kilson's help in finding promising boys from Black colleges in the South, so surely some of my classmates, like Bobby Gibbs or Travis Williams or Charlie Frazier, were among Kilson's "finds."

Monro was not the only white liberal who played a part in our arrival at Harvard. Another was Felice Nierenberg Schwartz, a wealthy white Smith College graduate who joined forces with Harlem minister James Robinson to form the National Scholarship Service and Fund for Negro Students (NSSFNS, usually

*John Usher Monro,*
*dean of Harvard College*

pronounced NISS-fins) to "increase and broaden opportunities for Negro students in interracial colleges." The two assembled an interracial and influential board of directors, including John U. Monro. Rather than attack the policies and practices of colleges, NSSFNS decided to flood them with qualified Black applicants. To achieve that, they would make sure that talented Black students were well informed and well prepared. A team of counselors scouted for prospects and made sure that those prospects had plenty of information about their options, step-by-step advising through the preparation process, access to a good prep school if needed, and help in finding a good "fit" in higher education.

Fred Easter's parents went to NSSFNS on the advice of some bridge club friends after Fred's guidance counselor had told them that their son was probably not "college material." NSSFNS told Fred to take the Scholastic Aptitude Test (SAT). He did, and he scored well. His scores were sent to his high school, where nobody even knew that he had taken the test, let alone done well. He remembered being in a class one day when the head of the math department came to the door and motioned him to come to his office. "Where have you been?" the teacher asked. Fred scratched his head. "Well, I've been right here." Although Fred no doubt would have been admitted to many different colleges at that point, his NSSFNS counselor had another suggestion. The organization's director of counseling at the time was Lois Rice, who had graduated from Radcliffe just a few years earlier. A first-generation American whose parents had emigrated from Jamaica, Rice would go on to a long career in higher education and become known as the "Mother of the Pell Grant" for her tireless work to create the Basic Educational Opportunity Grant Program, the federal higher education subsidy. Rice had a different idea for Freddy. He would turn sixteen just a few weeks before high school graduation, and she suggested that he "recapture those two years" by going to a quality prep school before college. Fred thought that Rice was a wonderful person—"If she had told me to go stand in a burning building I would have done that." Rice arranged for Fred to spend his next two years in prep school at The Gunnery in Washington, Connecticut. By the time she recommended the school to Fred, as he recalled, they were looking for Black students. As it turned out, Fred would be the only one there. And as NSSFNS hoped, he did gain facility with the kinds of tasks and questions he would face in college, plus he got a taste of what life with so many whites would be like. Then NSSFNS stepped in again to be sure he had support in applying to and paying for Harvard.

From inside and outside Harvard, people were working on getting us there. I was surprised to learn that some of us suspected it at the time. Ron Blau wrote in "Bright Shadows" that among us "there are quite a few who believe that being Negro was a definite influence in favor of their acceptance. Most thought that this is true solely because the administration is quite aware of the world situation of today and is trying to do its part to help." The key person in the administration was John Monro, that "progressive upper-middle-class WASP" who called on Kilson for help, the same man who had felt compelled to warn EPIC picketer Tony Robbins of the pitfalls of being a protester, but who admitted that, were he in Tony's shoes, he would definitely go ahead with the demonstration. The same guy who would soon leave his cushy job at Harvard to teach struggling students at a southern Black college.

Monro was also the man who convinced Wesley Williams to come to Harvard. Wes had told me that while he was still deliberating about where to go to college, he'd been summoned to a meeting on the Taft campus. He figured he'd be meeting with a local alum or two from the local Harvard Club, who traditionally volunteer to recruit and interview applicants. Entering the room, Wes saw a dark-haired man with a narrow face, sharp features, and bushy dark eyebrows over intense and friendly blue eyes. He wore gray slacks, a button-down shirt, tie and tweed jacket, cordovan shoes, and, Wesley noticed, mismatched socks. The man shook Wesley's hand briskly and introduced himself—John Monro, dean at Harvard College. He did something that would never have been done at Taft in a meeting like this: he doffed his jacket and loosened his tie. He opened a window. He liked fresh air, Monro explained. Wes found the informality, if not the cold air, refreshing, and as they talked he felt increasingly comfortable. Wes didn't remember exactly what they talked about, but by the end of the conversation he had decided to go to Harvard.

John Monro died just a few years before I started the journeys that would lead to this book; I would love to have met him. He came to Harvard in 1950, but it was his leaving that made news; his *New York Times* obit bore the headline "John U. Monro, 89, Dies; Left Harvard to Follow Ideals." Apparently choosing to leave a deanship at Harvard is that rare, and to leave to do unglamorous work in a small southern Black college with underprepared college freshmen is nigh on unfathomable. Monro had pursued his ideals at Harvard too, though: he really did set out to "increase diversity," before the phrase had been invented, and in order to achieve that he was implementing "affirmative action," before that term was being used.

*Fred Lee Glimp Jr.,*
*dean of admissions and financial aid,*
*Harvard College*

Another diversity advocate was Fred Glimp, whose obituary named him a "Harvard legend." In our day he was director of admissions and financial aid and he too fought hard against the faction who wanted to simply attract the biggest brains. I had the privilege of meeting and interviewing Glimp before he died; his *Crimson* obit describes him as having an "open and unassuming manner," and I found him exactly that way on the blazing July day when we met in Cambridge. When I asked why "so many" of us had been admitted to our class, he told me simply, "It happened because we started working on it." John Monro and he and a few others had simply made a decision to get out and "beat the bushes" for good Negro candidates. Glimp caught himself up when he said that, hearing the echoes of an old racial slur in the phrase, and suggested, "Well, we also beat the urban sidewalks." And why did they do it? From a belief that it was "the right thing to do. It wasn't right that we weren't getting a fair number of Black students, so everybody agreed we ought to do that." Not quite "everybody," Glimp admitted: "There were obviously a few people who didn't feel that way, but they weren't willing to fight with us, or if they did, we wouldn't listen to them. There were just people who for personal reasons weren't sure that this part of the population had anything unusual to offer us."

That they were able to pull this off was all the more remarkable given that Harvard was in the midst of a long and acrimonious fight over admissions, which is described in detail in Jerome Karabel's 2005 book, *The Chosen: The Hidden History of Admission and Exclusion at Harvard, Yale, and Princeton.* At Harvard in the 1950s, there were those among the faculty who objected to the admissions advantage afforded local Boston boys, athletes, the sons of wealthy families, and the sons of alums. While that faction was insisting that Harvard select only top academic performers, the post–World War II generation of admissions officers was aiming for a wider variety of boys in each class. They specifically tried to find candidates from outside New England and the Mid-Atlantic and boys with unusual interests or experiences, even if they weren't at the top of their class. Additional pressure to admit only the brightest of the bright came from Cold War fears that the Soviet Union was getting ahead of the United States in space and military advances; therefore, the reasoning went, Harvard should emphasize preparation and talent in science and math over all else and not worry about decorating the class with boys who could play the trombone or wrestle cattle—or, conceivably, with Negroes. Nonetheless, people like Monro kept working behind the scenes, "actively (if quietly) seeking to increase the number of African-American students on campus." Glimp told me that despite the controversy, "we never got great opposition to our efforts." In the days after the earlier, quieter efforts at recruiting Blacks, the opposition must have given way even more, since by the time we were seniors Glimp, now dean of admissions, would announce forthrightly that the college had undertaken a "talent search" for "applications from Southern Negroes."

According to Karabel's sources, between 1865 and 1941, Harvard enrolled an average of two Blacks a year; between 1941 and our year, that figure jumped to about six a year. And then came our time, with the unprecedented increase to eighteen.

Freddy speculated that Harvard might have been planning ahead for the centennial of the Emancipation Proclamation, but there was a more predictable explanation: money. Harvard got $50,000 (more than $400,000 in today's currency) to spend on efforts to enroll more boys from low-income families. The money, as Karabel details, came from the Taconic Foundation and wasn't specifically for Black students but nonetheless helped many of us, even providing some of us, like Freddy and Bobby, with a year or two of prep school between high school and college. Karabel notes that "between 1959 and 1961, ten low-income (family income under $5,000) black students entered Harvard." The nickname for the project was "The Gamble Fund," and one of their "gambles" was me.

As the spring semester of 1962 wore on, it didn't look like that gamble was necessarily going to pay off. Besides part two of Chem 20, I was in semester two of an intro-level course in physics that was equally tough. I was still doing my job over at the Educational Development Council, and I'd taken on an additional job down in Eliot House's basement Grille, where guys could go for late-night sustenance and companionship. Several nights a week from ten until midnight, I'd tie on a white apron and take orders: fry a burger, slide a slice of pie onto a flimsy paper plate, punch down the 20¢ and 5¢ keys that flung the cash register drawer open with a *ka-ching,* take the money, slam the door shut, and move on to the next guy. Besides the hourly pay I sorely needed, I could have a burger myself, talk to guys, and sometimes read a little.

Looking back on that spring, I can see the many signs that were right there on campus that the sixties were under way: TOCSIN, the antiwar and disarmament group, was one of the largest and most vocal groups on campus; Timothy Leary coined the term "psychedelic" and threw the conventional psychological world for a loop; folk concerts by the Weavers, Theodore Bikel, the New Lost City Ramblers, and Joan Baez popped up among the usual classical and pop options; and Lamont Library announced that it would be open to women for the summer. For me, just keeping up was a challenge. I was never one to waste energy worrying, so I just tried to keep focused and move forward. I had enough to do without tackling a twenty-four-page questionnaire about being Negro.

Lucky us, we again were to be the stars of an undergraduate Soc Rel research paper: "The Rising Son of Darkness: A Study of the Negro at Harvard." The budding sociologist this time was a year ahead of us, David R. Branon, class of 1962, whose 145-page thesis would contribute to a *summa cum laude* notation on his diploma that June. Branon had been working on his paper for almost two full years, starting with a pilot study during the 1960–61 school year. His adviser was Dr. Thomas Fraser Pettigrew, the social psychologist whose course on racism would be called "the academic stronghold of the civil rights movement." Pettigrew, a native of Richmond, Virginia, had come to Harvard to study racial prejudice under the author of the classic text on that topic, Gordon Allport. Pettigrew would continue to study the subject for the remainder of his long career, earning prizes and medals all over the world and publishing prodigiously. When Branon was working with him, Pettigrew was just four years out of his doctoral program and two years into his career as a Harvard professor. Sitting in class, Branon remembered, he would sometimes ponder what it would be like to be one of the few Negroes there at Harvard. So the idea for his paper was born, and once again we would be studied, categorized, analyzed, interpreted—and given a clever name. The year before we'd been "bright shadows"; now Branon labeled us "sons of darkness." Each author was making the spurious connection between our darker color and some kind of somber mystery. And each name, too, suggested that we were outliers, rare specimens of an alien tribe, which I suppose was true in some ways.

Branon's paper is an impressive piece of work for an undergraduate. He described a long process of developing the initial questionnaire, piloting the study, testing questions for reliability, and refining and expanding the questionnaire. He enlisted the aid of a couple of Negroes with whom he was already friends, including Bobo Gray and Booker Bradshaw, who helped him refine questions and wordings. In the end, the thing was gargantuan: the study had forty-eight Likert-Scale items (the familiar 1–5, from "strongly disagree" to "strongly agree"); over forty multiple-choice questions (many with one or more subquestions with spaces for "If yes, explain"); and dozens of other types of items, like rankings, sentence completions, and the like. One page required us not only to give our opinion but also to provide (or guess) the opinions of others ("my parents," "Negro Harvard men," "upper- and middle-class whites," "Harvard administration," and so on) about various "racial organizations." A "matching" page asked us to pair a long column of names and events from Black history with their correct descriptions; another section required us to evaluate thirty-three occupations as being "excellent, good, average, below average, or poor." Then there were three vignettes of racially charged interactions between characters, each with several open-ended questions to answer, and finally a couple of pages of demographic data. Branon hand-delivered a copy of the questionnaire to forty-two Harvard Negroes, and with the exception of the freshman respondents, he interviewed each boy when he went back to pick up the completed questionnaire. He must have had a mountain of data!

But what was he actually trying to find out? I'm not quite sure, and it seems to me that he wasn't either. This is, after all, the intellectual exercise of an undergraduate, an enthusiastic gatherer of data, a young man apparently genuinely curious about his Negro classmates. Branon punched cards and ran them through the IBM, submitting the data to an astonishing number of statistical manipulations, figuring percentages, testing for statistical significance, and using the data to classify us. Among Branon's findings were that Harvard Negroes placed "a high value on education," for the most part didn't think Harvard was a hotbed of discrimination, were inclined to seek out and get to know their fellow Negro students while avoiding looking "clannish," and "has not forgotten that he is colored."

Like Ron Blau's paper, Branon's offers some real insights about us that had little to do with his intentions at the time. For one thing, I think it shows that we were nice guys to submit ourselves to the ordeal—Branon himself said that it took several hours to do the questionnaire, and then there were the interviews. Some of us even told Branon that it had been "fun." Others told him that they hadn't thought about such issues before completing the questionnaire, and it's likely that the experience provoked some good conversations.

I'd found a copy of Branon's paper in the Harvard Archives, and skimming the table of contents, I was excited to see that pages 61 through 98 would deliver a chapter titled "A Qualitative Look at Negro Harvard Men"—four case studies. Good old ambitious Branon! I got to page 60, turned the page expectantly, and saw page 99; someone had removed the case studies, probably for confidentiality reasons. So I went looking for David R. Branon and discovered that he was retired, living in Florida, and writing crime mystery novels. And he still had the paper. He sent me a copy of the excised pages, the case studies that described in detail four of his "subjects," each one illustrative of one style of race-consciousness.

As with "Bright Shadows," I needed to decode the pseudonyms, and in this case it was more difficult, except for "Alex," the student Branon chose to illustrate the "impatient" Negro: that was Jack. As Branon characterized him, Jack was "the most concerned and involved Harvard Negro in terms of the peculiar problems which the Negro in America faces in this day and age," and Branon opined that "if there is such a thing as the 'new Negro,' perhaps [Jack] qualifies as the 'newest Negro.'" Here, again, in taking the time to really talk to us, Branon got on to something, discerning a nuance that was beginning to shape our identities and recognizing Jack as out in front of the curve for our class. Jack told Branon of his commitment to leadership, his "moral obligation to help his brothers," his frustrations with the pace of change, and his conviction that the scope of racism in the United States was both wider and deeper than whites knew or were owning up to. And he talked of racial pride—what Branon characterized as "love of his race"—of a need for awakening, and of the growing role of militancy. Jack told Branon without hesitation that the group he most strongly believed in was the Black Muslims, and that he was an advocate of Robert Williams's doctrine of violence for self-defense. Jack, Branon said, took no pains to hide his "bitterness and anger" and was outspoken about his hostility.

In closing his sketch of "Alex," Branon spoke of Jack's intention to start a publication for campus Negroes and to try to awaken his fellow Negro students to the cause of liberation. Branon commented that "Alex" was held in a "high degree of respect and admiration" by the rest of us, quoting an unnamed boy who said, "When I first came here I didn't have many or any opinions about the problem. Then I met Alex and got to know him in the House. By talking to him, and listening to him, I was able to form a lot of opinions. As a matter of fact, most of my views on this racial issue are the direct result of my association with Alex." I don't know for sure that that guy was me, but I think it must have been.

Jack came down to the Grille most nights when I was working. He'd struggled with his weight since adolescence and was often on some kind of diet (once it was an ice cream diet, no kidding), so the Grille wasn't the ideal place for him. Maybe he kept talking to avoid eating. I'd look up to get the next guy's order and there was Jack, leaning on the chest-high counter and chatting to the guy in line, waiting for me to have a minute. If it was a busy night, he might just entertain me with a little gossip, tease me about some girl, or throw around some ideas for the weekend. And if I had anything to talk about, he would listen, and he would listen like I was the only person on earth.

One night in late winter, Jack came in and flashed a copy of the *Crimson* at me. All weekend, nobody had seen John Hartman—our friend from Kirkland House who had gone with Jack to hear the Black Muslim talk on the night of the bomb scare—because he had been arrested at a sit-in down in Maryland. He'd gone down with a group organized by the Northern Student Movement, was arrested for trespassing, got bailed out by the NAACP, and was back by Sunday night. Jack read me John's remarks dramatically: "Morally, I am right. And I don't feel badly about the arrest because the law is morally unjust." Hartman was convicted of the charges, but the conviction would be eventually overturned by a higher state court. When I spoke with John Hartman more than fifty years later, he would tell me that he "majored in civil rights" at Harvard.

Our admiration for John and other white liberal civil rights activists was strong and sincere. At the same time, though, the lessons from Malcolm X were pushing hard on one of the pillars of our confidence in the conventional civil rights movement: the idea that whites could be trusted over the long haul to work for our best interests.

On my slower nights down at the Grille, Jack parked himself with both forearms on the counter and held forth. He could be like a locomotive, starting off at a slow pace, picking up speed, and then just cruising, with animated finger pointing, ironic laughter, arguing both sides, playing his own devil's advocate. Jack talked about organizing at Harvard, about making our presence known through a Black magazine or organization, he talked about something that felt broader than eating at a Woolworth's lunch counter, and he talked about Africa—not just as some kind of "awakening" world that everyone else had to contend with, but as our homeland. Many a hamburger was burned as I leaned over the Grille counter, getting my brain around all of this. I don't think I had ever really thought of myself as African. Africa was "over there," and I was from Brooklyn, and before that from South Carolina. And before that I was from . . . well, more South Carolina, from people and places I knew little about, and although I must have known where "slaves" came from, I hadn't made any personal connections to it all.

Some of Jack's thinking about Africa had been influenced by a growing friendship with a Ghanaian student, Ayi Kwei Armah, known to us as "George"; before the end of the decade he would become famous as a writer and social critic.* Born in what was

---

* Various other spellings/versions of his name were used at this time: Ai Kwei Armah, George A. K. Armah, Aryeequaye Armah, and Aryee Quaye Armah.

then the British colony of Gold Coast, Armah had a youth that spanned Ghana's long struggle for independence and the early chaotic days as the first African nation to gain sovereignty. He was from a well-off family and went to good mission schools and then to the first-class Prince of Wales College and School in Achimota, not far from Accra, Ghana. There, ironically, he became much more familiar than many of us American Negroes were with the upper-class British style of schooling and the kind of campus life that we'd found at Harvard. He was a brilliant and creative student at a time when some American schools and colleges were getting on the "Africa has come of age" bandwagon and looking for "suitable boys" from the continent. Groton prep school had been casting about in Ghana for a couple of years when they came upon Armah, and they brought him in as their first African student; at Groton, he reportedly "shattered the rigid thought structures of nearly everyone who entered into conversation with him." Presumably, one of those "rigid thought structures" was the assumption that an African boy couldn't succeed at highly selective and competitive Groton. He not only succeeded, however, but excelled, as a student and an athlete, and especially as a writer: his three essays published in the school publication put Ghanaian and pan-African issues in global perspective and quite possibly shattered, or at least bent, some "thought structures" in that way too.

After his *magna cum laude* year at Groton, he went back to Ghana for a short time. In the fall of 1960, he joined Harvard's class of 1964 as a literature major and got into the swing of campus life. He played soccer and made friends, writing later that, "from my first minute in America I'd been treated courteously and kindly," and calling his time in the United States "an idyllic spell of youth." He would later write, too, that his year in Cambridge changed his life. It was at Harvard that he began to think more seriously about what his life's work might be, and "my centre of interest shifted from the contemplation of arrangements of symbols, images, and words, to a scrutiny of the arrangements of the social realities buried under those words, images, and symbols." One of those social realities was that "if we Africans were to rise from the abyss of exploitation and contempt, we would be obliged to do so against murderous opposition from the West, America in the lead." It's no surprise that Jack found in Armah a like-minded soul and a man to pay attention to.

The "Africa coming of age" train had passed through Harvard too, spreading the notion that Africa, now presumably being ushered out of childhood by its benevolent colonial parents, might be a suitable subject for academic study. Added incentive came from the perennial fear that Harvard might seem to be behind the times; a *Crimson* survey of seventy-seven higher education institutions showed that while there were slim pickings for the study of Africa, many colleges nonetheless were ahead of Harvard, including (shudder) Yale! Harvard already had graduate programs in the study of East Asia, the Middle East, and, of course, the Soviet Union. In 1960, the first two courses on Africa appeared in the catalog, and the college began to at least talk about the possibility of a formal program in African studies, announced as appropriate for "some future date." It was far too early to get going, though, said the college, since the program would need time to find qualified faculty. One faculty member was more forthright: "Only in the last five years did we realize that Africa had a history."

Counterbalancing Harvard's push to keep up with the Ivy League Joneses was its equally persistent concern for rigor, for circumspection, and ultimately for control. Training for potential Peace Corps volunteers had brought a teacher of Swahili to campus the previous summer, but an appeal to develop a credit-bearing course was denied. The college had no way to evaluate the course, they said, and the course would have no academic home until an Africa department could be created; that was surely going to happen, but it still "await[ed] a proper man around whom to build." Besides, said a dean, the college "can't give credit to every project which students proposed, no matter how constructive it may be."

Meanwhile, Harvard had joined a multi-college project to bring more African nationals to study at the United States on scholarship. One of the first to come was our classmate Chuma Azikiwe.

Another few Nigerians would arrive in the fall of 1961, perhaps most notably the Olympian and soon-to-become Harvard sports legend Chris Ohiri, who scored thirty-six goals in nine games on the freshman soccer team and went on to glory not only in soccer but also in track and field. It was inevitable that some of the African nationals would encounter some of us, but according to Bobo Gray, early encounters didn't necessarily foster a sense of brotherhood. As he remembered it, the African boys tended to look down on American Negroes. John Woodford also remembered that sense of haughtiness at times, and he reminded me that many of those first African boys who came across the world to study were the sons of the high-born. Maybe they had good reason to feel superior too, since the competition for one of those US scholarships was much fiercer than it was for admission to Harvard; the boys who made the cut may well have been far superior to many of us academically. But they were also boys, and they laughed and played and studied and goofed off and played soccer and ran track more or less as we did. So our paths crossed, and we learned about each other's lives. But some of the things they found out about our country weren't so nice.

In May 1962, Chuma was out late one evening in Cambridge, walking along the street at about 2 a.m., when he was approached by two police officers who asked what he was doing and demanded identification. Chuma paused and insisted that he was doing nothing—after all, Harvard boys had been roaming Cambridge's streets late at night for over three hundred years—and turned to walk away. "Come here, you prick," said one officer. "Get in the car, you son of a bitch." They grabbed Chuma and arrested him for loitering. Like African diplomats subjected to police harassment in and around Washington, Chuma was appalled and infuriated, and down at the station, once the police saw his ID, they suddenly went all courteous and released him. A behind-the-scenes international incident ensued that eventually involved diplomats and politicians from both countries. It was settled in the spring: the apology of the police was accepted, and that was that.

In the spring of 1962, I was still trying to climb the steep and slippery slope of organic chemistry. Using the laws of chemical bonding and reactions to solve complex problems felt like working in a foreign language, and I was never adept with languages. Between my two jobs and all the time I was spending studying organic, my grades in physics were suffering. I would end up with Ds in both courses—a passing grade but not, by Harvard's calculations, "satisfactory." I needed 17.0 "courses passed" to graduate, but that had to include 11.0 "satisfactory grades," and those Ds didn't make it. I'd have to go to summer school, which meant no summer job plus the extra expenses of tuition and board for six weeks in Cambridge. To make matters worse, in February summer school tuition had been bumped up by a hefty 20 percent, so I would have to come up with a total of $240, not including books and board. My parents were patient and generous, but it would be a struggle.

Poor old Harvard was struggling that summer too, in the way that only the ultra-rich can. Over the Fourth of July weekend, thieves broke into the university museum and made off with some gems, including an eighty-four-carat diamond that would be worth half a million dollars today. Why an institution with that kind of wealth would insist on squeezing an extra 20 percent from my parents was beyond me. Dad and Mom had scraped up the money, and I found an affordable place to live with a couple of other guys on Trowbridge Street. I got down to business with two courses that looked like ones I could enjoy and do well in: History of American Political Institutions since 1789 and Sociology of Religion. Campus in the summer was odd, quiet, with a lot of unfamiliar faces and no bull sessions up under the eaves in Eliot, no Jack to talk my ear off, no grapevine to spread the word about a great party or a hot jazz band over in Roxbury. But I had met a really nice girl that spring at a party at Northeastern, and I still had her number. My parents would have swooned over Sophie Clark—a girl from a nice home, studying to be a nurse and active in her community and her church. She was light-skinned, with dark brown eyes, sweetly pretty but also no-nonsense strong and hardworking: she was holding down a full-time job as a medical technician and completing her nursing studies at night. We could date only on weekends, and that kept me focused on my own schoolwork. I suspected that she had another guy out there somewhere, a guy she really cared for; meanwhile, those relaxed summer dates were just what we both needed to ease the loneliness.

Jack Butler was in Detroit with his dad for the summer. Despite his resentment about his father's leaving the family, Jack spent lots of his off time there. So at that pivotal stage in the development of his race-consciousness, Jack landed smack in the birthplace of the Nation of Islam. It was in Detroit in 1930 that W. D. Fard Muhammad first preached the "true religion" of Blacks, first decried the hypocrisies of white Christianity, and first attracted the men and women who would start a movement. In Detroit, Muhammad established the first Nation of Islam mosque, Mosque No. 1 on Hastings Street, together with the small private school that was raided by police in 1934, prompting hundreds of Muslims to take to the streets. Mosque No. 1 had moved to Linwood Street in 1954, and in the summer of 1962, Jack went there. Our friend John Hartman, the white civil rights activist, was home in Detroit too that summer. John had access to a car, and Jack asked him to drive him over to the mosque.

Jack's brother Rick remembered that Jack became "involved" with the mosque, and also with one of the women who was a secretary there. In fact, he said, Jack "came pretty close to joining the NOI."

After Jack's illness and death, I was left with just these few clues about what that summer might have meant to his evolving sense of self and his expansive and visionary thoughts about us "Negroes" at Harvard and beyond. What I did know was that some WASP liberals had seen to it that Harvard would take a "gamble" on bringing us there; that the college had hired its first Black administrator and first Black professor; that we Negroes had arrived, stood out and blended in, and submitted ourselves to the white establishment's scrutiny with admirable forbearance; that we had looked at the Africans and they had looked at us.

Hey, there were "rising sons" all over the place.

# 9 *Afro Americans: Fall 1962 and Spring 1963*

*During the few weeks between summer school and my senior year, I waxed* floors with my dad to make up for lost time and assuage my guilt over the extra money my parents had had to come up with. Then it was fall and we were shuffling bags and boxes out to the steadfast Pontiac again. I had no problem ramming around in it when I was home in Queens, but my fickle car lust had settled on sports cars—tiny, zippy, sophisticated, maybe even foreign. An Aston Martin in British Racing Green or a bright red MGB.

The usual tableau assembled at the curb for my trip back to Cambridge: the back half of my father stuck out from under the hood, where he was checking on something or other, and the back half of my mother stuck out from the trunk, where she was arranging and rearranging, pulling out a bag here and pushing in a box there, swapping things around like a pro. It was a capacious trunk, but this time we had twice the cargo because Velma was on her way to Boston University.

As older brothers do, I had a hard time looking at Velma as her own person, let alone her own woman. What happened to the skinny legs, and when did she stop sticking her tongue out at me every time we passed in the hall? Whoever she was, the girl was headed out, sixteen years old, spirited, fearless, and eager to get away from the strict Garrett family upbringing, especially when it came to dating and boys. My parents would have preferred a city school, with Velma commuting from the safe confines of Queens, but there was no way she was going to do that. A reasonable com-

*Velma Garrett, Kent's sister, 1962*

promise was Boston, since I was there. It may have been reassuring to them, but I found myself thinking about the BU guys I'd met at house parties and what those parties were like. She was too young to get into that scene, wasn't she?

Like me, Velma had been in the city's Special Progress program and skipped grades. She, too, won admission to a good high school, plus college counseling, and she'd been offered a scholarship good enough that she didn't have to take a campus job, as I'd had to. But there was still a balance payable for Mom and Dad, who now had two kids in college, one of whom had just had to make up two courses in summer school. My parents didn't sit me down in front of a ledger, but I was aware that there were money pressures and this year would be tight. Next year, though, I'd be out on my own, working. Maybe. Harvard guys seemed to have started talking about graduate school all the time, and as we embarked on our senior year, it turned serious and urgent. Maybe because I couldn't think of anything else to say when friends started talking about the future, or maybe because my mother pressed the issue again, medical school had crept back into my mind.

Another arrival in Boston, just the four of us, all more relaxed this time. I'd been on the BU campus once or twice, so I had a little swagger in my stride and was quietly hoping I'd run into someone I knew and could show off my cool a little. Velma already knew a few girls who would be among her classmates, and she was a lot more eager than I'd been to get out on her own. Whereas I'd fumbled nervously as the time came for Mom and Dad to leave, Velma couldn't wait to wave good-bye and set out looking for fun.

Back at Harvard, I resumed my routines. The previous year had been my toughest, but now I knew I was going to graduate, on time, and although I was no dean's lister, "I had played with the big boys," as my classmate George Jones would say, and I hadn't been beaten up too bad.

John Woodford had an apartment over on Massachusetts Avenue, sharing with two white roommates, one of whom was "Bright Shadows" author Ron Blau. John's sweetie, Eliza, still lived on the Radcliffe campus but spent plenty of time at the Mass. Ave. apartment. The previous spring, Eliza and John had hitchhiked to Syracuse and caught a bus out to Ohio to meet Eliza's family. Soon after that, John's family had met Eliza in Cambridge when they made a trip east to visit family. Neither set of parents was overjoyed at the prospect of their child being in an interracial relationship, but neither was ready to raise the roof over it either.

John and Travis continued to be involved from time to time with the Boston Action Group (BAG), the umbrella organization that brought together civil rights groups from the area colleges and NAACP and CORE to challenge racism from a legal standpoint. Now Lowell Johnston got busy with those groups too. That year BAG organized a successful boycott to pressure the local Wonder Bread company to hire Negroes in higher-level jobs (not just as janitors or drivers), and they conducted investigations into housing discrimination, raised money for SNCC, and demonstrated against the violence and police brutality against civil rights workers.

Freddy Easter was back from his year of finding himself, and he embarked on his junior year with a new determination. He had a new girlfriend too, Mary Hardie Moore, a senior studying dance at Sarah Lawrence College. He had met her at the Penn Relays, an annual track and field competition that drew several thousand competitors and several hundred thousand spectators, the great majority of them Blacks. It was the "Negro Olympics" and one of the premier Black social events of the year. I remember hearing about it because Boys High won the high school 4 x 100 relay while I was there in 1956, and that was super-important for our school. Penn was also a gigantic party for the Black community—with five days of races and social events, it was one of the biggest Black bashes of the year—and of course my parents had never let me go. A friend of Fred's had invited him that year and set him up on a blind date with Mary. They'd been seeing each other ever since.

Bobby Gibbs was back for his junior year too. He'd made enough money at his magazine job in New York City to finance a few courses in summer school, but still had a lot of academic work to make up. He was an economics major and was ready to buckle down and, not incidentally, continue to keep the closet door firmly shut.

Jack and I were comfortably situated back in Eliot House, and he was scanning the horizon for his next opportunity to raise Black visibility at Harvard. Before classes even began, he found it. The President's Committee on Equal Employment Opportunity—the precursor of the Equal Employment Opportunity Commission (EEOC)—had issued an executive order to all entities with government contracts to report on how many Negroes they employed. Harvard had refused, falling back on the Massachusetts Fair Employment Practices Act, which forbade the recording of such information. When that rationale didn't satisfy the feds, the administration went highbrow, claiming that it had never kept such records because doing so would constitute an "outrageous invasion of privacy." The government shot back with the suggestion that somebody might just go around campus and look at people, counting heads. That would be even worse, said Harvard, "surreptitious, unhealthy, and repugnant to the dignity of the individual." Besides, they whined, they were already doing so much, "bending over backwards not to discriminate," with many programs to "help the Negro." Still, the EEOC didn't relent, so the university decided to comply, and the personnel office set about doing a "visual check," recording results without names attached.

Jack was on the case immediately, objecting not to the counting but to Harvard's unwillingness to comply. Together with a couple of white liberal collaborators, he wrote a letter to the *Crimson,* accusing the college of dodging. "Discrimination," they pointed out, "has become a very subtle and refined skill in the North. Only the naive take the fact that a firm keeps no records about race as proof of fair employment policy. Only a color-conscious count of heads can discover de facto discrimination . . . A social problem is not solved by ignoring it." Jack was truly in his element speaking up and speaking out.

Hobie Armstrong was back in his element that fall too: easily qualifying for first string on the varsity football team, he was ready for the 1962 season opener pitting the Harvard Crimson against the Lehigh Engineers. The odds for this particular game favored Harvard, but the prospects for a repeat of 1961's Ivy League Championship season were dim, with only five boys returning from the winning squad and a slew of preseason injuries. Still, even cautious Coach John Yovicsin held out some hope, in part because a few of the injured players were back and would give the Crimson one of the strongest backfields they had had in years. The Engineers' coach was worried about that backfield and about Hobie, who, he said, "will kill you coming around end if you're not careful."

Game day morning, September 29, was all fog and drizzle, but fans streamed into Harvard Stadium, carrying blankets and wineskins, a few damp felt Harvard banners poking out here and there through the cover of umbrellas. Over in Dillon Fieldhouse, the players got taped and suited up, and Yovvy reminded them of what they needed to do, though he made no particular effort to inspire his boys. In typical Harvard style, Coach Y believed less in pep talks than in engendering smart play. As the team filed out toward Soldiers Field, the rain abated and the fans furled their umbrellas, cheered, and waved those Harvard pennants as the home team won the toss, received a long kickoff, and star lineman Hank Hatch dodged and spun his way to Lehigh's 35.

Then Hatch fumbled and Lehigh took the ball all the way back for a touchdown. A few minutes later, Hobie fumbled a punt, and before the end of the quarter Mike Bassett had fumbled too. It was looking, in the words of one writer, like "the Crimson might not always prevail in 1962, [but] it would at least lose in interesting ways." Coach Yovicsin strode up and down the sidelines with a scowl, his big tan overcoat flapping in the wind. With the help of a lot of "fight-fight-fight" from the crowd and backflips from the cheerleading squad, Harvard managed a touchdown and a two-point conversion, so it was 8–7 as the teams ceded the field to the Harvard Marching Band for its halftime show. The sun peeked out in the second half, and Harvard surged for the win, 27–7, via three more touchdowns, albeit not without two more fumbles.

And then the usual partying began, with beer and girls and bands. Football was at once a big deal and nothing much at Harvard, more pageant than serious athletics, a spectacle to brag about when we won and dismiss as frivolous when we didn't. Appearing to be above certain things was a carefully honed skill at Harvard. Officially, the college didn't recruit athletes, but unofficially and in plain sight, the alumni network did, though not particularly effectively. As Coach Yovicsin once remarked, they tended to "get good boys, though never exactly what we need." Harvard's athletes weren't there primarily for sports, anyhow; not infrequently, boys took a year off to work harder academically, study abroad, or try another sport. That was post–World War II college football for you, a period when the Ivy League's dominance was fading as the huge midwestern and southern powerhouses took center stage.

At one of those Big Football schools some twelve hundred miles away, on that same day, September 29, 1962, another team would also stir up the fans and leave their field triumphant. Unlike the Crimson eleven, those boys would go on to an undefeated season capped by a Rose Bowl win on New Year's Day and a national championship. The powerhouse team was the 1962 Rebels of the University of Mississippi, Ole Miss, and at their home opener, they faced the Kentucky Wildcats. The weather was fair, the crowd was excited, and thousands of flags waved in the stands—not those little triangular school pennants but Confederate flags. As the home team advanced down the field, the crowd roared and the band in their Confederate Army uniforms blared out "Dixie." As had happened far away in Cambridge, the home team was ahead at halftime, and now the field swarmed with a marching band and out hopped a squad of cheerleaders—not handspringing boys wrapped up in slacks and wool sweaters, but pretty girls in skimpy spangled outfits, each one waving her own little Confederate flag as a gigantic one was tugged across the field.

It was an ordinary Ole Miss halftime until the music faded. Fans then craned to see what was going on down on the field. A couple of kids were dragging a microphone out to midfield and a dozen or so men in business suits strode toward it, followed by a gaggle of radio and television crews. From the front rows, a chant arose and took hold in the crowd: "We want Ross! We want Ross!" Stepping to the microphone was Governor Ross Barnett. He waved a hand, and the cheers slowly subsided. "Mr. Chairman and my fellow Mississippians," Barnett began, and the cheering rose again. "I love Mississippi!" he yelled, and he raised a clenched fist. The crowd screamed and waved their flags even harder. "I love her people! I love our customs! I love and respect our heritage!" According to one reporter, the crowd "went nearly berserk in a delirious, sustained ovation." The people Barnett swore he loved were, of course, the state's white people, the beloved custom was segregation, and the sacred heritage was racism. Barnett was riding an intoxicating wave of adulation because he had defied the courts and literally barred the doors of Ole Miss to James Meredith, the Negro who had tried to enter.

Like the Crimson had done earlier that day, the Rebels went on to victory in the second half and carried their coach off the field. They would go on to their parties too, but instead of awaking to mere hangovers on Sunday morning, Ole Miss students found themselves in what looked like a battle zone poised for action. The main campus building was surrounded by armed federal marshals, and outside that ring, students soon started to gather, first a hundred or so in tentative curiosity, then several hundred strong. When the news filtered out that James Meredith was on campus, more students arrived—a thousand, then more, waving signs and Confederate flags. And then it wasn't just students. Groups of armed segregationists streamed in from all across the country to help "save Mississippi."

Around dusk, US marshals smuggled James Meredith onto the Ole Miss campus and into Baxter Hall. He spent that night in his corner suite, alone but for the two dozen armed marshals who surrounded the room, and sleeping peacefully, as he would later recall. He read for a while and then went to bed, wakened only a few times overnight by the sounds of the violent riot that erupted on the Ole Miss campus around sundown and lasted through the night. What started with taunts and curses moved to bricks and bottles, then gunfire, tear gas, Molotov cocktails, and fires; it was a war, and it left two dead and dozens injured.

I spent that Sunday night safely up on the fifth floor of Eliot House, probably catching up with Jack about our summers, unpacking and reorganizing, adjusting our work and class schedules, maybe playing some cards or a game of Risk with some of the regular visitors. Monday was October 1, the first day of classes at both Harvard and Ole Miss. A little before eight in the morning, James Meredith brushed shards of windshield glass from the seat of a federal marshal's car and got a lift to his first class, surrounded by armed guards, inching through the rubble of spent tear-gas canisters, bricks and bottles, and burnt-out cars. Meanwhile, I breakfasted amiably with whatever Eliot boys happened to be around, most likely white guys, and enjoyed the walk to my first class as a light fog lifted through the fall leaves. I was at Harvard, in the bubble of genteel liberalism, where disagreements were resolved by reason, actions were guided by stoic and practical idealism, and it was assumed that good character and democratic values would prevail. I and the other Negroes in our class were on target to become the "rising sons" we were expected to be.

I don't remember the precise moment when I heard about James Meredith's awful experiences; it wasn't burned into my memory like seeing Emmett Till's gruesome remains in that magazine photo. I do remember feeling a little stupid for having gone along in my comfortable world, naively assuming that this integration thing was going to be as easy for the rest of the country as it seemed to be at Harvard. Now what might happen? Maybe the segregationists would prevail. Maybe James Meredith would be lynched, and soon I'd see a photo of his ruined corpse in *Jet* magazine. A boy who was a lot like me was suffering the bitter hatred and murderous violence of whites who were a lot like my classmates. At times, this awareness made me relapse into the wariness I had when I first arrived as a freshman, the gnawing idea that I didn't really belong there. I didn't have any thoughts of leaving, but I was reminded of what a tiny minority I was at Harvard. I wasn't exactly afraid for my safety, but if Martin Kilson had come up behind me with his "Hey, Spook! Hey, Negro!" I'd probably have jumped.

Other than that, it felt like an ordinary Harvard fall, but in hindsight I see that the college was rushing headlong into social change. Timothy Leary and Richard Alpert were continuing their "research" on hallucinogens, and in late November, Dean Monro issued a stern warning about the short- and long-term psychiatric dangers. Predictably, Leary and Alpert loudly defended their work and even the drugs themselves, which were no more dangerous to the mind, they said, than four years at Harvard. My Chem 20 professor, Dr. Fieser, accepted a prestigious post on the surgeon general's commission to investigate the health risks of smoking. A few years later, Fieser would quit smoking, but only after he was diagnosed with lung cancer. The Law School Forum held a panel on "the moral problems of sex" that included information about abortion and "the Pill." Biology professor James Watson and his associates won the Nobel Prize for their research on the structure of DNA, college students were offered the oral Sabin polio vaccine, and the Radcliffe president drew fire for predicting that within a short time "Radcliffe will fade into Harvard," which it indeed soon did. One clear afternoon, a helicopter thumped over campus, scouting sites for the JFK library, and another Kennedy brother, Ted, declared his candidacy for a senatorial seat from Massachusetts.

Beyond the walls of Harvard, President Kennedy vowed that we would put a man on the moon by the end of the decade. A few weeks later, in a Chicago title fight, Sonny Liston sent Floyd Patterson to the moon with a knockout in two minutes of the first round. Bob Dylan's "A Hard Rain's a-Gonna Fall" was moving up the charts, and many interpreted it as a warning against nuclear war. In her book *Silent Spring,* Rachel Carson issued another warning—that the environment was being destroyed by chemical companies and pesticides. On October 14, a U-2 plane flew over Cuba and found nuclear weapons installed by the Soviet Union, initiating a couple of long anxious weeks of fear that would come to be known as the Cuban Missile Crisis.

In the international literary world, James Baldwin was a rising star, gaining attention for not only his novels and plays but also for his eloquent and uncompromising essays about racism in the United States. In November, his *New Yorker* article "Letter from a Region in My Mind" spiked the magazine's sales and was the talk of the town. The *Crimson* carried a long-winded review of the article, titled "A Black Man Talks to the White World," and in the next few weeks Martin Kilson went back and forth with the reviewer, arguing in the classic Harvard style of formal decency, but still unflinching in making his points. Even at this sensitive time in his professional career—he was still a mere "lecturer," on trial every day—Kilson came out swinging. As he put it, Baldwin "seeks to shock the White American from his insulated world of false satisfaction about what little has been done to alter basically the Negro's human situation . . . from his belief [that] nothing really earthshaking will occur among Negroes if their reality is not transformed in the near future." The process of shocking whites, he said, was a good and necessary thing, but it would doubtless engender "confusion, threats, and perhaps much worse."

In the *New Yorker* article that sparked the exchange, Baldwin used the term "improbable aristocrats" for James Meredith and the dozens of other students, some of them only five or six tender years old, who walked through screaming, spitting mobs to go to school. Their predecessors in history were also "improbable aristocrats": "that unsung army of black men and women who trudged down back lanes and entered back doors, saying 'Yes, sir' and 'No, Ma'am' in order to acquire a new roof for the schoolhouse, new books, a new chemistry lab, more beds for the dormitories, more dormitories." On New Year's Day of 1963, the centennial anniversary of the issuance of the Emancipation Proclamation, Baldwin celebrated by going to meet one of those aristocrats. He spent the day in Jackson, Mississippi, partying with James Meredith and enjoying the company of Negroes and a fine meal of "hog jowl, black-eyed peas and cornbread."

Back in Queens for the winter holidays, I was comfortably back in all-Negro company too, with cousins, aunts and uncles, neighbors, and people whose names I couldn't remember, and of course chitlins and black-eyed peas. Uncle Elisha was in town, his forty-foot tractor-trailer parked over in Hempstead after another year spent hauling produce up and down the East Coast. His updates on relatives and friends down in South Carolina helped keep the ties with our rural roots strong. Uncle Elisha was the uncle I leaned on and learned from when the father-son thing just wasn't clicking for me. He had taught me to drive and to love driving and cars. Some of my earliest memories are of being swung up onto his lap and staring at his smartly trimmed mustache while he told me stories about the excitement of the open road. When I got too big for his lap, I was no less interested in his adventures, but now his commentaries inevitably led us into lively debate, each of us comfortable with giving or getting a good verbal thrashing now and then.

The educated college boy, I flaunted my cleverness, waxing all multisyllabic and analytical, probably even throwing down the occasional "define your terms" gauntlet that Harvard boys so loved. Uncle Elisha was no intellectual, but he was a master of wry sarcasm and humor, and he gave me the raised eyebrows that meant *Come on down off that high horse, young man, you are speaking to experience.* Like my father, Uncle Elisha hated Jim Crow and made no bones about the racism in our country, but he refused to let it get him down, refused to be bitter or to love life any the less for it. He kept on hauling those watermelons and onions, using his *Negro Motorist Green Book* to scope out where he could safely eat, sleep, fill a prescription, or get a haircut in little towns along the way. The courts may have pried open some restrooms along his routes, and whites may have reluctantly stowed away some WHITES ONLY signs, but he wasn't going to venture anywhere he wasn't sure about. He played by the abhorrent rules he knew so well, to make his living and raise his family. He was an "improbable aristocrat" in my eyes.

My older cousins Harold and Charles promised that we three would go to the Newport Jazz Festival that summer as a kind of graduation celebration for me, which sounded like a fabulous idea. They also took me to New York City and snuck me into a Harlem nightclub. There was a vibrant web of connections among New York City Black college students, always some friend of a cousin of a roommate who could pass on a morsel or two of news, some of it reliable, some not. I wasn't sure whether to trust the story I got just after New Year's Day: Fred Easter had gotten married? I knew he and Mary were tight, but to my way of understanding the world, there was only one reason they would have married quickly like that. It turned out that the rumor was true and my reasoning was sound. The baby was due in late spring or early summer, and Fred would finish his two years at Harvard commuting from an apartment in Cambridge, a married man and before long a father.

More news came around that time too, but not through the grapevine. Dad usually had a *New York Daily News* under his arm when he came in from work, and I'd grab it and sprawl out somewhere to read, often from back to front, starting with the sports pages. One afternoon I turned a page and noticed "Boston" in the headline. The murderer who was being called the Boston Strangler had struck again, murdering a woman on Park Drive on New Year's Eve. The article printed photos of several of his victims, and I idly glanced at each one in turn and then drew back in disbelief. Number seven, killed at age twenty on December 5, was Sophie Clark, the girl I'd dated while in summer school. Why her? Why a sweet, harmless, hardworking girl? As sad and horrified as I was for Sophie, I worried about Velma. We all did, but Velma herself was cool; she'd received all kinds of warnings and instructions from BU officials, and she wasn't stupid, she insisted. Neither was Sophie, I countered. I'm surprised my parents let Velma go back to Boston after the winter break.

As nearly as I can figure, when the spring 1963 semester began, there were between sixty and seventy Negro undergraduates and probably several dozen Negro graduate students at Harvard. Nobody really knows for sure. To try to make a reasonable guess, I used the fallible "visual check" method on the freshman *Registers* for the classes of 1964, '65, and '66. By my reckoning, there were forty-three, and so, with the eighteen of us, the total was sixty-one —fifty-two American Negroes and nine African nationals. That's probably an undercount, but still, it amounted to just a little over 1 percent of the undergraduate enrollment. The administration was correct when they said they weren't attracting as many as they had back in 1959, so our class's record of eighteen would hold for a few more years. Still, the general trend for subsequent freshman classes was upward.

Some of us spent the majority of our private time with brothers, while others hardly ever did. Aside from the temporary Black Table of each new freshman class, there was nowhere you would see any concentration of Blacks on campus. In fact, there were so few of us, and we were so dispersed, that you could probably go days wandering around campus, going to classes and events, even sports contests, and not see one of us. Nowadays when I page through the old college publications, I'm surprised at how invisible we were. Crowd scenes at games and concerts and meetings, candid snapshots of boys peering into microscopes, listening to lectures, costumed up for plays, taking exams, pouring beers, walking arm-in-arm with girls, strumming the folk guitars that were showing up everywhere—all white. Even the athletic teams were white. It's one thing to see crew, squash, tennis, swimming, ice hockey, sailing, and skiing teams without a single Black. But year after year Harvard's publications show, for instance, all white basketball players on its team and on all their competitors' squads. The soccer teams at times had their one or two star Africans or West Indians, and in one photo from 1962, Lowell Davidson stands half a head taller than even the tallest of his teammates on the track team. In photo after photo, the varsity, JV, and freshman basketball and baseball teams pose with their coaches and team managers—all white except Hobie.

So it was mind-blowing to walk into a common room in Winthrop House one evening that winter and see a whole room full of thirty or forty Black students—far more than seven or eight freshmen eating together in the Freshman Union, even more than some of the house parties off-campus—and no whites at all. But it happened. Jack posted a couple of hand-lettered notices of a meeting for "All Africans and Afro-Americans" and made sure that word spread by grapevine. For years he'd been talking to me, to Lowell Johnston, to anyone who would listen, about starting a publication about Negro life at Harvard and getting us all together for some kind of collective action or organization. And now he did it.

Like many African Americans at Harvard and across the country, Jack was growing disillusioned with the integration movement, and while not exactly ready to run off and join the Nation of Islam, he talked about voluntary and activist self-segregation. At a panel discussion at Cabot Hall earlier that month, on the topic of "Integration and Separatism," Jack said that he favored a kind of separatism that was not isolationist, but rather directed toward an "increase of race identification," a separatism that could raise race-consciousness and build specifically Negro leadership. Now he had teamed up with the Ghanaian George Armah to convene this series of meetings and serve as leaders and spokespersons for what would soon emerge as a new student group. Between Jack and the very persuasive Armah, they pulled in not only the activists but also those of us whose race-consciousness was just shifting into gear. Based on what I remember and have gleaned from reports of the day, most of the Blacks at Harvard came to at least one of those early meetings. Some decided to stay out of it, others became the active nucleus of the group that would survive our graduation and beyond, and still others stayed on the periphery.

We heard a call to become more than just "Bright Shadows in the Yard" or "Rising Sons of Darkness," more than mere curiosities at Harvard, exceptions to the rule, and tolerated "others," and instead to be part of something to which we undeniably and proudly belonged. We weren't particularly disaffected—we all had white friends among whom we were happy to spend the majority of our time—and we were willingly, successfully, and often enthusiastically integrating Harvard. We were succeeding academically. But in some important ways, there was a restless energy going around, no doubt influenced by our impending graduation but also by the dramatic events outside the gates of Harvard, by our changing sense of ourselves as "guests" in that precious world. There were enough of us, and we were confident enough, that getting together felt like a natural thing to do. And it was exhilarating.

We had no real agenda, but discussions burst out. It was one thing to sit on our beds, or in lecture halls or dining rooms, analyzing current events with our Black and white friends. It was another thing entirely to sit in a room with dozens of Blacks and no whites at all and have at it. George Wallace was determined to follow Ross Barnett's lead and bar the doors of Alabama's "public" university. In Birmingham, children half our age were facing Bull Connor, police dogs, and fire hoses. Martin Luther King wrote from the Birmingham jail that he'd grown tired of the white moderates who were "more devoted to 'order' than to justice . . . who paternalistically believe that [they] can set the timetable for another man's freedom." There was so much to say, much of it anguished, some of it angry.

Meanwhile, the Africans talked about independence, about forming Black governments, about self-rule and Black nationalism. And Armah relentlessly pushed one message—enough with the talk of "Negroes," we were Africans and Afro Americans. In comparison to what was happening in Africa, the US civil rights movement made me think of the old saying "been down so long it looks like up to me." It was in those days that I got my first sense that being Black was something to be treasured. I think if Ron Blau or David Branon had come to me with his research questions at that point, I'd have had a lot more to say about that "reborn" question, if I'd gone along with the foolishness at all.

Over the course of that late winter and early spring, at least some white Harvardians had seen or heard that the Negroes were up to something. Then, in April, we went public as the African and Afro American Association of Students—AAAAS. The headline appeared on the front page of the *Crimson:* "Africans, Afro-Americans Form Club." Jack told the reporter that about seventy Negroes, including some two dozen grad students, had been meeting regularly. At any given meeting I remember maybe thirty or thirty-five in attendance, but over the weeks, probably about seventy individuals had shown up at one or another time. Jack's comment about that first meeting—"the response from Negroes of all viewpoints was overwhelming"—jibes with my memory very well. We'd come together, Jack said, out of a "desire to be ourselves."

Archie Epps, at the time a grad student and lecturer and soon to become Harvard's first Black administrator, was a prominent early member, and he took particular interest in the prospect of a Negro publication. He announced that AAAAS intended to start a college journal to address issues "facing both our peoples"—civil rights in the United States and independence in Africa. The journal would include scholarly articles, poetry, and short stories by students, and Epps had already been in touch with American and African colleges to solicit submissions.

Lowell Johnston had been working closely with his senior honors thesis tutor, Martin Kilson. Besides talking about Lowell's thesis on South Africa, Lowell told me, the two also enjoyed discussing "who we were as Blacks, how to get out from under, and how to make it better for everybody." So Lowell was pretty sure he'd get support when he and Jack and George Armah went to Kilson and asked him to be the group's adviser. Kilson agreed, and on record he praised "the greater aggressiveness of young Negroes in attacking their problems," as well as "the greater self-consciousness of the American Negro and his greater sense of identity."

Although this would be the first group of its kind in decades at Harvard, and the first officially sanctioned one, it wasn't Harvard's very first Negro group. In the 1920s, the few Negroes at Harvard —one estimate is that there were about a dozen, more than half of them grad students—called themselves the Nile Club and met in dorm rooms and at homes off-campus to share ideas and support one another. Students from other area colleges joined too, and in the Nile Club they found "academic motivation and general intellectual and social maturation." Spencer Jourdain's father, who had spearheaded the resistance to President Lowell's barring of Negroes from the dormitories, was a member, just one among what Spencer would later write was an "impressive roster of brilliance." Former members of the Nile Club went on to illustrious careers: Spencer's father, Edwin "Gint" Jourdain, was a writer and publisher; Charles Houston was dean of Howard University's law school and a founder of the NAACP's Legal Defense Fund; and Ned Gourdin was Massachusetts's first African American superior court justice. By the end of the 1920s, however, the club was dying out; the scholar and diplomat Ralph Bunche, who completed his master's degree in 1928, was part of the last generation of Nile Club members.

In AAAAS, though, we would be Afro Americans, not meeting in dorm rooms or off-campus but applying for official status as a Harvard-sanctioned organization. With official recognition, we could use college facilities and recruit members at registration each semester. Plus, this would be a pan-Africanist group, open not just to invited American Negroes, like the Nile Club, but also to Africans, whom the college had been actively recruiting. Bobo Gray said that the administration had tried to get the American

Negroes and the Africans together a few years earlier, but the effort hadn't been very successful; now we'd achieved it on our own. And AAAAS would be even more inclusive; among its members were Afro Caribbeans, for instance, like my classmates Barbadian Ezra Griffith and Cuban Larry Galindo, who only partially identified as American Negroes and who also had African roots. The idea of the organization seemed so great, and so timely, that at first I think we expected to be approved and maybe even commended for being so forward-thinking. A hint of how wrong we were, however, came from Dean Watson, who thought that the group could not be sanctioned because it sounded "discriminatory" to him. There was no actual written rule against that, he said to a *Crimson* reporter, but that was only "because we don't feel like we need anything like that at Harvard."

Unfazed, AAAAS submitted a request for formal recognition to the Harvard Council on Undergraduate Affairs (HCUA), which took up the issue in early May. The preamble to the AAAAS constitution read, "We, the students of African descent at Harvard and Radcliffe, in order to promote mutual understanding and friendship between African and Afro-American students at Harvard and Radcliffe; to provide ourselves a voice in the Harvard and Radcliffe community by means of a publication and by means of periodic statements; and to develop the leadership capable of effectively coping with the various problems of our peoples, do hereby establish the Harvard Association of African and Afro-American Students." Lofty and admirable? Definitely. Almost daring for its day too. The idea should have made the administration proud. After all, Harvard loved being out in front of the curve, and this would put them out there. True, there were other early signs of a rising Black campus movement at other colleges, but they were new, few, and far between. Besides, hadn't the college been talking about attracting more Black students and faculty and also moving forward with studies of Africa? All of these efforts, it seemed to me, would be strengthened by the AAAAS, right? None of those points got any attention. Instead, this is what got all the attention: "Membership in the Association shall be open to African and Afro-American students currently enrolled in good standing at Harvard and Radcliffe."

HCUA met on May 6 and debated our request for approval for two hours. George Armah, representing AAAAS, explained that membership was not determined specifically by race, but rather by relationship to Africa. All Africans, he said, could join, except those who had come there as colonizers. Therefore, it wouldn't be open to Afrikaaners, but it would be to a white person who moved to an African free state. Several HCUA members wondered why AAAAS had to put it in writing—wasn't it possible to just choose members and achieve whatever group composition it wanted? "We do not wish to sink to that moral level," he replied. Armah was a compelling speaker; a sophomore who was a regular attendee at AAAAS meetings remembered that Armah could "tease, chide, and coerce within the space of a few minutes. The experience of talking with him left many quite shaken." Notwithstanding how shaken some of them may have been, HCUA voted 14–5–1 against approval.

Black alumnus William Harrison '32, the radical communist editor of Boston's Black newspaper, the *Chronicle,* wrote to the *Crimson* right away to say that he thought that AAAAS was "a capital idea." He wished that there'd been a group like that in his day. Dean Monro called a press conference to announce his support for the membership clause, saying, "I don't personally think of this as discriminatory in the sense in which the term is usually applied." Unlike just about everyone else, Monro tried to focus on the good that might come out of AAAAS. He hoped that the issues would be ironed out because of the organization's "constructive purpose." "I think one has to look very hard at what's being tried here, and what the purpose is," he said. "African students and American Negroes have got a lot of things to talk about and work over. It doesn't distress me to think of their assembling for this purpose."

Despite HCUA's refusal to recommend AAAAS for approval,

the door wasn't closed yet. According to university rules, the Faculty Committee on Student Activities (FCSA) could override HCUA, but their next meeting wouldn't be until the fall. So that left us with the question of what to propose in the fall—should we stand firm, or should we change the membership policy? The question sparked wide-ranging discussions, at AAAAS meetings and elsewhere across campus. Harvard had been preparing us to debate topics into the ground, so there was plenty of hair-splitting, appeals to history, playing of devil's advocate, challenges to define terms, definitions of terms, and well-constructed lines of logic. Why bother with Harvard's approval at all? some wondered. The answer was that being able to use college facilities and recruit on campus was crucial to keeping a group moving forward. Lowell Johnston reminded us that official status would also make us eligible for funding to bring in some big-name speakers on racial issues. Jack argued, too, that we shouldn't let Harvard off the hook so easily: "This is a way of establishing and legitimizing ourselves on campus. We are sending a message here, that we are to be recognized as a force." As tempting as some found it to just turn our backs on official status, we would press on.

What about the charge of "discrimination" on the basis of race, then? Could—or should—whites join? We heard through the grapevine that some white liberals wanted to join. Paul Cowan, for instance, who had just received an award for his reporting on the sit-ins in Maryland, and John Hartman, who'd been arrested down there—what if they asked to join? Freddy had just come back from a road trip to the SNCC conference in Atlanta with his white roommate, a sincere guy who was interested in joining. As much as he liked and admired the guy, Fred said, "there are just times when I don't want to have to be explaining shit to white people." John Woodford spoke in favor of excluding whites if and only if we had a clear purpose for doing so. And what was that purpose? Jack said there was "nothing malicious" about it, and he talked about being free to "be ourselves," and that resonated with me, the feeling of ease and freedom we had had at the Black Table. Someone else thought that if whites were involved, they would "take over," and we needed to keep control and also to cultivate our own leaders. Travis Williams thought that we needed time to sort some issues out and for too long we'd been "too hung up on integration."

Armah's argument about African heritage versus race proved convincing to the *Crimson* editorial board, which came out with a recommendation that the FCSA approve AAAAS. And even if the FCSA were to find the clause discriminatory, the *Crimson* said, the committee should still approve it. The difference was that in other circumstances—and they named the Final Clubs as the most obvious example—discrimination had "social aims" that were "uniformly pernicious." In AAAAS, the discrimination was "incidental and subordinate to creating a homogeneous intellectual community." Three subsequent letters to the editor expressed the "minority view" of the *Crimson* editorial board. The first saw the issue as simple: the regulations said no; therefore the answer was no. With barely disguised disdain, that writer recommended that AAAAS leaders "calm themselves" and find better ways to express their "revolutionary zeal." He said that we were being immature by "insisting so stubbornly on their special privilege to maintain a technically unacceptable clause." The second minority opinion called us out for "hypocrisy," insisted that "the viciousness of discrimination is not transformed because the discriminators are a minority," and argued that we would make the "atmosphere of the University less tolerant." Up to there, he'd gone out on a limb but hadn't quite begun sawing himself off. Then he did, with a stroke of hypocrisy that shocks me even now: while the university should never "attach its name to explicit, premeditated, and flagrant exclusion based principally on race," it was "not practical to stop covert discrimination practiced by groups like the final clubs."

For generations, the Final Clubs had excluded Negroes—and Jews, Catholics, Italians, Slavs, midwesterners, boys from "new money," and guys from categories that I can't even imagine. The Final Clubs looked down upon the masses and selected their own to dine and lounge and play with, to become brothers who were destined to rule together as bank presidents and senators and members of boards of directors. Harvard sanctioned all of this because those boys would indeed soon rule—and they would earn, and they would donate. How could anyone condone that kind of discrimination because it was "not practical" to stop it?

It was argued that maybe we should fight fire with fire, choosing our members one by one, as the Final Clubs did. This argument was emotionally appealing. But Armah spoke against it again, as he had at HCUA. No, we didn't want to sink to that level, and we certainly didn't want to be anything like the Final Clubs. We were staking out a certain moral high ground, and it felt very satisfying to state our membership criteria outright. We went around and around, but the majority was never in favor of giving in. Armah was particularly frustrated by the withholding of approval. He missed Africa, wanted to be in on the struggles there, and had been losing patience with Harvard, the United States, and the Western world, which he believed "did not want to see potentially creative Africans in power." The author of a biographical sketch of Armah thinks that the controversy over the AAAAS was the last straw: before exams had even started, Armah and his Radcliffe girlfriend were bound for Algeria—by way of Mexico—where they would train to fight in the resistance.

There were so many angles and arguments, and the conversations were fascinating. I also was often just plain angry that we'd been turned down so flatly. As usual, I was more the observer than the fighter. Now, as an old man, I find myself wanting to go back in time and walk my skinny self up there to stand before HCUA and say, "You are wrong. Here we are, finally in this place that for more than three hundred years was closed to us, and the first time we say we might want to close you out for a couple of hours a week, you get up in arms. You accuse us of 'reverse racism.' To suggest that our desire to have a Blacks-only club is somehow the same as Jim Crow is intellectually indefensible, historically wrong, morally weak, and just crazy. AAAAS is not part of an elaborate and centuries-old machinery of laws and customs specifically designed to oppress you. The subtext under our membership clause is not 'You may not be with us because you are inherently inferior and you will never be otherwise.' We have lived for hundreds of years by rules you made up, rules that never had our best interests in mind. Now you say you've seen the light, and things have changed. You will have to forgive us for not quite trusting that every minute of every day. Sometimes, for some things we want to talk about, things we need to talk about, we just want to be alone. Is that so hard to understand?"

Those of us who were graduating couldn't carry the AAAAS forward. It would be the younger guys who had to do that, so we elected officers and entrusted them with our most potent arguments for recognition. There the matter would have to lie while we scrambled to write our exams and papers, fill out forms, rent our caps and gowns, pick up tickets for the various activities and ceremonies, and try to have some fun as we slid into our last few days at Harvard. Thursday, June 13, would be the Big Day, except that at Harvard, graduation is the better part of a Big Week, once described as "an orgy of accumulated tradition and ceremony . . . splendid, ridiculous, touching, pompous, brilliant, dull, frenetic."

The alums started streaming in on Sunday—fifty-five hundred of them by one count. The twenty-fifth reunion is the "big one," so hundreds came from the class of 1938, along with thousands of others, including one man from the class of 1890. Alumni activities started Monday with a morning of golf, followed by two full days of all manner of amusement: orations and processions, tours of some of the new buildings and facilities, shuttle buses to the beach and the Manchester Yacht Club, bus tours of local historical and cultural sites, a lobster dinner, an evening at the Boston Pops, a comedy performance by the "Dunster Dunces," an auction to raise money for the Class Gift, and symposia on the topics of "The Communist World" and "Frontiers in Science."

For us graduates, Monday afternoon was devoted to a nondenominational church service in our honor, and that evening there was a formal dance in the Eliot House courtyard. Tuesday morning, grads and families and dates could take a cruise on the SS *Yankee,* plus there were interhouse games and Glee Club performances and various kinds of frolicking all over the place. Until our year, the festivities had stretched out over five days, but participation had been declining, I guess because of people like me. I skipped everything until Wednesday, which was Class Day—the less serious version of Commencement and traditionally one of the highlights of the week.

We assembled for Class Day at 9:30 that rainy Wednesday morning at the John Harvard statue—which, perhaps fittingly, isn't John Harvard at all, but some anonymous guy who posed for the sculptor. From there, we marched in a brisk and drippy procession to Lowell Lecture Hall, led by the class marshals we had elected earlier that semester: the first class marshal was my suitemate David Rockefeller, and the second class marshal was our Black classmate Wesley Williams. The two were friends, each securely at the top of our class's social hierarchy. Once we were all reasonably well settled in our seats and the inevitable happy buzz was shushed down, someone prayed and the speakers began. Over the course of the next couple of hours, we would hear a humorous oration on the subject of the "Wonk" at Harvard and a reading of the Class Poem, which included a reference to John Woodford's fence post-smashing back in our freshman year. Various adults made the usual comments about character and perseverance, and Dean Monro presented a couple of awards. The only really serious part was an oration by a self-described white, Anglo-Saxon, Protestant southerner. He spoke on the racial situation in the United States, lamenting that a hundred years after the bloodshed and violence over race during the Civil War, there we still were with bloodshed and violence over race. The speech was covered in the Boston papers, one of which ran a large full-color photo of our class marshals with a caption that said their faces reflected "the faith and hope of America."

The weather cleared for Commencement the next day. My parents came in just for the day, not being exactly the type for lobster dinners or symposia. But they did like fanfare and ceremony, and I imagine they were well satisfied in that department. I wasn't fully aware of just how much of it there was all around me, and now, when I look back at descriptions of the day, it seems pretty ridiculous. For instance, that morning, eighteen mounted members of the National Lancers, a state militia, all suited up in scarlet and blue, met Massachusetts governor Endicott "Chub" Peabody, class of '42, at the State House and escorted his Victorian-era horse-drawn carriage across the Charles and down Massachusetts Avenue to Johnston Gate, where they presented arms and paraded through campus.

The Yard bristled with wooden folding chairs in neat compact rows. The band cranked up "Pomp and Circumstance," and we graduates lined the route to stand in reverence as the procession passed us—phalanxes of men in top hats and tails, faculty gowned in black with colorful satin hoods, tassels flopping and swishing in the breeze. We fell in behind, the 1,094 capped and gowned seniors along with some 2,500 more students who would receive advanced degrees. In an astonishingly short time, everyone was in place. The officials sat on a platform under a huge tent in front of Memorial Church, the graduates packed in densely down front, and guests surrounded it all. The sheriff of Middlesex County pounded a staff on the floor of the stage and declared the ceremonies open. A pretty ordinary series of events followed: an invocation, a song, the official awarding of degrees en masse, and more songs, speeches, and orations, most with some reference to Commencement as a beginning.

And so it was. In a turn of events that probably surprised me more than anyone, I'd been accepted at NYU's medical school for the fall. Bill Exum would be at NYU too, but in the far-off world of graduate-level sociology. Larry Galindo would also be in New York, working at City Bank, and Jack Butler had taken a job at the Carver Federal Savings Bank, one of the premier Black financial institutions of the time. George Jones would continue his studies in biochemistry at UC Berkeley after staying on for the summer at Harvard as a research assistant. Kent Wilson would stick around for the summer too, to take the last course that would complete his degree. Then he was headed off for a long tour of Eastern Europe with a group called Experiment in International Living. Four of our Black classmates would go directly to law school: Lowell Johnston would stay at Harvard and focus on civil rights law, Gerry Secundy would start at Columbia in the fall, Wesley Williams was going to the Fletcher School of Law and Diplomacy at Tufts University, and Deck McLean would take up legal studies at Boston College. Hobie Armstrong and Ezra Griffith didn't know it, but they would receive draft notices in the near future; meanwhile, Ezra would stay on in Cambridge doing underwriting for an insurance company, and Hobie found a position in computer programming with IBM in his hometown of Kingston, New York.

Besides the drama of beginnings, the day marked an ending too. The eighteen of us would never be in one place at the same time again. Maybe we even realized that as we sat through the speeches and songs. What I don't believe any of us realized was that we were living through the last days of being "Negroes": soon there would be no more Negroes, or even "so-called Negroes," at Harvard. We had heard and seen and spoken the phrase "Afro American," and the AAAAS controversy had splashed it onto the front page of the *Crimson* and sprinkled it into official college documents. Although it took a few years for the word "Negro" to die out completely, we, like our brothers and sisters across the country, were charging or stepping or being pulled into new self-chosen terms—including the sharp, powerful "Black"—with all the changes in thought and identity signaled by a new vocabulary.

Meanwhile, we were just proud and grateful graduates who were musing over endings and beginnings of a more prosaic sort, I feel sure. The sun was hot and the ceremony was long. At last, somebody up on the platform said one more profound thing, another prayer was prayed, and the sheriff pounded his staff on the wooden platform again, declaring the end of the ritual. A short burst of applause, a few mortarboards flipped into the air, and then the tidy rows dissolved into an enormous murmuring crowd. I knew my family was behind me and to my left somewhere, and I was eager to get to them. I turned and cut through a row of chairs, stumbled past clusters of hugging white people, sidled politely behind a weepy mother, and circled around a group of guys chanting some kind of brotherhood song. I wedged my way toward my people, bearing up under the all-too-familiar embarrassed stare and the occasional blazing glare of a white liberal smile. Finally, there they were, Mom and Dad and Velma, as pleased to see me as I was to see them. My dad snapped a photo of me. No hugging or kissing, no weeping or snuffling—we weren't that kind of family. We just stood there, a little stiffly, a little self-consciously, but glad to be together. Slowly the groups dispersed and began strolling toward the various houses, where we would each individually receive our diplomas (small size, and in English) that afternoon. I led my family over to Eliot.

Half a century later, I found the family photos of Commencement. One afternoon when I arrived to visit my dad at his apartment, I stepped over the threshold and was cornered by two big blue plastic storage bins full of photo albums that he planned to unload on me. Velma had already turned them down, and after all, I was the one asking all the questions about family. Among the hundreds—no, thousands—of pictures my folks had taken over the years, on ocean cruises, at birthday parties and graduations and weddings, at the big family reunions both sides of my family hold every two years, I found a battered green loose-leaf binder. This was where my mom had assembled the ephemera of my childhood: a snapshot of me riding a mule in South Carolina; a certificate for "meritorious service rendered" on the Safety Patrol in 1954; a photo of me and my boyhood friend Mickey from the projects, kitted out in our cowboy gear; junior high school academic commendations—two of them from my inspiration, Mrs. Rutledge; a news clipping showing me on the television set of *Spotlight on Youth,* a daily half-hour of student news on New York's WPIX; clippings with newspaper photos of me on the winning team at a Boy Scout hobby show, as an officer on some kind of student council, and as salutatorian of my class at Boys High; the program (doodled on by a bored Velma) from the ceremony that admitted me to membership in the New York City schools' version of the National Honor Society; and the program from my high school graduation at which I gave an address as salutatorian and received seven awards, none of which I remember. Then there was my Certificate of Admission to Harvard and, finally, the program and tickets for Commencement, clipped to an envelope that enclosed ten small color snapshots from the day.

*Graduation Day, June 13, 1963*

The pictures from the morning ceremony show just a sea of the backs of heads. Then there's the moment after the end of the ceremony, when Mom and Dad found me and I found them, and I'm smiling broadly, my cap already doffed, my gown and tie loosened.

*Graduation Day, Eliot House, receiving diploma*

And then there I am walking up onto the terrace of Eliot House, toward Master Finley, who was reaching out for a handshake. In another shot, I'm coming back down the steps with a crimson folder in my right hand. And then there's Jack in the same pose, with his diploma, a wide smile, and cool-looking sunglasses.

*Graduation Day, Eliot House,*
*Jack receiving his diploma*

One snapshot captures Velma, Mom, and me enjoying the after-ceremony refreshments at a small cloth-covered table in a sun-dappled Eliot quadrangle. My mother is in a pillbox hat and a pale dress, with Dad's jacket draped around her shoulders. Velma is in a pastel blue suit, and I've got my mouth full. Dad's straw hat is on his wooden folding chair while he snaps the picture. Of all of us, my mother spent the least time with white people and was probably the least sociable to begin with, and I can almost see the tension in her face as she is once again marooned in the white world. It was an easier day than Arrival Day, but only by a small margin. It was still difficult to sit there, at our little table island, and feel that we belonged.

Mom and Velma had gotten up to stretch their legs before the long drive home, and Dad thought he'd better escort them. I noticed Jack dragging a chair over to join us, and as he passed my family, he managed a handshake with Dad and they exchanged

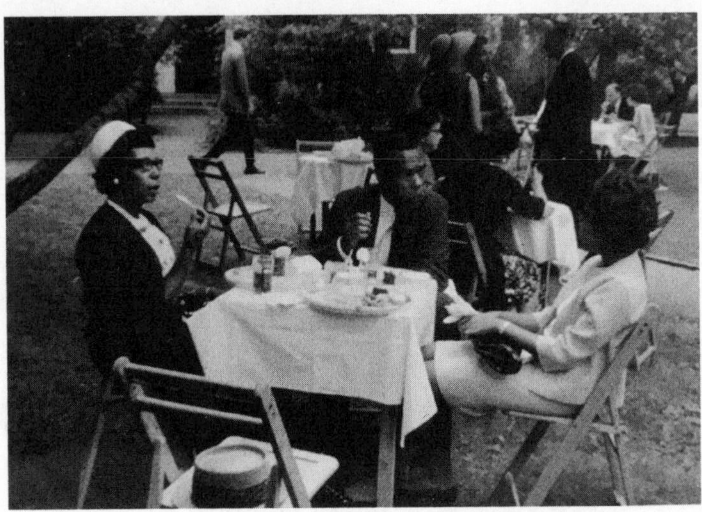

*Graduation Day, Eliot House,*
*Kent at lunch with his mother and sister*

the customary greetings and congratulations. I let out a sigh of relief to see the two men part. Jack might have started in with Dad about the AAAAS struggle, and I just didn't want to get into it. I needed time and the right circumstances to tell Dad about it, to assure him first of all that we weren't going to get in any trouble over it, and then to explain that we are Afro Americans. It would take some considerable explaining, and then I'd be in for the whole thing all over again with Uncle Elisha.

Jack abandoned the chair he'd been carrying and slumped down onto Velma's, looking like something was wrong, and it was. In all the craziness of the past day, he told me, we'd missed a big news story. Medgar Evers, hero of the Mississippi civil rights movement, had been gunned down by a white supremacist in his own home in Jackson, Mississippi, bleeding out on the floor of his garage while his pregnant wife and two little children looked on in horror. My dad must have already known, being an early morning newspaper reader, a news-on-the-car-radio guy. But it wouldn't have been like him to bring it up and dampen anyone's spirits, least of all his own, not on that fine proud day.

While we were high on our own glories on the night before

Class Day, President Kennedy had gone on television to talk about the country's "moral crisis," and make a promise to end segregation and work toward equality. Medgar Evers had listened to the speech with friends and then gone to a meeting to discuss the speech and to prepare himself for the next day, when he would testify to the House Judiciary Committee in favor of civil rights legislation. Just after midnight, Evers pulled into his garage and stepped out of his car and into the sights of Byron de Beckwith's high-powered rifle. While we were at Class Day laughing over the inside jokes we'd accumulated in four years of comparative leisure, hundreds of Blacks were facing down white police in the streets of Jackson. The years of assassinations and riots had begun.

That's when I should have told Jack my dad's story about standing in the circle down in South Carolina, about Granddaddy saying that when all the brothers stood together, they couldn't be knocked over. But I paused, and my best friend and I said our simple good-byes, as if we were going to wake up the next day under the eaves in Eliot.

# 10 *Alumni*

*During the first week of classes in the fall of 1963, Ononeze "Martin"* Anoche,* the Nigerian whom we had elected AAAAS president the previous May, sent a six-page letter to the Faculty Committee on Student Activities, reiterating the arguments in favor of approval of the organization with the original membership clause intact: "open to African and Afro American students currently enrolled at Harvard and Radcliffe." It was mid-November before the FCSA took up the issue, and then they refused to approve it, once again on the grounds of what they saw as racial discrimination in the membership clause. People have told me that over the next few weeks there were intense negotiations between the administration and the club, with Archie Epps as the uncomfortable mediator. In early December, AAAAS relented and deleted the phrase "African and Afro American," but added: "membership shall be by invitation." This, they realized, could achieve the same end. But it was just what Armah had tried to avoid when he kept saying, "We can't lie. Don't lie."

At least it was done and over with, and the real business of the group could begin. But AAAAS ran afoul of the administration again almost immediately, with their first public event in late Jan-

* Anoche, like many of the other Africans at Harvard at the time, had his name butchered repeatedly and, it seems, also wrote it in a variety of ways. His January 14, 1964, letter to the *Crimson,* for instance, was either signed or misprinted as "Omenese Martin Ameshia."

uary 1964. James Baldwin had been contracted to speak on "The Cultural Implications of the Negro Revolt." Admission was to be free to AAAAS members, fifty cents for members of civil rights organizations and residents of the local Black communities of Roxbury and Dorchester, and a dollar for everyone else. Hold up there, the dean said, you can't do that, or if you want to, you can't use Sanders Theater. That's discrimination. AAAAS argued that the sliding scale was intended to make it affordable for Harvard's low-income neighbors. Boston's de facto residential segregation meant that those paying half-price would be virtually all African American, and the dean argued back that "under no circumstances could we allow a group to discriminate on the basis of residence in a particular city, or the type of clothes worn, or race, religion, or creed." All of which, of course, the Final Clubs had been doing, openly and without compunction, without interference or veto from the college, for years. AAAAS would soon concede and a flat fifty-cent fee got everyone in to hear Baldwin, but not before President Anoche blasted out a long and strident letter to the editor that presaged things to come in race relations at Harvard and beyond. He talked about a "Negro Revolution" and explained that AAAAS's purpose with the sliding scale was "not just to soothe the cares of the big-handed intellectual hypocrites in universities, but rather to enable all the people in the Boston area who are committed to the struggle to hear whatever suggestions Mr. Baldwin might have." Those people, Anoche pointed out, were Black and white. He went on to recall the membership controversy: "And the big club with which they smash all such worthy endeavors is always the same: frantic charges of 'reverse racism,' 'black supremacy,' and 'black paranoia.' Staunch members of our Association will not be bothered a tiny bit by the hypocritical efforts that are being made to present us as 'the bad guys.' All of us know that if we wanted to be thought 'nice' we should know better than to join a principled and determined Association such as the AAAAS. An intelligent and intellectually honest Afro-American must forget the idea of being considered nice."

I had heard that AAAAS had relented on the membership

clause, and I recall feeling sold out, that the guys we'd elected and entrusted with our plans had caved. I don't think I heard about the sliding scale issue for the James Baldwin lecture, and only all these years later have I read Anoche's letter to the editor. I now see that whatever compromises they made, the group at least had fought the good fight.

That spring small groups of students participated in various demonstrations in support of the civil rights movement in the South; others raised money for SNCC legal expenses, rallied to commemorate the *Brown v. Board of Education* decision, and protested the war in Vietnam; still others raised their voices against cutting down the sycamores that lined Memorial Drive, against making house assignments by computer, or against the removal of cigarette machines from university property. Roy Wilkins spoke on campus, Malcolm X came again, Martin Kilson criticized liberals for hypocrisy, and in April a graduate student named "Mr. Barack OBama" (his name looking strangely Irish) presented his views on "East Africa—The Economics of Non-Integration."

And then it was another flowery spring at Harvard, another Commencement. Once again, a procession of shiny top hats, tasseled mortarboards, velvet tams, military caps, and even a few bare heads bobbed along past the ivied walls, under crimson VE-RI-TAS flags. Near the end of the procession, the lowly bachelor's degree candidates let decorum lapse a little, chatting excitedly and waving to friends and family. As the gowned boys rounded a corner, a young man in street clothes called out, "Easter, is that you, Easter? You sonofabitch, you made it!" He jumped the ropes to go up and shake Fred's hand briefly and then dutifully stepped back into place. The guy was a section man in geology, the course that Fred had flunked back in his fateful sophomore year. Not only had Fred made it to graduation, he'd won a public speaking contest just a few weeks earlier. And after the last prayer was prayed in the formal Commencement ceremony, Fred stood up and dodged and weaved his way back to his family, as I had done the year before. His family now included his wife, Mary, and their eleven-month-old daughter, Allison Garner Easter. They'd soon be moving to New York City, where Fred would enter an executive training program at Time, Inc.

Also in the procession that day were Travis Williams, Bobby Gibbs, and John Woodford. John and Eliza had "officially broken up" the previous summer, and she had spent a year in Germany, working on her master's degree and, her parents hoped, getting over John. But the two exchanged letters, and they would soon give up on "getting over" each other.

I had spent the school year living on East Eighteenth Street near Third Avenue in Manhattan and learning that I was neither suited for nor interested in medicine as a career. It had always been more my parents' idea than mine, but I had no better ones to counter with. NYU had decided to take a chance on me, so I took a chance on NYU. I got an apartment with another med student and bought my books and the white lab coat that some of the guys just seemed to love putting on every morning. Right away, the coat was a poor fit for me. I was not as well prepared or as driven by passion as my classmates, many of whom were sons of doctors or boys who grew up wanting nothing more than to be a doctor. All the classes were tough, especially when it came to dissecting a cadaver, even more so after we somehow found out the name and life history of the human being who'd lived his life in the body we were hacking up. NYU was next to the New York City Coroner's Office, and when word filtered in as we sat in the cafeteria at lunch that an interesting murder or accident victim was down in the morgue, there'd be a stampede downstairs to catch a look. At first, I joined in, but later I dodged the crowd. NYU was also near Bellevue Hospital, with its famous (and infamous) psychiatry department, and we first-year med students had to go over there once a week. I soon dreaded Thursday mornings, when we would meet in a grim little conference room and listen as the instructor brought in the first "case" and described the unfortunate person's affliction. I began to think that if I stayed in med school, I might wind up as one of the "cases."

So I quit and crossed one career off the list of possibilities. To clear my head, I took off with a friend on a cross-country road trip and even considered staying on in Los Angeles to study acting. That odd idea evaporated quickly, and I crossed another career off the list. Back in New York, I shelved the idea of "career" and just looked for a job. I found one without much trouble, and suddenly I was living the modest dream I'd had as a kid: every morning I put on a dark suit, white shirt, and tie, picked up a sleek briefcase, and rode the subway uptown to the offices of Ted Bates Advertising Agency. I don't remember how I ended up there in an account executive training program; Ted Bates might have been under some pressure, either from within or outside, to hire Blacks. I know that the agency had a strong Ivy League presence, and I'm sure that argued in my favor. The work typically involved researching and writing market reports, which was fine, but what I liked best was spending time on the television commercial sets. I asked for a transfer, but the Ted Bates Agency didn't have a spot for me in that department, so I left there for the Grey Agency, which did have a job for me as a producer of TV commercials. There I learned the trade and gained skills with cameras and lighting and actors and technicians, all of which would actually become my path to the elusive "career."

It was fun, but the absence of some larger purpose often nagged at the corners of my mind; trying to make breakfast cereal appear to float out of the box—with pretty much no special effects—wasn't exactly a calling.

Like me, John Woodford had spent the mid-1960s trying out options for a future. The summer after graduation, he was the only Black member of a group of Harvard graduate students who went to Mississippi to teach summer school at Tougaloo Southern Christian College. The organizers saw the trip as a pilot project for "assistance to Southern Negro colleges" that would someday involve faculty and grad students from many northern schools, as "a more efficient use of talent" than voter registration drives or sit-ins. Although he was driven to act in the civil rights movement, John said that he didn't "have whatever it takes to face armed attackers with no matching weapons of my own." During the first weeks when they were in Tougaloo, Martin Luther King came by and announced that CORE field workers Michael Schwerner, Andrew Goodman, and James Chaney were missing, and everyone feared the worst. By the time John finished his summer teaching, the bodies would be found: the two white men had been shot through their hearts, and the Black man was shot, beaten, and castrated. One could hardly overestimate the dangers.

John came back north in one piece to begin graduate school in an interdisciplinary sociology program at the University of Chicago. He loved living in the city, where he had a lively circle of friends and activities, but he soon found that he'd made the wrong choice academically, so he quit grad school and got a job with the Chicago-based Black publishing house, Johnson Publishing, first writing for *Jet* magazine and then for *Ebony*. Eliza was working in Cleveland, and as far as her parents were concerned, the two had parted ways permanently. But in fact, John and Eliza continued to write to each other regularly; then in late 1964 they met, as John described it, "clandestinely" at the Cleveland Museum of Art. The outcome of that meeting was a decision, again in John's words, that they "might as well get married." And despite some last-minute attempts to dissuade them, they did marry, in January 1965, at John's place in Chicago, with just family and a few friends in attendance. His freshman roommate and great friend Travis Williams was John's first choice for best man, but he feared that Travis was drinking to excess in those days, so he chose someone else.

Jack Butler's first job in the "real world" was as an administrative assistant at a bank. After about a year there and another working as a market analyst for *Sports Illustrated,* Jack went back to Cambridge to get his MBA at Harvard. He would later write that he was "pursuing an ambition that took root during my years at Harvard." That ambition was to move to Africa and start a business. He had become, he remembered, "really convinced at that point that African Americans had a limited future in this country and that Africa was the place where more of us were going to have to pursue our opportunities. And I guess I considered myself a part of the vanguard of African Americans who would go over there, make connections with our African brothers and sisters and prepare them for the onslaught of African Americans who would be following me."

While Jack was dreaming of Africa, Ghanaian Ayi Kwei Armah was already there. He had set out with passion and commitment, expecting that he and his Radcliffe girlfriend would help rescue his home country from the political chaos into which it had been descending since independence. One biographer described his trip as "an idealistic quest for self-fulfillment through self-sacrifice and revolutionary action." Armah worked as a translator for *Revolution Africaine,* but before a year was over, he'd come back to Harvard, having suffered "a debilitating setback." Sketches of his life tend to brush past this time in Armah's life, but several people told me that he'd had a "nervous breakdown." Whether that is the right phrase or not, it is certain that his physical and mental health had taken a beating; back in Cambridge, though, he regained his strength and finished his Harvard degree. He also decided there that it was through his writing that he would make his way in the world and help build modern Africa, and in a few years he would establish himself as among the foremost modern African writers with his first novel, *The Beautyful Ones Are Not Yet Born.*

In contrast to those of us who were taking some time to figure out where we were going, Lowell Davidson followed his passion, music. Although he was also vitally interested in the biochemistry he was studying at Harvard, it was music—jazz in particular—that was consuming him. He played in various groups and at different venues in the early and mid-1960s, displaying his virtuosity and experimenting with new sounds, new instruments, and original compositions. Somehow, in the summer of 1964, he came into the orbit of jazz saxophonist Ornette Coleman, who had risen to the forefront of the new wave of improvisational jazz that came to be known as Free Jazz. Playing with Coleman pushed Davidson's improvisations and explorations into a new phase, and he found like minds in drummer Milford Graves (my old Boys High School pal) and bassist Gary Peacock. Coleman caught the ear of a producer at ESP Records, who urged him to record the new Lowell Davidson Trio. On July 27, 1965, they spent the day in a recording studio and laid down their tracks. According to Milford, it all happened in one exciting session, "no take one, take two—we just did it. How? Some things you don't know, like the origin of the universe."

However, Harvard was losing patience with Davidson's academic progress, or lack thereof. In his sixth year as an undergraduate, he'd been sucking down a large scholarship every semester but not spending very much time on campus, let alone in classes. So they asked him to leave—or that's how Milford remembered it anyhow. But maybe they didn't. Others I spoke to thought that he did accumulate enough credits to graduate, and then got a job (or was it a graduate assistantship?) in a lab at MIT . . . or maybe it was a private firm on Long Island . . . and somehow he was involved in a tragic lab accident . . . that left him with lifelong injuries . . . or the story of the accident was created to cover for his drug problems. I stopped trying to piece together Lowell Davidson's life story out of the many rumors that swirled around him. Few deny that he was using drugs at the time, but it doesn't seem like drugs were using him. What is undeniable is that the Lowell Davidson Trio made a memorable piece of jazz history.

By the mid-1960s, George Jones and Bill Exum were deep into the graduate studies that would lead to their careers in academia. Wesley Williams was in graduate school too, collecting the first of his many advanced degrees. Several of my classmates' careers were temporarily sidelined by either war or peace. Hobie's lifetime career with IBM was interrupted by a stint in the Army. Bobby Gibbs was drafted and served his two years, like Hobie, stateside. Ezra Griffith put in two years, one of them in Saigon, before he took up his studies in medicine. Three of our Black classmates joined the Peace Corps: Kent Wilson went to Ecuador to work in something called "rural community development," which for him translated into coaching the Ecuadorian national track team. Gerry Secundy was placed in Peru in a development program that, among other things, aimed to help the locals grow potatoes—something they had been doing for centuries quite well, thank you. He then took up the direction of a youth center. For two years after finishing law school, Lowell Johnston was in western Venezuela, working with city government "in a program with lawyers, city planners and architects sent over to try to 'improve' local public administration."

And then it was 1968. It's been described as "the year America unraveled," "one of the most tumultuous years in history," "the year that changed the nation," "the year that rocked the world." Death and destruction in Vietnam were escalating, and so were antiwar protests; the assassinations of Martin Luther King and Robert Kennedy, just two months apart, were tragic in themselves and also set off new rounds of rioting; violent clashes between students and police broke out at the Democratic National Convention in Chicago, in Paris and Mexico City, and in dozens of other cities worldwide; Tommie Smith and John Carlos medaled in the Mexico City Olympics and raised their fists to Black Power in the awards ceremony; the first two African Americans to be elected mayors of major cities took office; while in Orangeburg, South Carolina, young protesters trying to integrate a bowling alley were shot at and three were killed.

Lowell Johnston got back to the United States from Venezuela late that year, and within a week he was hard at work for the NAACP Legal Defense Fund, whose offices at the time were at 10 Columbus Circle in Manhattan. On one of his first days on the job, Lowell stepped onto the elevator and found himself face to face with his old suitemate from the fifth floor of Eliot House—me. I was also at a new job, coincidentally in the same building. For the past ten months or so, I'd been a producer on the groundbreaking public television program *Black Journal*.

Lowell had planned on traveling around for a while after the Peace Corps, but the Legal Defense Fund job wouldn't wait, and he'd been thrown into a case immediately. While I'd been making TV commercials and Lowell had been in Venezuela, civil rights actions and violence had continued in a South unwilling to relinquish segregation, and racial tensions had erupted violently in northern cities. In 1964, for instance, there were riots in Rochester and Chicago and Philadelphia and several New Jersey cities. Watts exploded in 1965. As the summer of 1966 approached, it was clear that this wasn't going to quiet down anytime soon. The rioting continued into 1967, which might have brought a "Summer of Love" for white youth, but for Blacks in Tampa, Minneapolis, Detroit, Milwaukee, Washington, DC, and dozens of other cities, it was the summer of anger and violence, tear gas, broken glass, and bullets. Newark, New Jersey, was the site of one of the ugliest riots, and soon Lowell would be working on a case there, when labor unions challenged New Jersey's affirmative action plan.

The riots played a role in my life too. National Education Television (NET), the forerunner of the Public Broadcasting Service (PBS), allocated funds to do a show about the rioting and put a white producer, Al Perlmutter, in charge of a documentary project. With cities still burning, President Lyndon Johnson appointed a commission to find out what was causing the unrest and what could be done about it. In February 1968, the commission released its report, citing white racism as the root cause of the violence and issuing its famous warning: the country was "moving toward two societies, one black, one white—separate and unequal." The report also criticized white domination of mass media; from staffing to programming to implicit messaging, television was all about "the white man's world." In response, NET decided to reallocate the funds for the Perlmutter project to a new show that would be "of, by, and for Blacks." Perlmutter would still be in charge, and a number of other in-house white producers were assigned to the show. There were exactly zero Black producers at the station, but they pulled a man named Lou Potter from the research department and made him an associate producer. Beyond that, NET would have to go out of house to find Blacks to work on the show. By luck, I met one of the white producers, Phil Burton, at a party, and when he learned what I'd been doing, he sent me to Perlmutter. In early 1968, I left TV commercials behind forever and started applying my skills to something that mattered.

On a Wednesday night in mid-June 1968, on Channel 13 in the New York metro area and on about 150 public television stations around the country, the Black comedian Godfrey Cambridge walked into frame in a house painter's overalls, holding a paint roller and a can of paint. He rolls thick black paint up and down, back and forth, onto a glass between himself and the viewer, seeming to paint the screen black. He leaves a smaller and smaller window through which the viewer can see his face, and finally that's painted over too, making the screen all black. A strong jazz theme comes up, heavy on the horns and with a distinctly Afro-Cuban flavor, and the words BLACK JOURNAL swipe in. Cut to a slim Black man—Lou House—standing at a small podium in a pale sports jacket. He announces, in a perfect standard-English newsman voice, "Good evening. This is *Black Journal*, program number one. It is our aim in the next hour and in the coming months to report and review the events, the dreams, the dilemmas of Black America and Black Americans."

The very first feature on the very first show took viewers to, of all places, Harvard. Martin Luther King had agreed to speak at Class Day for the class of 1968, but he had been murdered just weeks before. Coretta Scott King addressed the graduates in his place, and *Black Journal* covered it. Later in the story we see five young Black men from the class of 1968 talking about their future plans, about how and why they planned to serve the race. They are members of the Harvard African American Society—the name had been slightly altered, but this was our AAAAS, carried forward, growing in strength and number since we'd left.

Program number one also featured a human-interest story about a Black jockey, a summary of news stories involving Blacks, and an extended piece about the Black Panther Party that included an interview with Huey Newton in jail, where he was awaiting trial. Also airing that night was a report on New Breed, an "organization of some 150 Soul Brothers" that had launched stores in major cities to "offer a new direction in men's clothes—the Afro American look." The organization was, in one man's words, "quietly building a nation" that one day would meet "all Black consumer needs." As my parents watched at home in Queens, they saw WRITER AND PRODUCER: KENT GARRETT scroll by in the credits. But it almost hadn't been that way. Perlmutter had originally given the New Breed assignment to Phil Burton, but when Phil showed up at the Harlem store, the company representatives refused to work with a white man. That's how I got the story.

That first broadcast of *Black Journal* concluded with Godfrey Cambridge again, this time in a comedy skit with two white men. The three play television producers, charged with dreaming up an idea for a TV show that will "portray the average Negro in a realistic and courageous manner." The two white guys come up with one idiotic idea after another. They ignore Cambridge and cut him off every time he tries to speak. That skit—and also what had happened with the New Breed story—said a lot about *Black Journal.* It was supposed to be, as NET proudly promoted, "*of, for,* and *by* Blacks." But the executive producer was white. And so were a lot of the producers, and they made most of the editorial decisions. In fact, I didn't know about the Harvard story until I saw it on air.

All summer in the cheap little diners and bars where Black staff hung out, we vented our frustrations. We had no personal gripes with the white individuals we worked with; they were smart, liberal, decent guys whom we liked, but we still had to fight them. It felt to me like the AAAAS controversy all over again. Sure, Phil Burton could have done a creditable job with the New Breed story, and he did have more journalistic experience than I did. But we would have ended up with a different story. The brothers at New Breed wouldn't have acted with Phil as they did with me, and Phil wouldn't have seen or understood them as I did. Like Freddy in AAAAS, the brothers at New Breed didn't "want to have to explain shit to white people." Neither did we at *Black Journal.*

Blacks all over the country and the world were standing up to white power. Even the guys at New Breed, we realized, had put themselves on the line and risked forgoing some free national publicity in order to make their point about Black control of Black institutions. We needed to do something to make the same point. So we went to the management and demanded a Black executive producer, recommending Lou Potter. NET didn't bring up what Jack Butler referred to as "the old canard of reverse racism," as Harvard had done with AAAAS. Instead, NET insisted that Lou simply didn't have enough experience to "assume at this time the role of executive producer, a most complicated organizational job ranging from budget control to the last details of scenic design." And although they had looked, they insisted, they couldn't find anyone with the qualifications. Well, then, we countered, change the promotional copy, because it's false. A few Blacks working under the direction of a white man didn't make it "*by* Blacks." With whites making the top-level editorial decisions, it couldn't even be said that the program was "*of* Blacks." That left the phrase "*for* Blacks" carrying all that patronizing stuff about "uplift" and deficiency.

We should be doing it ourselves, and we knew we could, so in August 1968 we went on strike and called a press conference. "NET has deceived the Black Community by advertising the program series as being 'by, for, and of the black community,'" we announced in our official statement. On a bright hot summer afternoon, we assembled on the stoop of the West Twenty-First Street building where I had a loft apartment, and we made our case to a news crew. To cover the story, WABC sent Gil Noble, their sole Black on-air guy—each of the local stations had one. We all fielded calls from reporters, stressing the hypocrisy of the promotional language and also our feeling that we were "being used as a front" to maintain the illusion that Blacks controlled the program. I complained to one reporter, "Right now it's cool at all the networks to have Black shows, but we're at the stage where Blacks will have to have control." I don't remember making that remark, but I found a brittle yellowed clipping in that scrapbook my mother kept, my name double-underlined in pencil.

Going to the media worked, and Bill Greaves, one of just two seasoned Black filmmakers whom NET would accept, agreed to come aboard as executive producer. We went back to work. On the September show, the change was announced on air. It was also made brilliantly visible. Greaves and Lou House—now Wali Saddiq—open the program sitting in director's chairs, relaxed in their dashikis, no doubt bought from New Breed. Gone are the podium, the sport jacket, and the self-conscious white newsman voice. Saddiq is in shades, a cigarette dangling from his lips and a cup of coffee in his hand. He introduces Greaves and gives a brief description of our strike and the new arrangements, and he raises his fist in the Black Power salute.

I wasn't exactly the dashiki type, but I did buy a slick leather jacket and left the dark suit jacket and tie in the closet. The work, the brotherhood, the power—we were making a difference, raising consciousness, and it was exhilarating! We were proud to be in the struggle, publicly and conspicuously in charge and making history. I often traveled with the talented cameraman Leroy Lucas, and we'd show up in Black communities that had never seen any newsmen, let alone young Black ones asking them questions about their lives, about race and racism and injustice. We basked in the adulation of a public who finally felt heard. Especially after the September episode with the dashikis and the Black Power salute, we would unload our big silver cases of gear in a city and get rock-star treatment, including the parties and groupies.

Besides the pleasures of celebrity, we of course saw our share of racist reality. Greaves once sent Leroy and me to New Orleans to do a story about the racial dynamics of economic development there. We'd found a local Black sound guy who met us at the airport, and we headed out in his car to do our first interview. Three young Black men in a car in the Deep South. We actually made it almost twenty minutes before we were leaning against the car with our hands on the hood, nightsticks and growling cops at our backs. After a quick call to NET in New York, they got their lawyers on it in short order, and the cops were soon claiming the predictable "mistaken identity." I think the cops might even have apologized, surprised that they had come upon some niggers with a little bit of clout. Of course, without the white establishment behind us, we wouldn't have had that clout, and who knows where we'd have ended up.

My next big *Black Journal* project was an investigation of the dilemma of the Black police officer. What was life like for Black cops who were trying to do their jobs but were often criticized for working for "the man"? For three weeks I rode around Harlem in the back of a police cruiser with a white/Black police duo who'd been selected for us by the NYPD. Dave Walker, the Black cop, was a nice guy with a serious but gentle demeanor. He'd been on the force for about two years and was deeply conflicted about how to do his job well while maintaining allegiance to and relationship with the Black community as the Black Power movement gained steam. The fifteen-minute segment called "Black Cop" aired in the fall of 1968. I went on to assignments all over the United States and the world, including Vietnam, where I produced the hourlong "Black GI" episode, which exposed discrimination and inequities in the armed forces. I met key Black leaders, like Andrew Young and Kathleen Cleaver, plus dozens of local leaders and hundreds of everyday brothers and sisters from across the country and the world. *Black Journal* would last for just a few more years, always marginally and contentiously funded, before it morphed into *Tony Brown's Journal,* which was more of an interview show. I then left NET to go into mainstream TV news.

I didn't know it at the time, but by 1968 my Harvard classmate John Woodford had landed in journalism too. After his first brief time at *Ebony* and *Jet* magazines and a couple of years in a master's program in literature at Harvard, John took a stab at law, enrolling at Yale. In the spring of 1968, he summed up his present life situation for the Harvard five-year reunion book: "My feelings about the country are that right now it's run by some of the most vile, bloodless, deceitful, egomaniacal men who ever defaced an era . . . This country has hit the proverbial fan. Those who don't wish to get stained, or to become janitors, had better head for the door. That, at least is my plan." Here John was referring to his and Eliza's plan to go to Canada if John was drafted. He wasn't. "I hope my reaction to the times is wrong," he continued, "but I doubt that it is. I've looked 'long and strong' at the mess; I've got a better wife than I deserve, and a day-old beautiful son to take care of: What can I do but follow my judgment and feelings?"

John's judgment and feelings said that law school wasn't the right path, and he quit that and for a time worked at the *New Haven Journal.* As racial strife continued to heat up, John yearned to write more about civil rights, Black liberation, and the antiwar movement. So he returned to Johnson Publishing, thinking that he'd get that chance writing for *Ebony.* Instead, he ran up against resistance there too. As he would later write, "H. Rap Brown was in jail in Louisiana on trumped-up charges. The Black Panther Party was striding around northern California declaring it the right and duty of our ethnic group—the African-American people—to defend itself with arms against brutal police. And there sat I, in what I thought would be a good position to cover the freedom movement, as an editor/writer for *Ebony* magazine in Chicago. The problem was, in 1968 both Rap Brown and the Panthers were strictly *verboten* as topics for our country's biggest magazine aimed at African-American readers." Johnson publications, like other mainstream media, were dodging important issues, John believed, and following "pocketbook-first principles." So he decided to "seek an employer with more guts to cover stories that needed to be told." He had read *Muhammad Speaks,* the newspaper of the Nation of Islam, when he lived in Chicago, and at the time he'd "enjoyed reading [it] only for its kookiness." But when he went back to it, he found that it dealt in depth with the very topics he most wanted to write about. He heard that they were looking for writers, and after a minor dustup sparked his exit from *Ebony,* John got a job at *Muhammad Speaks.* It was, he said, "a matter of covering what I wanted to cover and giving utterance to radical opinions at full throat." Never a member of the NOI—one of the "mentally dead," as Elijah Muhammad called non-Muslim Blacks—John nonetheless was soon editor-in-chief and would spend four interesting and exciting years there.

In 1968, Freddy Easter found what he would come to consider his life's most important work. Sometime the year before, a friend had asked Fred to come to Carleton College in Northfield, Minnesota, to be part of a summer program for promising kids who needed a boost to be able to go to college. As NSSFNS had done for Fred back in 1959, A Better Chance, founded in 1963, was finding good students in poor schools and arranging to have them go to quality boarding schools to prepare for college. Fred's friend needed someone to help him run the summer program, someone "who had talked to a Black kid before." That January, Fred traveled out to Minnesota to interview the young counselors with whom he'd be working that summer, and then went home to New York.

After the assassination of Martin Luther King, the small number of Black students at Carleton rose up and challenged the administration to find more Black students and faculty. It was going to be very difficult, the administration countered, but they were willing to make some efforts, one of which was to offer a job to Fred. He took the position at Carleton that would soon give him four titles: Associate Director of Admissions, Associate Dean of Students, Director of Minority Affairs, and Director of the Better Chance Program—all at the same time. "Four titles," he told me, "for about fifteen thousand dollars a year." Fred went to work and was successful: "In three years," he told me, "eleven percent of the college population was Black and brown. Some of them flunked out, but I said when I was questioned about it, 'Hey, ten percent of the kids who come to Carleton don't finish. I don't think I'm unsuccessful if ten percent of the Black kids ain't finishing." For counsel and for leads, Fred turned to none other than the man who'd been so important to our arrival at Harvard, the college's unofficial minority recruiter, Dean John Monro, who had left Harvard the year before to take a position at the small, historically Black Miles College near Birmingham, Alabama. There he would fashion English and social studies curricula for the bright but underprepared freshmen who came out of chronically under-resourced high schools.

By 1968, Jack Butler had already completed his master's in business administration at Harvard. Over the summers he had worked as an intern at Mobil Oil doing audits that sometimes took him overseas. On one trip to Hong Kong, Jack saw a chance to fulfill a childhood ambition to visit Africa, and he rerouted his return through Nairobi. Working for Mobil, Jack told me, "I was just marking time before there would be an opportunity for me to go to Africa." He left for Nairobi in late 1968, and for the next fifteen years he would spend the majority of his time living and working in Kenya, where he established the Kiambere Land Development and Building Society, which built multi-unit housing and set up mortgage and financial infrastructure. Jack lived there with his wife, Leslie, whom he had met way back at our first freshman mixer. She told me that Jack always saw "Africa as the motherland, the home."

The year 1968 was pivotal for Black Harvard too, and it all started with AAAAS, by that time usually referred to by its nickname, "Afro." For the first few years after it was finally recognized, Afro served mainly as a discussion forum and a sponsor of lectures. It also produced four issues of the *Harvard Journal of Negro Affairs,* thanks in large part to printing funds provided by Martin Kilson and Archie Epps. African nationals, who'd taken Afro leadership roles early on, drifted away from the group, and US racial politics increasingly took center stage. As early as 1967, maybe earlier, they started talking about the still tiny percentage of Blacks at Harvard—we had been about 1.5 percent of our class, and that had barely budged in the midsixties. Kilson and Epps, although they were now on the paths that would keep them at Harvard through their careers, remained the only Blacks on the college's faculty or in administration. Afro members also talked about the continued absence of anything pertaining to African American history or culture in the curriculum.

Then came April 4, 1968, and the murder of Dr. King. A few days later, President Pusey presided over a packed house at Memorial Church in a tribute to the civil rights martyr. About eighty members of Afro stayed outside on the steps in protest. The Afro president explained, "If they come out of there with tears in their eyes, we want it to be plain that we don't want their tears. We want Black people to have a place here at Harvard." "If they're really sorry," another Afro member said, "they'll change this school." Later that day, Afro presented to the administration "Four Requests on *Fair* Harvard": that the college "establish an endowed chair for a black professor, establish courses relating to black students, hire more lower-level black faculty, and admit more black students to Harvard." In response to the fourth request, the college immediately increased (some say doubled) the number of Black students admitted for the fall of 1969. In response to the first three requests, Harvard did what institutions do: they created a commission. Eventually, after a yearlong fight and "threats of militant confrontation" by Afro, the African American Studies Department, the Black Cultural Center, and the W. E. B. Du Bois Institute for African and African-American Research were established.

## *May 23, 2018*

I finally got myself to a class of 1963 reunion. Before getting into this project, I'd spurned the invitations. During my days at *Black Journal,* I'd come to think of Harvard as part of the "establishment" and not worth my valuable time. Besides, I couldn't imagine what I would actually do at a class reunion, never having been to one, nor was I particularly curious to find out. But then, around the time I started tracking down my classmates, I got a phone call from a young woman who wanted to ask me about my days at *Black Journal.* She was researching a book she would title "Black Power TV." Her book came out in 2013, and pretty soon I heard from another young person, this one planning a film festival—he had read the book and wanted to include "Black Cop," "Black GI," and a piece I'd made on Ethiopia in a film festival at Lincoln Center. That led to another film festival, and then a third, this one at Harvard. Then I got a call from *Harvard Magazine:* could they do a story on me? After all these years, here I was, climbing up on stages to talk about my work and those times, and then there I was in full color in *Harvard Magazine.*

In the interview for the article, I mentioned this book. That led to a call from a classmate asking me if I'd do a panel discussion at our class's fifty-fifth reunion. By the end of our conversation, I'd agreed to do it and even offered to show an edited version of some of the video interviews I'd done with class members. The plan almost fell apart when I found out how much it cost to go to one of those reunions. About $500 to attend, and even the "special" rate at the hotel was more than I think I'd ever paid to sleep anywhere. But the alumni group had money to pay my way, given that I was doing the panel (Harvard always has money). They would bring Freddy out too! So once again Freddy and I were headed for Harvard . . . on scholarship.

Our reunion dinner was held at dear old Eliot House. The dress code had been announced as "business casual," and I took that to mean no necktie. Fred texted me that afternoon to see if I could pick him up later and drive him over; he wasn't well enough to make the walk. I agreed and realized that I still had time to make it to our class's church service to honor those who had passed on since the last reunion. On an ordinary day, the walk across campus to Memorial Church would have taken just a few minutes, but with Commencement two days away, the campus was jammed. Rows of folding chairs were squeezed onto every inch of grass, and workers were still carrying in more; I paused to watch the setup of the dais, projected live on a number of giant TV screens strategically placed throughout the grounds. The only space without chairs was ceded to commerce—big crimson tents surrounded by people handing over their credit cards and leaving with armloads of Harvard shirts and hats and I don't know what else. I wove and dodged through excited families with their graduates, groups of capped-and-gowned friends, and even clumps of tourists—just about every person had a smartphone at the end of an outstretched arm.

I had to hurry, and by the time I got to Memorial Church I was a little bit late and a little bit out of breath. A young person creaked open the door, and I got settled in the back row as quietly as possible. I couldn't see the man in the pulpit, but I could hear him, and oh yes, it was definitely Wes Williams, his sonorous voice leading us through a simple service. Members of the class read a list of those who'd left the planet since the last reunion—a long list, I thought. Wesley closed with words from Martin Luther King's final speech, the one about the mountaintop and how we as a people will get to the promised land, and then led us in the Negro National Anthem, "Lift Every Voice and Sing." It was the kind of beautiful time in church that makes me believe—maybe not in God, but in my fellow humans, especially my fellow Blacks and my Black forebears. "Let us march on till victory is won!"

Fred was waiting for me on the corner of Kirkland and Oxford Streets—apparently, to his mind, "business casual" included shorts and a T-shirt. He was every bit his vibrant, witty self. We shared news as I drove in and out and around through the narrow streets, trying to get us as close to Eliot House as possible. He was staying, he said, with his old friend from back in the projects in Harlem, Bob Moses, the famous SNCC man and lifelong activist. A few more turns, dodging the cones that were probably meant to discourage me, and there we were. I dropped Fred off at the door, parked the car, and walked toward Eliot. Up the steps and into the entryway, I was half-expecting to have a monitor peer out from the little office to make sure I wasn't sneaking a girl in, and then I went on into the dining room, for the first time in fifty-five years, and the first time without a tie. The furniture had been rearranged for our dinner, but otherwise, it was the same grand place. I thought of Jack and the hours we'd spent talking there, I thought of Malcolm X dazzling me that December night so long ago, and I looked around the room without recognizing a soul until I managed to find Fred and John and made my way to their table.

The next morning was warm and clear, worthy of the class of 2018's Class Day, and I fumbled my name tag lanyard over my head and walked from the hotel to the luncheon that would precede our panel discussion. Bob Moses had delivered Fred and would stay for the discussion, Fred reported, and right after that, Bob would take Fred over to Mass. General. The hospital? Well, yeah, Fred said, he was pretty sure he had a pulmonary embolism—he'd had one before—but he was not going to miss the panel. It would turn out that he was right, and he wouldn't get back to Minnesota for a week.

The small stuffy lecture room in Emerson Hall was pretty much packed with gray-hairs, members of the Harvard and Radcliffe classes of 1963, along with a few from other classes, notably 1968, who were at their momentous fiftieth. Scattered here and there, giving up seats to their elders and looking shockingly young, were a few current and recent Black graduates. Fred Easter, John Woodford, Wesley Williams, Ron Blau, and I sat self-consciously behind microphones at a crimson-draped table. I made a few introductory remarks and rolled the video—there bigger than life on the screen were George Jones in his lab, Kent Wilson with his family in Austria, Larry Galindo reminiscing about Cuba, Ezra Griffith remembering Barbados, Hobie talking about football, and me sharing memories of South Carolina; then we heard from Martin Kilson on John Monro's contribution to getting us in, Lowell Johnston on his work with civil rights, John Woodford on *Muhammad Speaks,* and Jack Butler on AAAAS. There was Wesley reminding us that we'd all been "richly blessed," and Freddy saying that we may have been admitted via some kind of affirmative action but "I earned that thing," pointing behind him at his framed Harvard diploma. All of this over Lowell Davidson's music.

The video faded to black, and I cut off the smattering of applause by saying that we were ready for questions and comments. Someone put a microphone into an eager hand, and they were off and running with reminiscences. Someone talked about Archie Epps, another marveled that Connie McDougald had been the only Black woman in the Radcliffe class, and another remembered how influential the Riesman Seminar had been. Every time one person relinquished the mic, a dozen others waved to be next, but soon we were out of time. I closed by thanking the crowd, and people still clustered around us with more to say, as well as bits of advice and words of encouragement. A very young Black student shook my hand and said how glad he was to know about us and our times, which must have seemed prehistoric to him. A few knots of people made their way to the door, and slowly the room began to clear. When I'd gathered up my stuff and reached the door, there were still people crowding around Bob Moses. I sat with Fred on a bench in the hallway while he waited to make his trip to the hospital. What do you think? I asked him. "Well," he said, "we played our positions, we carried the ball and didn't fumble." With that, he pushed himself up and hobbled off with Moses.

Maybe Freddy was referring to our not having "fumbled" the panel discussion, but maybe he was talking about the whole thing —about what the Blacks of the class of 1963 could claim as our accomplishment at Harvard.

We weren't foolish enough to believe that there was nobody who saw our presence as ruining Fair Harvard, no classmates who would have refused to share a table or a backseat or a locker room with us, no boys cracking up over nigger jokes behind closed doors. Of course, we were devalued, even despised, by some of our classmates, professors, and Cambridge neighbors. Others, if they thought of us at all, saw us as anomalies, as strange geniuses plucked from the ghetto. Still others were curious about us or eager to test their liberalness by hanging out with us. But we also had genuine white friends and allies, particularly among the active liberal Jewish circle. We had dates and joined clubs and horsed around and studied and made good use of the superabundance of Harvard. Racists could easily avoid us, and they did so, as Fred said, "by staying the hell away." It was a more innocent time, I think, when despite the horrors of violence and ossified racism, there was still hope. We lived out our Harvard years comfortably for the most part, in a bubble of civil rationality, erudition, genteel politesse, and liberalism.

I don't think anyone in the administration considered the possibility that we might rock the boat, that we might want not only to fit in but to stand out, that we would gravitate toward each other and our younger and older Black and African classmates, or that we would go off together and start talking, finding common cause and feeling the power of our unity, the possibilities of pride and brotherhood. Harvard probably did not suspect that we would ultimately put its liberalism to a test by showing it what exclusion felt like. But that's what happened.

We were optimistic, we were young, and we believed in a changing and changeable world. And one of the changes would be rejecting the name for us that had been in use and choosing our own name. We chose our organization's name not so much as a rejection of "Negro" but as a step forward into the possibility and power that "Afro American" seemed to embody. There was no magic moment when all eighteen of us said, *Okay, we're not Negroes anymore.* But in important ways, we weren't, through the accident of being alive in our times and through the influence of the many voices of the civil rights movement and African liberation. When we came to Harvard, despite the wild diversity among us, despite the fact that some of us were biologically more white than Black, we were all called "Negroes" because a social convention rooted in racism said that we were. I think of us as the "last" Negroes at Harvard not because one or all of us specifically rejected the name, but because we saw that there was another option for naming ourselves and for our very identity as human beings.

Although the administration may not quite have seen it that way, by starting the AAAAS, we put the college out in front with regard to one of the biggest campus movements of the coming years. The new boys who carried their suitcases into Harvard Yard when we left would soon reject the word "Negro" altogether, and they would demand of Harvard things we couldn't yet imagine. The eighteen of us were out in the world by then, some of us making similar demands of the larger society.

Pushing Fred's football metaphor a little further, I'd say we did more than not fumble. I'd say we left our team in scoring position.

Another class dinner was on the reunion agenda, but to me it felt like the right time to go home. My car was over there somewhere, so I set out across the Yard, probably for the last time.

# *Epilogue*

*No longer can I claim that I "hardly ever think about Harvard." Not only* have I thought about it a lot in recent years, but I've read about it, spent time there, gone to reunions, and pored over the anniversary books. (I have yet to give money.) I still get my *Harvard Magazine* these days, and I still flip right to the obituaries. I'll make sure Robert Edgar Gibbs is on the list in the next issue. One wintry morning as I was revising these pages, I thought I'd give my new old friend a call to check up on him, as I'd been doing for the past few years. No answer, no answer, and so I emailed John Woodford, who said he couldn't get through either. We checked with Carter Wilson, who called Bobby's sister and soon emailed to report that Bobby was in the hospital. Less than a week later came the news that he'd died.

When I started this project, my curiosity about my Black classmates was mostly centered on who had done what and who was still on the planet. All that was settled pretty easily, but the larger questions about race and class, about privilege and power, proved much more complicated. I asked everyone why they believed there were "so many" of us in our class. Nobody mentioned "affirmative action," but I've come to know that affirmative action is exactly what it was, though that was before the term had been applied to college admissions and before it acquired the contentious history it carries now. At least half of us were there because we were Black, but more so because we were Black and very capable—we had the "talent" that the National Scholarship Service and Fund for Negro Students was out to find. Even if guys like Glimp and Monro hadn't "beaten the bushes," a few of us probably would have ended up at Harvard, but the total number of Negroes in the class would undoubtedly have been more like the average number for those days—in the single digits.

Glimp and Monro had a vision. If all went well—if we all measured up and blended in and kept smiling—presumably Harvard could just go on finding a small number of good Negroes like us and the college would be pleasingly integrated. It would remain the same old revered institution, but with a few good Negroes sprinkled around, Harvard would look and feel forward-thinking. That sounds cynical, but I don't believe it's inconsistent with what Fred Glimp told me about himself and John Monro and others—that they knew that "it was the right thing to do." Glimp also told me that there were those who thought it was unnecessary—if not pure folly—to make a special effort to bring Negroes to the college. Judging from the fact that they called that scholarship money the "Gamble Fund," it seems clear that even those at the center of the effort had their doubts. They believed that they were taking a gamble on us, that we might flunk out, scare the whites, or upset the alumni.

But really, who was taking the gamble? Nobody seemed to have given a second thought to whether we would be the targets of racism—whether a cross might once again burn in Harvard Yard, or white boys would ask for separate dining rooms. No one seemed to have considered how unnerving it might be to find ourselves the subject of thousands of stares and at least two sociological studies. That was the gamble we ourselves had taken by coming to Harvard at the end of the 1950s. We were left to fend for ourselves in a job that we hadn't signed up for—to integrate lofty white Harvard, to answer questions, to be given clever names and slip seamlessly into the fabric of the college. I don't believe anyone at Harvard was particularly concerned that by recruiting specifically in the South and the ghetto, they had pulled some of us into an unknown world. Young Charles Frazier of Mobile, Alabama, may have been a casualty in that gamble. His widow still believes he was.

Still, by Harvard's terms, the gamble paid off. Everyone who stayed got his degree, except possibly Lowell Davidson (who made jazz history instead). Nobody got in any real trouble. Did we change Harvard? Well, except for those freshman meals at the Black Table, we did mix in happily with the white boys. Both our mixing-in and our self-segregating, I believe, changed the class of 1963; our mere presence and our competence surely changed a few minds among those boys who looked at us but kept their distance, and I feel sure that we profoundly changed some of our closest white friends, like Ron Blau and Frank Bardacke. Having a Black class marshal made a statement too.

Our legacy in the institution is the African and Afro American Society, originally AAAAS and later just "Afro." The group we started would grow in numbers and strength, make demands, and even threaten violence in order to get a significant Black presence on campus, more Black administration and faculty, a Black studies program, a dramatic increase in Black enrollment, and the W. E. B. Du Bois Institute for African and African-American Research. AAAAS was a small start from which future generations of Afro grew. More than that, our membership controversy was an early sign that the liberal integrationist image for the United States—institutions, neighborhoods, workplaces, and play places unchanged but newly speckled with a few happy Blacks, pleasantly and evenly distributed—might not be the way things were going to go.

In 2018, I met one of the later Afro leaders at yet another reunion, though not of my own class. Shortly after our class's fifty-fifth, I got an email from Sylvester Monroe, who introduced himself as a Black member of the class of 1973. He had read about my project in *Harvard Magazine.* Would I join him and a few classmates on a panel at their forty-fifth reunion to talk about being Black at Harvard? I agreed to come, having gotten used to saying yes to these invitations.

The panel discussion was held at the old Brattle Theater not far from campus, where we had taken in the big movie hits and odd little experimental films back in the day. I didn't have a great deal to add, I soon found out, because our experience was so different from that of the class of 1973. They were the freshman class who arrived in the fall of 1969 with about a hundred Blacks, after the administration had agreed to most of Afro's strident demands about admissions. The Blacks of '73 on the panel remembered race relations as tense and strained at Harvard. Separatism had become the order of the day. Sylvester Monroe commented that it was possible—indeed, it was probable—that Black students would spend the majority of their time with other Blacks exclusively. For him, it had been "a wholly Black world." By then, I'd been working on this book for a long time, and I had never imagined that.

Although I think I can understand the separatist urge, I'm glad it wasn't that way for me. People often ask me what I got out of going to Harvard, and over the years I've blabbered on about "learning how to think." Which I did. I also benefited from having some professors who were famous and at the top of their field, and I know that my Harvard degree brought my résumé near the top of the pile when I applied for jobs and posts throughout my life. That I didn't come out with the "twenty-five friends for life"—part of Harvard lore—says more about me than about Harvard.

After spending these last years immersed in pondering those years and how they changed me, I've come to believe that living and dealing with whites was very useful when I went out into the world. For the first seventeen years of my life, I spent almost no meaningful time with whites. When I got to college, it was high time that I did, and Harvard might well have been the best place on earth to do it. At meals and in classes and bull sessions, I got comfortable being with them. Even answering all those nutty questions from Branon and Blau gave me a window into the white world, and their weird curiosity made me think about whiteness in new ways. Maybe I should have asked some white guy, as Gordie Main did with Freddy, "What's it like to be white?" He might have even let me touch his hair.

Besides that, in going to college with whites, I held my ground with some of the most gifted, which gave me confidence in my ability. I lived with some of the most powerful, and I found out that they were decent and ordinary. There was no reason I couldn't walk up to a Rockefeller or a Vanderbilt and look him in the eye, even feel myself to be his equal, joke around with him, bullshit him, or ignore him. But I also learned that in the end even decent, liberal Harvard could be hypocritical when it came to protecting the moneyed classes upon whom it depended. It took all of a day for the administration to denounce the AAAAS membership clause, while for more than a hundred years, they had bowed before the Final Clubs, never challenging their open discrimination.

It's a long process, this learning about white people, especially when your family doesn't talk about them openly. I'd been learning about them all my life without actually knowing it, and Harvard offered some new and potent lessons.

Jack Butler's older sister Beverly and I were talking on the phone one afternoon about the good (and bad) old days when she said something that brought this home to me again. We were talking about those questions that crowd in on folks of our age, the issues around declining health and maintaining independence. In "the next few years," she said, using that phrase we all seem to be overly fond of and underspecific about at this point in our lives, she would sell her house and move to a retirement community; she had, in fact, found one that she liked very much, in North Carolina. It was all white, but she reassured me that she'd be fine: "You know how it is, Kent—I know them better than they know us." I'm still struck by the elegance of her statement, and yes, I guess I do know how it is. W. E. B. Du Bois wrote with regard to white people, "I am singularly clairvoyant. I see in and through them. I see these souls undressed and from the back and sides. I see the working of their entrails. I know their thoughts and they know that I know." When I talked to Fred Easter about Bev's remark, he agreed, adding, "I don't think you can get to this age and be Black in America without understanding white people very well." It was, he said, something almost unconscious, "like looking both ways when you cross the street."

The perfect complement to my education about whites was the time I spent with my fellow Blacks—and with Jack in particular. It was his insights and friendship that nudged me toward seeing the promise of brotherhood and the need to stand up and fight as I did at *Black Journal.*

After my days at *Black Journal,* I seem to have lived a life of tens: ten years producing the news at CBS, ten years at NBC, ten years working as a dairy farmer. Then there are the ten years I have spent working on this book project. When I started my long trip down memory lane in 2008, going around the country and the world, reconnecting with Freddy and John, Wesley and Jack and the others, it seemed like the perfect era to be reflecting on those long-gone days. The possibility of a Black president of the United States was on the horizon, and as I started my journey it became a reality. People were talking about a "postracial society," and I felt a guarded optimism, a recharged belief in a changeable world. As I talked to my Black classmates, although we'd all been hardened by the injuries and frustrations of our long years of being Black in America, I don't think there was one of us who was not in some way seduced into feeling hopeful again.

By the time I was in the final days of this project, and as I write now, that hope has all but vanished. It seems to me that our lives have been bracketed by the hard realities of racism in America—the obscenities of Jim Crow defined our childhoods and the obscenities of Trumpism are defining our old age. In the years between, there have been ups and downs, but until recently there have been many times when it has seemed that the moral arc of history, as King put it, might just be bending toward justice. But those better days, if they ever were really better, feel very long ago now, and I wonder how I could have been optimistic at all.

As I write today, there are twelve of us left here on earth, now that Bobby Gibbs is gone. Bob beat the life expectancy for Black men in the United States by a couple of years but didn't quite make it to the average for white men. Meanwhile, educational achievement gaps have failed to close substantially, white supremacy has regained power and legitimacy, and the injustice system has stepped in where lynching left off. Until we moved a year ago, Jeanne and I lived across the street from a house with a Confederate flag in the front window.

So here I am at age seventy-seven, and like Freddy, I'm "a pissed-off Black man." But I'm my father's son, and so I'm not going to just sit around being pissed off. As I write, Dad is ninety-seven. He was pushing ninety when he took on an enormous project, as cochair of a committee from Calvary Baptist Church in Queens to build an affordable apartment complex for grandparents who were the sole caregivers for their grandchildren. After the committee raised millions of dollars and plowed through miles of red tape, it finally one day broke ground and the building of the complex was under way. The formal ribbon-cutting took place on a warm September morning in 2016. I was there to hear the speeches and applaud as we watched my dad and others wield big ceremonial scissors and declare that the CGG complex—the Covington-Garrett-Glover Intergenerational Homes—was now open. Covington for the woman who cochaired the committee, Glover for the ten-year-old Black boy shot by a cop on that block back in 1973, and Garrett for my father.

When the time came to apply to the City of New York for a tax exemption, I drove Dad into Manhattan to testify before the City Council, and they agreed to a thirty-year exemption. Dad thanked them and replied, "Okay, and then I'll be back." I wouldn't be surprised.

So now, yes, I am a pissed-off Black man, but one with enough fight left for at least the next twenty years. I've taken the producing and reporting guns off the shelf, saddled up, and joined the resistance. I now write a blog and produce a radio news show here in rural, conservative upstate New York. One of my recurring commentators is John Woodford, and I'm working on Fred Easter and Lowell Johnston to do guest spots too. Maybe I can do some good, change some minds and attitudes, before I ride off into the sunset.

# *The Gallery*

## *Hobart Glenn Armstrong Jr.*

***Born:*** *Kingston, New York, 1941*

***Prepared at:*** *Kingston High School, Kingston, New York*

Hobie Armstrong is the quintessential hometown sports hero in Kingston, New York. When I visited to do our first interview, Hobie showed me into his den to talk. It was what I'd describe as a serious personal sports bar, fitted out with a giant captain's recliner with a cup-and-snack holder, facing two televisions. By the side of the chair sat a set of hand weights—I could picture Hobie taking in two football games at once while lifting his hand weights, but he refrained from picking them up as he told me about his family. Not surprisingly, Hobie's conversational style often resembles "athlete-speak," that pattern of Q&A that you hear on television when the commentator down on the field grabs the quarterback as he's headed into the locker room.

Hobart Glenn Armstrong Sr. was born in 1896 in Gastonia, North Carolina, and Ethel Marie, Hobie's mother, in 1900, just across the border in Clover, South Carolina, making them a full generation older than my own parents. They escaped the South in 1928, coming to Kingston to work in the brick-making industry, which had made money from the veins of fine rich ice-age clay in the Hudson River valley since the late 1700s. Hobie Senior was a big, strong man who was famous, his son remembered, for being able to hold four bricks in one hand. Hobie Junior was the youngest of eight children, all of whom were also strong and tended to use their power on the athletic fields.

As a first-year Little Leaguer, Hobie led the league in home runs at the age of nine, playing against boys as old as twelve. He is remembered even today as "probably the greatest athlete Kingston ever produced." Folks in Kingston use the word "legend" when they talk about Hobie. In high school, he lettered in four sports, but his star performances were as the outstanding player on the varsity football team that went 23–0–1 during the three years Hobie led the team. As of 2017, he still held the school record for most career touchdowns (37) and points scored (237).

Hobie was the first in his family to graduate from college. At Harvard, he was in Adams House, and he excelled at football and track and graduated on time with a concentration in physical sciences. Right after graduation, he took a job as a computer programmer at IBM and came back to the Kingston area to work and help his family. Drafted three years later, he served in the Army from 1966 to 1968, working in an engineering science program for weapons testing at the Aberdeen Proving Grounds in Maryland. Back at IBM, he moved up into middle management, often doing minority recruitment and, of course, playing on their football, basketball, volleyball, and softball teams. Hobie retired in 1993, and since then he has played on three New York State championship softball teams and become a deacon at his New Jerusalem United Baptist Church. Plus, he told me, "if you look around, I've got a yard to take care of, a house to take care of."

A few days before I arrived to visit him, the city newspaper had run a feature article titled "One of the Greatest: Committee Seeks to Honor Star Athlete Hobie Armstrong." Three years later, they did it. In a ceremony on the field where he'd played, they unveiled a monument in his likeness and presented him with the first Hobie Armstrong Excellence Award, for "commitment and excellence in athletics, community, education, and family." In 2017, Kingston High School opened its new sports Hall of Fame, and Hobie was in the first inductee class.

## *John Gordon Butler*

***Born:*** *Pittsburgh, Pennsylvania, 1941*

***Prepared at:*** *Schenley High School, Pittsburgh, Pennsylvania*

***Died:*** *2011*

Jack received his MBA from the Harvard Business School in 1966 and spent most of the next fifteen years in Kenya, where he established the Kiambere Land Development and Building Society, building low-cost housing estates. When he returned to the United States, he taught business courses at the State University of New York at New Paltz and stayed involved in a number of organizations. In 1998, he cofounded a nonprofit called the Partnership to Strengthen African Grassroots Organizations, and in 2004 he joined the advisory board of the Murunderera Project for HIV/AIDS Orphaned Children in Bikanka, Burundi. He died in 2011 of multiple myeloma.

There were three memorial celebrations for Jack, and I went to two of them. The first was hosted by the Harvard Business

School African American Alumni Association (HBSAAAA). Jack had served as the first treasurer and throughout the rest of his life he undertook a dizzying array of responsibilities for the organization. In a richly paneled meeting room at the Harvard Club in Manhattan, several dozen of us gathered to pay tribute. The larger memorial planned by Jack's widow, Roni, and his siblings took place a week later, on a windy May afternoon at the beautiful Mohonk Mountain House. The events at each of the memorials were similar, opening in a way that felt a little more religious than I believed Jack would have preferred, but who am I to say? Among the many who spoke was one of our older brothers at Harvard, Otis Gates, who talked about the time he and his wife and four children visited Jack and his family in Nairobi; a younger man, also a Harvard Business School grad, described Jack's fortitude in managing the many complications of doing business in Kenya in the 1970s; another seconded that and mentioned a scary road trip to Uganda he had taken with Jack; a very young man from HBSAAAA read words that others had emailed. I closed by reading a short, affectionate note from Ron Blau and then a longer one from John Woodford in which he credited Jack with helping "me and other classmates start filling in our ignorance and misconceptions about African history and current affairs." John went on to provide some comic relief, recalling that Jack did a great James Brown imitation that was "impressive for a slightly pudgy guy." I showed an edited version of the interview I had done with Jack two years earlier, and we all loved hearing his voice and his laughter once again.

The third memorial to Jack was a mass of remembrance at a packed stone church in Bikanka, Burundi, where the organization Jack helped found had helped so many, and still does. I've seen a video of the service—a recent photo of Jack, framed with red and white carnations, was propped on a vase of more carnations on a stool in front of the simple altar. There was a lot of great singing, and praying, but I didn't understand much, since parts were in French and most was in what I suppose was Kurundi. But I caught the word "Jack" clearly now and then.

In closing the many interviews I did for this book, I often asked my subject, “How do you want to be remembered?” For some reason, I didn’t do that with Jack, but given the fondness and respect I saw at all three memorials, I expect he’d be pleased at how he was remembered.

## *Lowell Skinner Davidson*

*Cover of Lowell Davidson's "Trio" album.*
COURTESY OF ESP-DISK

***Born:*** *Boston, Massachusetts, 1941*

***Prepared at:*** *Boston Latin School, Boston, Massachusetts*

***Died:*** *1990*

From a life sketch Lowell provided to a jazz publication, I learned that he was born and grew up in Roxbury, the Black community of Boston, where he started to study piano at age four; he went on to study composition and harmonics and to play the tuba, bass, and flute. At twelve, he became the organist at his father's church, Zion Temple Fire Baptized Holiness Church of God in Roxbury. As its name suggests, the church was a pretty radical one, and some believe that, although Lowell may not have been fire-baptized, his psyche was singed by his parents' ideas.

Lowell must have been an excellent student in elementary

school, because he was admitted to highly competitive Boston Latin School. He was slim and very tall—six foot four or five, or even six six or seven, depending on whom you listen to—and by his freshman year on the track team at Boston Latin he'd emerged as a star. In 1957, at fifteen, he broke the 600-yard record "to smithereens," wrote the *Boston Globe.* He continued to break and rebreak records and as a senior he was hailed as one of the city's best high school athletes and was chosen to speak at the tribute dinner.

At Harvard, although he was a standout on the track team, he was probably more recognized for his intellect and his eccentricities. He seemed to do well despite not going to classes very regularly, and he was well liked but difficult to get close to, to know in any depth. After Harvard, music was more and more at the center of his being. In his submission to our class's fifteenth anniversary book, he listed his occupation as "Music, and the making thereof; Composer, Pianist," and he closed by saying, "My piano, at least, is waiting for me. Good day." In between are passages that are garbled, and in his submission to the twenty-fifth anniversary book, very little is comprehensible. For instance, he wrote: "The institution of molar notation and stave extensibility coupled with the non-associative notion of gender instability mandates for concerns of commensurate metaphysic." I think maybe he was doing with words what he did with music—experimenting.

I talked with five of Lowell's artistic collaborators, and although each had different memories and feelings, there were strong similarities in what they said. Perhaps above all, they talked with awe about his creative brilliance and the absolute fearlessness with which he pursued his musical goals and visions. He was, said fellow jazz artist Joe Morris, "willing to step over the line of what was reasonable, to go completely into what he was thinking about. He was very courageous about giving up on normal things to be and think the way he wanted to." One musician said that Lowell "feared nothing," and another that he believed in himself and his music "against all odds." An artist friend chose the imagery of Lowell's height to explain further: "He was able to reach up to such high places, mentally and metaphysically, and artistically. He was like a tower of a sort. You have to take the elevator up to get to the penthouse, and it was fun to take that elevator up."

Up there in the penthouse, Lowell had a lot going on. Harvard recognized his brilliance in biochemistry, affording him lab space to pursue his ideas for a while. Friends recall that he spent some time working at MIT and at a lab on Long Island; at one place or the other, he suffered a "horrible accident," though some dismissed that as pure fabrication. Lowell was especially fascinated by the intersections of biochemistry and music; in Joe's words, "He often declared that new sounds had the capacity to reformulate the biochemistry of the brain. The rhetoric he used about music was rarified, dense, recondite, the highest and most inspired I have ever encountered." He experimented with music in all kinds of ways, one of which was shared with me by a musician who asked to remain anonymous and whom I'll call Cal. "As a drummer," Cal wrote, "he strung out long mike booms filled with everything from African percussion instruments to toys. He was so tall he could easily reach them. He held four thin timbale sticks between the fingers of each hand: he was playing his drum-set as he would play the piano." He also experimented with various methods for marking up musical staves to create "scores," such as this one described by Cal: Lowell had "a group of different colored ballpoint pens bound together and attached to a small motor with a rubber band. He would place music manuscript under the pens, turn on the motor, and the pens would create lines, wiggles, faint indiscernible marks on the music paper."

But there were demons up there in the penthouse too. Lowell suffered from mental illness exacerbated by drug and alcohol use, and also by simply living as a unique and gifted individual in an often hostile world. One friend believed that he was "unable to express his pain, and it would come out as anger and crazy things." By all reports, his parents and their radical Pentecostal religious ideas were a source of some of that pain and emotional affliction. Some speculated, too, that his constant creative impulses were a lot to handle, that he "didn't know how to exist in his extraordinariness," that his uniqueness put him in a "place by himself," a place where he was very alone. Joe said, "He was the kind of guy who seemed to be in a constant psychedelic state of mind. He would talk about his hallucinations, and I never knew whether he was tripping on acid or if he saw them when he was having a psychotic episode, and I don't know if he knew, and I don't know if he knew he was telling me these things." Once when Joe visited him in the psych ward of Boston City Hospital, he found Lowell at a chalkboard, sketching out some musical ideas and lecturing to other patients; two friends similarly remembered Lowell conducting what he called "bum junior college" on the street, giving presentations on color and sound to a little class of homeless men.

I heard other stories of hallucinations and creative outbursts, but also of rage and aggression. Joe remembered that Lowell "had moments when he was unbelievably lucid and incredibly hilariously funny and really kind, and other times when he would sort of turn on you and look like he was going to kill you." Others experienced violent episodes, but to a person, they preferred not to detail those; as another person said flatly: "Nobody found it easy to be with Lowell on a regular basis." Despite everything, they all expressed an abiding affection for him and a deep appreciation for his intellect, and said that he had inspired and influenced them as artists. As Cal put it, working with Lowell "was like being apprenticed to a shaman." All but one of the people I spoke to described Lowell's mental and physical decline as painful to watch, and his early death as tragic.

The outlier was Taylor McLean, a musical collaborator who met Lowell at Harvard, where he was two years behind us in the class of 1965. Like others, Taylor refused to dwell on Lowell's illness and decline, but he went further. He was adamant that Lowell's life was not a story of failure or tragedy, but rather was "positive and victorious." The man lived, he said, in an "alternative universe," and in that universe he was successful: "It is a form of success that is little understood, and that brings with it no comforts. The artist is driven to pursue and formulate successive objective forms. That is the only way to cross the river and stay alive in the current. It is a form of achievement and 'success' that is incomprehensible to the normative path because it comes at great personal cost, [does not] include social status, accumulation of material goods, praise and adulation, or even a supportive social network. Lowell was a champion in this area."

In Lowell's photo in the freshman *Register,* he is eighteen and staring directly at the camera. Looking into his eyes knowing what I now know, it feels, paradoxically, both obvious and unthinkable that so much was going on inside that mind and soul. Taylor was right. No, we don't have to think of Lowell's life as a tragic one, as unfathomable as it was, and in fact Lowell apparently expressed no regrets or wishes to "get better" or make money or record more or see the world. Music was enough for him.

## *Wilfred Otis Easter*

***Born:*** *New York City, 1941*

***Prepared at:*** *The Gunnery, Washington, Connecticut, and George Washington High School, New York, New York*

When I pulled up to Fred's house in Minneapolis, I parked behind a late-model Honda with a Harvard alumni license plate frame. I teased him about having become a Harvard gearhead. Fred laughed and said that he had put the bracket on his license plate "to piss off the cops," since he'd recently gotten a speeding ticket from a white cop. We made small talk for a while at the house and then got into the Honda to go over to the alternative high school. It was part of a broader social service and advocacy project of the Minneapolis Public Schools for at-risk high school–age kids called The City, Inc. Fred served as president of the project, and he took me on a quick tour of the sprawling brick and cinder-block school building, now and then stopping to trade easy banter with small groups of kids working or wandering around the building. Talking about the disadvantaged Black and Native American kids in his school, Freddy joked, "Harvard didn't prepare me for any of this shit."

Unlike the other Harvard classmates I'd interviewed thus far, Freddy slipped in and out of standard English, Black English, and everything in between, choosing the words, accents, and expressions that would best adorn whatever story he was telling. Also unlike all the other men I interviewed, before that day and after, Fred teared up a few times. He wore his heart on his sleeve, he knew that, and he wasn't afraid to have anyone see it.

Back at his place, I asked Fred to tell me more about his family, and he pointed out an old dim photo on the wall. "They are my two grandmothers," he said tenderly. "That's my father's mother, Idelia Garner Easter, and that's my mother's mother, Lula Belle Anderson Smith, born in South Carolina. My mother was born in Charleston, her father owned a grocery store, and he keeled over playing poker with his friends at the age of forty-two." His grandmother divided up her nine children and sent them to various places in New York City to stay with friends and relatives until she was able to come up and collect them all.

Fred's father was born in Harlem Hospital in 1912, and Fred was born there too, in 1941. Post–World War II Harlem was not the intellectual and artistic hub of Black life it had been in decades past, and drugs and crime were rife. The Easters, like my family, lived in the projects. His father managed a ladies' shoe store on 125th Street, and his mother helped out there at peak sales times. Later, his mother would go back to work as a telephone operator to help meet the college costs that weren't covered by scholarships for Fred and his older brother. His parents were avid bridge players—"My mother was a barracuda!" he told me. The couple played in tournaments sponsored by the Black National Bridge Association, which brought them into a wider and more intellectual circle than they might otherwise have encountered. His parents noticed that Fred was bright, and so did some of their friends, especially when they saw that he could read before kindergarten. Fred believes that his parents and the bridge club were largely responsible for his academic success: "They saw intelligence in me at an early age, and challenged it, nurtured it, and prodded it and goaded it, and tried to make sure it developed as fully as possible."

As a kid, Freddy didn't think much about race, as kids often don't. Other things were more important, like "who could beat who in a race, who knew the latest songs or had the best jokes." But the murder of Emmett Till would become a vivid memory and a turning point for him, as it had been for me. For Fred, however, it was not the murder itself that had the greatest impact, but the news that the jury had refused to convict the two obviously guilty men. Telling me about it, Freddy paused, took a deep breath, and teared up, "I saw my mother cry for the first time in my life." His voice shifted toward anger as he went on: "The kid was my age and died because he had whistled at a white woman, which was something I might have done, so it was a watershed event for me. And when I saw my mother cry, it helped me understand that this was not just a personal thing."

The bridge club intervened again when Fred's high school guidance counselor told him that, despite having been chosen for the SP program and despite having excelled in high school, he was "not college material." One of the bridge friends had heard of a counseling and scholarship service for Negro kids—NSSFNS—and that's how he wound up at Harvard, Fred explained.

After Harvard, Fred would go on to a career of helping disadvantaged, inner-city ghetto kids. From 1968 to 1976 as associate dean of admissions at Carleton College in Northfield, Minnesota, he was able to bring in and nurture hundreds of kids who would not have made it otherwise, kids who like him were not considered "college material." Within three years, 11 percent of the Carleton student body was Black or brown. He would have the same success as statewide director of the California-based MESA program, which supported and encouraged kids to go into math and science fields. And at The City, Inc., he was still doing the same thing—helping those kids who someone along the way had determined were "not college material."

When I asked Fred how he wanted to be remembered, he said that there were a few things that he might have done differently, but "those are bells I can't unring." He summed his life up with a football analogy: "I threw some blocks for some young people, and they have scored. I feel good about that." But he is still angry, at whites, and at American society: "No question in my mind that I am a pissed-off Black man today. Tomorrow, I expect to wake up pissed off. Yes, no question in my mind."

## *William Henry Exum*

**Born:** *Wewoka, Oklahoma, 1942*

**Prepared at:** *Franklin County High School, Frankfort, Kentucky*

**Died:** *1986*

Born in Wewoka, Oklahoma, Bill grew up in Kentucky and graduated from Franklin County High School in Frankfort. The family moved there when Bill's father joined the faculty of Kentucky State College, where he coached football and track and eventually served as head of the athletics and physical education departments. The elder Bill Exum was a track and football star at the University of Wisconsin, where he also earned bachelor's, master's, and doctoral degrees. He took the job at Frankfort when young Bill was about seven, and the family lived on the college campus. Like several others of us, Bill must have skipped a grade or two in school, because he started Harvard three months before his seventeenth birthday. No surprise, then, that the difference in

Bill's freshman and senior photos is striking; there's no doubt it's the same guy, but those four years transformed a gawky kid into a handsome young man. He was in Lowell House and a member of the Social Relations Society and the World Cultural Society. Beyond that, however, I don't know much about him. Nor did my classmates, and one reason might be what he told Ron Blau in the "Bright Shadows in the Yard" interview: although he loved the place—Ron commented that he was "uncommonly enthusiastic about Harvard"—and had a close friendship with his freshman roommate, he kept his distance from the rest of us.

After Harvard, Bill earned his PhD in sociology at New York University in 1974. He received the Founders Day Award from NYU in 1974 for "consistent evidence of outstanding scholarship." Bill was a professor of African American studies and sociology at Northwestern from 1977 to 1986. After short stints teaching at Sarah Lawrence and Williams Colleges, he took a professorship in sociology and African American studies at Northwestern.

As a scholar, Bill was interested in the phenomenon of Black student unions, presenting papers and publishing articles about the topic and then, just a year before his death, a book titled *Paradoxes of Protest: Black Student Activism in a White University,* which details the Black student activism on the Bronx campus of NYU while he was a graduate student and instructor. The photo on the book jacket shows the same wide smile as the photos from his Harvard days, but he'd traded in the horn-rims for the popular aviators of the '80s, and his hair had undergone a 180-degree shift—he was now bald up top with a full beard. The sociology department set up an annual writing prize to memorialize him, and a colleague who wrote his obituary for a campus publication called him a "great teacher and mentor," "sensible and imaginative," kind, gentle, and clever.

## *Charles Bernard Frazier*

***Born:*** *Mobile, Alabama, 1941*

***Prepared at:*** *Most Pure Heart of Mary High School, Mobile, Alabama*

***Died:*** *2001*

Charlie was a standout in high school academically, and he was captain of the football team. He came to Harvard having never been out of the South and was likely one of the southern boys recruited for Harvard as part of the push to find talented Negroes for the class of 1963. His Harvard classmates remember him as a nice guy who wasn't very happy at Harvard. His ex-wife told me that he hadn't been a drinker before college, but that he partied hard during that one year he was on the Yard and there was a family history of alcoholism. After he was asked to leave after the dorm fire, Harvard did invite him back, but Charlie chose instead to take a night job at the post office and finished college during the day. He was fascinated by computers and became particularly adept at working with them, so he got a job with the federal government, working in a department of human resources. He worked on but never finished his master's degree, but nonetheless rose to the pay level usually reserved for supervisors with advanced degrees.

## *Lazaro Rogelio Miguel Angel Galindo*

**Born:** *Havana, Cuba, 1940*

**Prepared at:** *Cardinal Hayes High School, Bronx, New York*

Larry was born in Cuba in 1940 and was the closest to slavery of all of us. His maternal grandmother was brought to Cuba as a slave at the age of seven and was sold on the piers of Havana to a very rich Cuban family with whom she would stay for the rest of her life. He told me that she "was very lucky, because that family was just looking for a playmate for their seven-year-old daughter and she never worked a day in her life."

Larry's father was an academic, and Larry grew up in a part of Havana he described as "right across from the sea, very nice, upper-middle-class." So it must have been a big change to move to Spanish Harlem when he was nine. There were very few Cubans in the city then, and the family chose to live among other Hispanics, so, as Larry said, "I was raised among Puerto Ricans." Larry remembered noticing that there were poor people around him, and the people he knew worked long hours at low-wage jobs or received public assistance. Even as a kid, he was aware of drugs and alcoholism on the streets. Now and then, he would get downtown and see a different life: "I went to the Metropolitan Museum on Fifth Avenue and the Eighties, and I saw the tremendous difference and access to the better parts of life, and it really hit me: why did this exist, this injustice?"

At first, the family's plan was to get Larry a good education and then bring him back to Cuba. They sent him to Cardinal Hayes High School, a solid Roman Catholic school in the Bronx. Larry loved the school at the time and appreciates it to this day: "We had a sense there of being Catholic, a sense of always fighting for justice, for the ideals that are incorporated in the New Testament and the Bible. It felt very comfortable there, and I took part in football and ran track. I excelled academically, and that was the buffer to the reality of Spanish Harlem."

Through the Boys Club, Larry got a mentor whom he described as a "Boston Brahmin." His mentor was also a Harvard alum, and he was the one who pushed Larry to go to Harvard; otherwise, he would have probably gone to Columbia, to stay near his ailing mother, or to his dream school, Notre Dame. Larry came up to Cambridge on that September day in 1959. Like me, he was pretty nervous that he might not make it at Harvard. "Boy, I was running scared," he said. At the same time, his vision for the future had recently shifted dramatically: that January, Fidel Castro seized power in Cuba, and it was soon clear that Larry would never be going back there.

He was a little taken aback when Ron Blau approached him for an interview as an "American Negro." But he was interested in learning about race in the United States, and sometime around junior year, he said, "I thought that somewhere in my life I would have to liaison with Black society and I wanted to know more about my Black roots." He joined Alpha Phi Alpha, the first African American fraternity, and "started learning about myself through some great friendships." Larry continued to succeed and graduated on time with our class.

After graduating, Larry took a position as a junior executive but soon decided to return to Harvard, where he earned a master's degree at the Business School in 1971, followed by a long career as a bank executive and investment manager. Larry traveled widely for business and also while doing humanitarian work for Catholic Relief Services, and he played competitive rugby well into his fifties.

## *Robert Edgar Gibbs*

***Born:*** *Atlanta, Georgia, 1942*

***Prepared at:*** *Booker T. Washington High School, Atlanta, Georgia*

***Died:*** *2019*

Bobby was born and raised in Atlanta, Georgia. His parents didn't go to college, but they let him know that it was the "only way out" for Blacks. At all-Black Booker T. Washington High School, Bobby got a solid college-prep education that included Latin and higher mathematics. He figured that afterward he would just go on to Morehouse or Clark and be stuck in Atlanta. But he really wanted to get farther away from home. A friend who was going to an elite eastern prep school in the summer to prepare to get into a top-tier university in the North suggested that Bob do the same, and so he did. Both boys most likely were able to do this through the intervention of the National Scholarship Service and Fund for Negro Students. At Andover, Bob told me, "those first two weeks were the hardest two weeks I have ever spent in any school setting." But he stuck with it, learned a lot, eventually applied to Harvard, and was accepted.

Bobby started out as a chemistry major, made a brief switch to Far Eastern languages and literature, and then "off to economics I flew and stayed." Although he was closeted for the most part, he was part of a small group of gay men that included several individuals in the theater arts, and as a sophomore at Winthrop House, Bob got involved in various theater productions. And he hit the clubs. Consequently, he became one of the many Harvard boys who were "advised" to take a year off and come back ready to buckle down, and he did, with the economist John Kenneth Galbraith as his senior tutor. Also during senior year, he got married and unmarried in the space of less than six months. After graduation, he worked for a while at Harvard's Loeb Drama Center doing the finances, then went south for a summer and taught African history in one of the Freedom Schools. Just as he was getting started on a career in advertising, he was drafted in 1967. Stationed in Virginia to do computer programming, he flew home to his New York City apartment almost every weekend.

Over his career, Bobby worked at a variety of companies in the fields of advertising, aerospace, and banking. He died in the late winter of 2019 in California.

## *Ezra Edward Holman Griffith*

***Born:*** *Barbados, West Indies, 1942*

***Prepared at:*** *Boys High School, Brooklyn, New York*

I discovered in Ezra's online CV that he was a research psychiatrist at Yale and that his studies included emphases on forensics, ethnicity, and ethics. Ezra had studied in France and earned an MD from Albert Einstein School of Medicine. He had won awards and had some impressive and intriguing-sounding titles: Professor of and Senior Research Scientist in Psychiatry, Deputy Chair for Diversity and Organizational Ethics, and Medical Director of Connecticut's Department of Mental Health and Addiction Services. Waiting for him outside his ninth-floor office on the Yale campus in New Haven, I was just beginning to wonder how he had found time to meet with me at all when he came around the corner.

Soon I heard again that British lilt, that careful pronunciation, that formality and reserve from so long ago. Still the light-skinned guy I remembered, he had kept the compact body that gave him speed and agility in soccer. The addition of a trim beard suited his professorial demeanor. Before we met that day, I learned that Ezra had written a book about his childhood, titled *I'm Your Father, Boy: A Family Memoir of Barbados,* and had enjoyed reading about his vibrant island boyhood. But the island was, in his words, "as polarized as any other society." Ezra's father, a clergyman and politician, could describe in detail the social power structure of the island and its clear correlation with color, and it was the wealthy whites, he explained, who were "pulling the strings that only the informed and the experienced could see." Had one of the children asked their mother about exclusion from the beach, Ezra explains in his memoir, she would have turned the question around, "Why, with all the beautiful beaches in Barbados, do you need to go play on a little stringy piece of white sand that a few white people need to feel they control?"

Despite the social segregation, there were integrated schools on the island that were, in Ezra's words, "the best on the island. I went there and I sat next to a white guy on my right and a white guy on my left. And I was not the only one, there were many Black students in the schools I went to." He went on to high school at integrated Harrison College; patterned after British prep schools, it was among the best schools in the English-speaking Caribbean. Ezra wrote later that he "ultimately came to appreciate this Bajan approach, this tropical form of British seriousness, where the effort was made to create in us youngsters self-confidence melded with the grasp of what our Black brains could accomplish." Looking back, Ezra believed that his life was marked more by class than by race: "What I felt was not having the money that the landed gentry in Barbados had in that agricultural society. My father didn't have that kind of money, and I certainly knew the difference."

At the time, many Barbadians who also "didn't have that kind of money" looked north for a better life, having heard stories of prosperity from those who'd already made it. When Ezra was twelve, his father left for New York to scout out the possibilities for emigration—he would be gone from the family for two years, preparing the way. Finally, in May 1956, when Ezra was fourteen, the rest of the family left their island home for Brooklyn, where he was placed in Boys High with me and wound up at Harvard as my freshman roommate. He excelled at Harvard, concentrated in Romance languages, played soccer, and felt, he told me, "protected" by the Boston West Indian community. There, too, he found a lifelong pastime in Afro-Cuban drumming.

After graduation, Ezra worked at an insurance company for just a few months before he was drafted and spent two years in the Army, one stateside and one in Saigon, working as a preventive medicine specialist. Back in civilian life in the United States, he taught high school for a few months and then decided to pursue a career in medicine, studying at the University of Strasbourg in France and then, for graduate training in psychiatry, at the Albert Einstein School of Medicine in New York City. Ezra joined the Yale University faculty in 1977; during his time there, he not only taught and published widely but also was an administrator and directed various special projects, including one that helped Granada rebuild after the United States bombed a psychiatric hospital in its 1983 invasion of the island. Ezra played organized soccer for years and didn't retire until 2016, but he is still very active in his field. His dream is to "visit Cuba and hang out with a few conga drummers for a month or so."

## *George Henry Jones Jr.*

***Born:*** *Muskogee, Oklahoma, 1942*

***Prepared at:*** *Manual Training High School, Muskogee, Oklahoma*

I met with George in the midsummer of 2009 at his office and lab on the campus of Emory University in Atlanta, where he was a professor of biology, teaching and doing research on things like "The Kinetics of Polynucleotide Phosphorylase." George was almost as bald as I was, but otherwise he looked great and entirely capable of hopping on his BMW R1200 motorcycle and zipping up the Blue Ridge Parkway, which he had recently done. We sat on high metal stools, and I put my tape recorder on a black stone lab table among beakers and microscopes like ones I remembered from science classes long ago, alongside other unrecognizable gear that I imagined being put to mysterious high-tech scientific purposes. There seemed to be a lot going on for summertime, and men and women in lab coats, whom I took to be grad students, came and went as we chatted.

Like many of our stories, George's begins with family migration away from the South, but not to the industrial North. When George's mother was a child, her family moved from Waco, Texas, up to Muskogee, Oklahoma. Some years later, George's father also relocated, from St. Charles, Missouri, to Muskogee, where he met and married George's mother. It's not difficult to imagine why they chose Muskogee. At the time George was born, the Muskogee, Oklahoma, Negro City Directory crowed about the fifteen thousand Blacks in the city: "Educationally and intellectually, it has been said that Muskogee Negroes enjoy a prestiege [*sic*] unequaled anywhere else in America . . . There's more Negro lawyers, doctors, realtors, etc. to the square foot in Muskogee than there is anywhere else in the world." During George's youth, it was a stably segregated town where, as he put it, "basically, Blacks and whites had established a sort of truce. They left us alone, and we pretty much left them alone."

George's father worked for four decades in what was then the prestigious position of a letter carrier, delivering mail to both sides of Muskogee. His mother earned a master's degree in music education from Columbia University and was the supervisor of music education for the city's Black school system. At the pinnacle of that segregated school system was Manual Training High School, founded in 1911 and made great by the constant efforts of parents, teachers, and the greater Black community.

Belying its name, Manual Training High had an outstanding college-prep division. Despite inadequate funding and the extreme poverty of many of its students, it sent 36 percent of its graduating class to college or university in 1954, when only 7 percent of the total US population and 2.5 percent of Blacks had college degrees. Despite *Brown v. Board of Education,* Manual Training remained a de facto segregated school through George's four years there; George saw no problem with that at all, however, in light of the high quality of the education he received and the sense of community and ambition instilled in him.

George leaned forward and his voice rose when he talked about his high school, and he brought it back into the conversation several times. He was clearly passionate about the education he received at Manual Training, which had excellent teachers, he recalled. "They were dedicated and committed, and they were not only there for us at school, they were part of the community, friends of our family, the same people we saw at church and in social contexts. We didn't have the kind of instructional tools that they had in the white schools, but my teachers had to try to make up for that in other ways, by spending more time with us and giving us experiences that we wouldn't otherwise have had, even if they had to support it financially from their own pockets." Equally important, George left Manual Training with a sense of indebtedness to the school and the community. "Failure," he told me, "was not an option, because too many people had paid and were paying too much for me not to succeed." Much has been written about those few high-quality all-Black schools that were the exceptions to the rule that Black schools were surely separate but rarely anything like equal. "You hear about them," George said, "with sufficient frequency to think that they are folklore, but it's true. I think my classmates would agree that we would not be what we are had we gone to an integrated school."

Although he had a fine education and the will to succeed, George wasn't sure he would get into Harvard, but he took a chance, applied, was accepted, and did well. His bachelor's degree was in biochemical sciences, and he went on to the University of California at Berkeley to obtain a PhD in 1968, which is also when he bought his first motorcycle. After two years as a visiting scientist at the National Institutes of Health, he did two postdoc years at the University of Geneva in Switzerland. Next came about ten years of teaching at the University of Michigan, after which it was on to Emory in Atlanta in 1989, where I caught up with him. George's area of research has been the mechanism and regulation of antibiotic synthesis in the bacteria Streptomyces. His CV includes various administrative titles, publications, grants, awards, and editorships.

Relaxing after the interview, I told George that I still lamented my D grade in organic chemistry. George said that he had loved Chem 20; he graciously told me that he didn't remember his grade, but he felt sure it was better than a D. George is one of those earnest, can-do types. Still playing a little basketball, he had recently had knee replacement surgery, gone on a diet and lost forty pounds, and had ridden his motorcycle some thirty-six thousand miles in the last three years. The slogan George used to sign his emails is unsurprising: "Never give up. Never slow down. Never grow old. Never ever die young."

## *Lowell Douglass Johnston*

***Born:*** *Washington, DC, 1941*

***Prepared at:*** *Kent School, Kent, Connecticut*

Lowell spoke with visible pride about his parents and grandparents, though with his characteristic reserve and precision. His paternal grandfather, James Hugo Johnston Sr., began his career as a teacher and rose through the ranks to serve as the second president of the historically Black Virginia State University. Lowell's father, Virginius Douglass Johnston, was a 1913 graduate of the Virginia Normal and Industrial Institute, another historically Black college. He went on to earn a BS in commerce and an MBA at Northwestern University. Virginius was commissioned as an officer in the 92nd Infantry Division in World War I, and then worked in the insurance business until 1931, when he was appointed treasurer of Howard University. In both positions, he traveled in the highest echelons of Black society, even exchanging correspondence with W. E. B. Du Bois. Lowell's mother, Hazel Bramlette Johnston, was born in Chicago, earned degrees at Chicago Teachers College and Howard University, and taught business and math courses for thirteen years at Randall Junior High School.

Lowell took pains to explain that he didn't feel cheated by not going to an integrated school; he was very proud of his all-Black school, especially the teachers. "In my generation," he said, "we were brought up to feel good about ourselves. We were given excellent training in the segregated schools we went to; even though we didn't have all the resources that everyone else had, we had these teachers who were so dedicated to passing something on to us, that I never had any doubts about my ability. I think if you ask any of us who were in school together at that time in Washington, they'll say the same thing. I have friends that I grew up with—one is an astronaut, one is a four-star admiral—we have done all kinds of things."

Lowell's parents sent him to a private preparatory school, the Kent School in Connecticut. In the very white world of the Founders League of prep schools, it had long been regarded as the most exclusive in the country. Unlike the other member schools, whose students were mostly very wealthy, Kent from its founding was meant to be a place where "young men with slender means could gain an education second to none." Lowell was hardly of "slender means," but he was one of the first Blacks to attend Kent. Overall, he rated the experience there as a positive one: "Kent gave me a whole series of experiences that have become part of my life and set out directions for me—my interest in literature, my interest in sports, my interest in living in the country as we do here. And I think there was a socialization process that helped me. I became familiar with the unknown, to see what the white community was like, and to test my feelings about my role among whites." Lowell smiled and added that, nonetheless, he sometimes sorely missed the company of Blacks. Riding the train from Connecticut home to Washington, he remembered, "we would get to 125th Street Station in Harlem, and I would have my face pressed against the glass, looking for Black people, because I hadn't seen any Blacks for so long."

Lowell went directly to Harvard Law School after graduation, with the express interest of pursuing civil rights law. As a law student, he participated in the March on Washington and the Boston school boycott in 1964, served as principal of a Freedom School, and worked with the Northern Students Movement. He went to Mississippi for short stints to work with the NAACP Legal Defense Fund. After two years in Venezuela with the Peace Corps, Lowell returned to work for the Legal Defense Fund in New York City, and he stayed there until 1989, when he went into private practice as a solo practitioner, doing commercial litigation and counseling and, in his words, "some civil rights work as could be found." He was also very active as a member of the board of directors of not-for-profits concerned about race and sex discrimination in employment, law enforcement, prison reform, and post-incarceration opportunities. He closed his practice in 2002 but continued to work as an employment and commercial arbitrator and with financial services regulation until he retired completely in 2014.

## *Lionel Deckle McLean*

***Born:** Jersey City, New Jersey, 1941*

***Prepared at:** The Peddie School, Hightstown, New Jersey*

Deck's father was a dentist who was born in Barbados and came to Jersey City, New Jersey, via Ellis Island, with his family when he was six years old. Deck's mother was a teacher. She was born on the Eastern Shore in Maryland, and her family moved to South Jersey, just across the Delaware from Philadelphia, when she was about seven. Deck came to Harvard from the Peddie School in Hightstown, New Jersey, where he was an excellent athlete, playing football and running track; a few years ago he was elected to the school's sports Hall of Fame. He was class president and very involved in the life of the school. Peddie was rigorous academically too, and Deck excelled. Peddie, he said, "prepared me for the drill."

When he visited Harvard, they "shuttled me off to meetings with Black faculty—some of the few. I was offended that they played my visit racially, and suspicious regarding what this indicated about the place." Nonetheless, he settled in at Harvard easily, rooming first with Pat Tovatt, who would tell me that Deck was "an excellent roommate." While Pat "went through the usual stuff of staying up late and drinking too much," Deck's days were disciplined and structured, with classes, sports, studying, and regular sleep. But, Pat went on, "Deck was perfectly accepting of my extreme behavior," including being patient and nonjudgmental even when Pat lugged that horrible moose head back to their common room.

I remember that Deck had a great sense of humor, which no doubt helped with the moose head fiasco. It was Deck, also, who in response to Ron Blau's "reborn" question had laughed and called it all "psychological nonsense." He also told Ron that he "could pass if he chooses," and that although he "never tried to hide the fact that he is Negro," some of his prep school friends only learned that he was Black in their sophomore year. His neighborhood and schools were predominantly white, he told Ron, and it was at Harvard that he had his first chance to hang out with Black peers. In fact, he said, he felt that "he has become slightly 'more Negro' while at Harvard."

After he graduated with a concentration in social relations, Deck received a law degree from Boston College Law School, but he never practiced law. Writing became his career—he worked as a newspaper and magazine journalist, wrote books on press law, the First Amendment, and invasions of privacy, and also produced a few mystery novels. He taught journalism and directed a journalism program, then retired in 2006.

## *Gerald David Secundy*

**Born:** *Washington, DC, 1942*

**Prepared at:** *Phillips Academy, Andover, Andover, Massachusetts*

Gerry went to public schools and grew up "definitely lower-middle-class, if not poor," in Washington, DC. His white dad was an electrical contractor, his Black mom a teacher, a homemaker, and later a social worker. It was his mother who was the educational mover and shaker in the family, it seemed to me. The first in her family to go to college, she had walked to Brooklyn College every day from her home in Brownsville because she couldn't afford the nickel subway fare. After she married Gerry's father and they settled in Brooklyn, she saw an ad for a government job in Washington at the Bureau of Printing and Engraving, applied for it, and soon received a letter saying she got the job. The family moved down to DC. But then, Gerry explained, "she arrived on the job the first day, and they took a look at her and said, 'Oh, my God, you're a Negro. You can't work here.' She showed him the letter and said, 'You accepted me at this job, and by God I'm going to work here." The administrators worked out a schedule where she could work a night shift after the white employees had left. She accepted the arrangement and took up her job running a printing press that made one-dollar bills.

Gerry, like Fred Easter, arrived at his segregated elementary school already a reader. But by fourth grade, his mother was dissatisfied—there had to be a better school for him in Washington. She found the only integrated private school in DC and enrolled Gerry. When more public options opened up after *Brown v. Board of Education,* she took him out of the private school and put him on the bus to integrate Taft Junior High School. It was a rough time for Gerry: "There were five hundred kids outside carrying signs and yelling, 'Two-four-six-eight, we won't integrate,' and 'Nigger go back to Africa'—the whole nine yards." He stuck it out, but he was getting beaten up, and his mother realized that he was not learning much. On the advice of the family doctor, Gerry's mom hauled the family off to look at New England prep schools. Phillips Academy in Massachusetts looked good and offered generous financial aid, so Gerry was off to Andover, where he was very happy. Although he started at the bottom of the class, he ended at the top, earned a college scholarship, and went to Harvard. It was at Andover, he said, that "I was really transformed. It taught me how to study and I was nurtured. By the time I got to Harvard, I pretty much knew the game."

Before the afternoon slipped away, I remembered that I wanted a nice photo of Gerry, so we stepped out onto his lawn. Right away Gerry went to stand in front of his favorite tree, which made for a great picture. Clearly, he had done this many times before, having had a high-profile career. After Harvard, Gerry went into the Peace Corps, serving in Cusco, Peru, then to Columbia Law School. He worked at the US Department of Justice, after which he spent twenty-eight years with the oil company Arco before retiring in 1998. He says he is now "giving back to the community" and works with the State Water Resources Control Board, the agency that controls water quality in California. In fact, during one part of our interview Gerry had to step out to take a call from the California governor.

## *Travis Jackson Williams*

***Born:*** *Durham, North Carolina, 1941*

***Prepared at:*** *Hillside High School, Durham, North Carolina*

***Died:*** *1968*

It's likely that Travis Williams was one of the Negroes found by Monro and Glimp's team of recruiters when they were "beating the urban streets" in southern cities. Travis attended segregated schools in Durham, North Carolina, where he was lucky to encounter some outstanding teachers. Travis mentioned to Ron Blau that one teacher in particular, a history teacher, encouraged him to write, and that two topics he had written about were "socialism" and "the necessity of black atheism." No small feat for a high school student! The son of a barber, Travis was not exactly part of the Black elite in Durham, but he had been elected class president. In Ron Blau's retelling of the story in "Bright Shadows," "the 'black bourgeoisie' (which are for him a class apart from 'Negroes') decided to 'adopt' him. But he did not adopt *them* and went to one of their formal dances in dungarees."

Among the classmates who had passed away before I started this project, Travis was probably the one most fondly remembered, and as I talked to people, there were two things that came up again and again. First, Travis was gregarious and well liked—Lance Morrow went so far as to say that Travis had a "gift for friendship." Second, everyone agreed that he was very smart. He was known for reading widely and deeply; "his mind," as Lance put it, "was a little hectic, yet he had a good mind and made very good connections intellectually." After graduation, Travis worked for *Life* magazine in New York until his death at age twenty-seven in 1968.

## *Wesley Samuel Williams Jr.*

***Born:*** *Washington, DC, 1942*

***Prepared at:*** *The Taft School, Watertown, Connecticut*

On a bright breezy Caribbean Sunday morning, Jeanne and I sat in the beautiful Cathedral Church of All Saints, Charlotte Amalie, St. Thomas. The church was built in 1848 to thank God for the parishioners' deliverance from slavery. The Rev. Dr. Wesley S. Williams Jr., in white vestments embroidered in red, bent from the waist, spread his broad hands, and laid them in blessing on the heads of two angelic-looking little island kids. Another overseas trip had taken us to the Virgin Islands, and Wes had just delivered his morning sermon.

Before arriving on the island, I'd learned that Wes had made a lot of money and spent most of his career in government, business, and finance: twenty-six years as director of Penn Mutual Life Insurance Company, membership on the board of directors of Salomon Brothers and later Bear Stearns, chairman of the National Conference of Federal Reserve Banks, and partner in the prestigious Washington law firm of Covington & Burling. In our email correspondence, Wesley had told me that he ended up in St. Thomas through his wife and her family, who had real estate, financial services, and insurance interests on St. Thomas.

After church on that beautiful Sunday, Wesley explained that he had left the world of high finance to run what started out as a small family island company and to pursue the priesthood. He had decided to leave DC, he said, because of "the 'Me Problem.' Everybody for himself. Here I think we are all dedicated to the islands. We are all dedicated to our community, and we try to be a family-friendly company. And I've been interested in religion all my life. I mean, my parents would tell you that they didn't take me to church, I took them to church. I liked the music and liked the preaching." I followed Wesley around the island while he visited the sick and toured a shopping center owned by his company, wearing his clerical collar wherever he went. It was all very impressive, as I should have expected.

I would be surprised to learn that anyone who meets Wesley remains unimpressed for long. He was probably the most sophisticated of our group, and certainly one of the "golden boys" of our class—outgoing, capable, serious, involved in everything. He would be edged out in the election for first class marshal only by a Rockefeller, serving as second marshal. Wes explained that he had used the freshman *Register* to keep track of his classmates, and by the time he graduated, he knew over eight hundred of them by name.

Wes was raised in the highest echelon of Negro society in Washington, DC. His parents were well educated, with extensive connections among the Negro intelligentsia. He grew up in what he called a "fantasyland" in which his parents tried to keep the realities of segregation a secret from him. For instance, to cover up the fact that the music halls and restaurants were off-limits to them, his parents explained, "Why go to those public halls downtown? We can hear classical music at church." Or, "People of breeding, of good character and background, do not eat in public places; we go to visit the homes of our well-educated, refined friends."

Wesley was brilliant and those well-educated and refined friends contributed to not only his excellence in school but also his developing love for all things intellectual. Like others of us, he was pushed ahead in elementary school and wound up the smallest and youngest kid in his class. So he was just twelve when his parents sent him to the Taft School in Watertown, Connecticut. Although Wes made some good friends at Taft, he had to put up with plenty of racist taunts and exclusion. "But on the other hand," he told me, "there was never any doubt in my mind, no feeling of inadequacy, it was just the opposite. Why, I wondered, am I subjected to this ridiculous world with these people who don't understand just how adequate I am?" Taft, he said, "taught me that everything can be overcome."

Academically, Wes was a standout, always at the top of his class. He planned to go to the historically Black Virginia Union College in Richmond, Virginia. Both of his parents were VU grads, and Wesley's godfather was John W. Barker, the VU academic vice president. It was Barker who had been foremost among the many adults who nurtured Wes's intellect and character throughout his childhood in Washington, DC, introducing him to the classics and biblical Hebrew. Frequently on Sunday afternoons after church, Wes had been quizzed on everything from Shakespeare to current affairs by one of his mother's former professors at VU, Arthur Paul Davis, who was by then a professor at Howard. VU was almost in his blood by this time.

But the Taft guidance counselor suggested Harvard, and Wes remembered having heard the Harvard Glee Club sing at the Metropolitan AME Church in Washington when he was a child. Wesley was musical, he had always loved singing, and so, although he still privately planned to go to VU, the Harvard idea began to take root. It was his meeting with Dean John U. Monro that sealed the deal, and Wesley joined the Harvard class of 1963. His four years there were predictably exemplary, and his degree was in Romance languages and literature. The graduation yearbook lists his activities as associate editor of a college publication, secretary and then president of the Glee Club, and member of the Young Republicans, the Music Club, the community service organization Phillips Brooks House, the International Relations Council, the Pre-Law Society, Quincy House Athletics, the squash team, the Hasty Pudding Club, and the Boston-area Black fraternity Alpha Phi Alpha. I suspect that space limitations required omitting at least a few. In a recent edition of our class reunion book, Wes said that one ambition has been to have more letters—i.e., degrees—after his name than in it. He may well succeed yet.

## *Kent Wilson*

**Born:** *Springfield, Illinois, 1942*

**Prepared at:** *Springfield High School, Springfield, Illinois*

We recognized Kent right away at the Vienna airport. A Black man in Austria is easy to pick out of a crowd, but also, Kent looked much the same as he had in college, more youthful-looking than a man of our age had any right to be. Kent was mostly retired from a career with IBM, he told me, and was just teaching the occasional summer course at Webster University in Missouri. It was via that college's website that I'd found him. He and his Austrian wife, Susie, had lived for years in Baden, where they raised their three children; when we arrived, they were in the last days of a long visit from several young grandchildren.

We arrived during Heuriger season, when the new wines are featured in dozens of seasonal "pop-up" restaurants, and over the next few days Kent took us to sample a few. Over glasses of fine white wine and plates of sausages at an outdoor table under a striped awning, Kent and I entertained his adult son, Mark, with stories about our dismal social lives as freshmen at Harvard. Kent remembered our forays to the "mixers" and how they rarely paid off. "You would go to a mixer, and first off, there were very few Black girls, and if you asked a white girl to dance, she would dance with you, but," Kent stuck his arms rigidly out over the table, "it was the straight arm, please don't get too close." We both remembered that distance as more than physical; there were always some white girls in these liberal northeastern schools who were eager to show their open-mindedness or were too well bred to refuse the offer of a dance.

Kent remembered another of the dances: "I walk into this mixer, and there are lots of white women, and all of a sudden a couple of girls come up to me and say, 'Stay right there because we have just the girl for you.'" He waited, and sure enough, a few minutes later they came back with a Black girl who had stayed in her room thinking there would surely be no Black boys there. "There we were, the two of us, and all these whites just standing there glowing, saying, 'Isn't it great?' It was very embarrassing for her and for me." We had been chuckling over all this, Kent and I and Mark, but suddenly it didn't feel so funny, and there were still wines to try and a little daylight left, so we changed the subject to Mark's favorite—vintage American jazz.

Over the course of the next few days in Baden, I learned the Kent Wilson life story. He grew up in Springfield, Illinois, in racially mixed lower-income neighborhoods where he was always in the distinct minority. He never knew his father's family, having been "born out of wedlock," as he put it. With regard to his mother's lineage, he, like so many of us, had only stories to document the mixed racial picture of his family. One great-grandmother, he'd been told, was Pequot Indian, and her husband was Black and Irish; another great-grandmother either was an illegitimate white child or was racially mixed and had been "put in with the slaves." She wound up hating whites, Kent said, so she "married the blackest thing she could find, and that was my great-grandfather."

Kent also heard stories about the early-twentieth-century race riots in Springfield. As his elders told it, before that, the oppression was fierce but predictable, but things got nastier after the riots—which weren't "riots" so much as white-on-Black violent mob actions that included lynchings and burning down whole blocks of Black residences. Henceforth his family had learned to avoid certain places. Kent learned "the rules" about where to go and how to behave, and he was also taught, "when you saw a Black in the street, to always say hello. You greeted each other. Even though you didn't know the person, it was a Black person."

In high school, Kent was the only Black chosen to attend a statewide student council conference, and when the delegation went to a restaurant, they were turned away for having him along. His first job, too, was washing dishes at Howard Johnson's, where Blacks were not served. "Of course, you get angry," he said, "but my grandparents ingrained in me that if somebody makes a dirty remark about you, just say that person has a problem, not you. Of course," he said, smiling ruefully at his son, "you do get angry."

When it came time to think about college, Kent's family wasn't much help because they simply "weren't attuned" to the idea of higher education. When he began applying to places like Harvard and Yale, Kent's uncle asked him point-blank, "Who do you think you are, applying to white colleges?" Nevertheless, Kent was determined to go to college, and to go as far away from Springfield as he could. He wrote away to the big-name colleges and prepared his applications, but everything he sent in was late, plus he hadn't yet taken the SAT. In the end, he took the test and Harvard accepted him late and gave him a scholarship. So he took the train east and arrived in Cambridge with the rest of us on that same day in September 1959. He settled in with a roommate and went to classes, studied, and ate with us at the Freshman Union.

Harvard broadened Kent's horizons, he told me, and as I heard more about his life after graduation, I realized that he kept right on broadening them. First he traveled through Eastern Europe with a group called Experiment in International Living, and then he spent two years in the Peace Corps. His post was in Ecuador, where he found himself coaching the national track team. He was only back in the States for a short time before he set off for Europe again, this time to study at the University of Vienna, where one day in the cafeteria line he met the woman he would soon marry. When they had two little boys, the family spent two years back in Boston while Kent did his MBA at the Harvard Business School. They returned to Austria soon after and have lived there since. Kent still sings with a local church choir.

## *John Niles Woodford*

***Born:*** *Benton Harbor, Michigan, 1942*

***Prepared at:*** *Benton Harbor High School, Benton Harbor, Michigan*

When we pulled up to John and Eliza Woodford's home in Ann Arbor, Michigan, I noticed a motorcycle parked in the garage, which didn't surprise me, knowing John's predilection for risk-taking. As it turns out, John and our classmate from Muskogee, George Jones, had remained close over the years and had done a lot of motorcycle touring in Canada and the United States. Over the course of the next few days, we interviewed John and his wife, whom he met in our freshman year when she was a freshman at Radcliffe as Elizabeth Duffy. On another visit with John, I tagged along to his high school reunion in Benton Harbor, about two hours away, and over the course of that day John told me a lot about his childhood.

He grew up in Benton Harbor, Michigan, a small town on the southwestern cuff of the mitten part of the state, not far from

Lake Michigan. Benton Harbor attracted its share of Blacks coming north in the Great Migration in the first half of the twentieth century, but John's roots had been northern for at least a generation before that: his father grew up just fifty miles east of Benton Harbor, in Kalamazoo, and his mother was from Massachusetts. Both families were middle-class and included many college graduates.

John remembers that Benton Harbor was racially mixed and roughly segregated geographically, with most of the Blacks living in an area known as the Flats. The city was still in relatively good shape economically when John was growing up. Postwar prosperity, the baby boom, and the emerging suburban lifestyle demanded thousands of the Whirlpool washing machines and refrigerators that were built in Benton Harbor, and the city's fruit market was the largest in the state. As John described it, "Kids of all backgrounds got along well; industrial and agricultural jobs were plentiful then." The decline would begin in the 1960s and continue as Whirlpool stopped making appliances there; today Benton Harbor is about 90 percent Black and has the lowest per capita income in the state. John's high school reunion committee had rented a bus to take everyone on a tour around the city, and I couldn't miss the look of sadness on the faces of the alumni as they looked out the windows at their hometown.

John has thought a lot about his father's race-consciousness through the years. He sees his father's ideas about race as having been conflicted, as illustrated by a story about his military service. John's father joined the Army during the Second World War and was assigned to a post in North Carolina; at the time, John said, "they didn't know he was a Black doctor, and when he got there they were stunned and they made him stay in the barracks all by himself and he was incensed." Eventually, John's dad joined the military pilots and support personnel who fought in the 332nd Fighter Group and 47th Bombardment Group of the US Army Air Force, better known as the Tuskegee Airmen. On the one hand, his dad was angered by the discrimination and segregation in the Army, and he would say that "he was glad he didn't have to go overseas and risk his life for these bastards." But then, later on, he would say, "Oh gee, being with Tuskegee Airmen was the greatest thing in my life, serving the country; I'm going to be buried in the Arlington Cemetery."

John had a complicated relationship with his father, he told me: "I disagreed with my father on a lot of stuff; we got along but we had a kind of edgy relationship." Benton Harbor was steeped in Jim Crow realities; as John sees it nowadays, his father and uncles were "accepting of a certain kind of separate social institution. They had to be a certain way to get through the world in their generation, and they were trying to pass it on. It usually had to do with 'don't make waves,' and try to get along, especially with people with power and influence." John's father had faced restrictions in the medical community, and instead of using organizational processes, John recalled, he "knocked down the segregationist practices in the hospital, using personal authority and persuasion."

After Harvard, John told me, he had made a few false starts in graduate school, married Eliza in 1965, and wound up with a career in journalism, doing stints at *Ebony, Jet,* the newspaper of the Nation of Islam, *Muhammad Speaks,* and later the *New York Times.* John and Eliza moved back to Michigan to raise their family, and there John worked first as editor of Ford Motor Company's magazine and later of University of Michigan publications. He was now retired, and the last time I spoke with him, he told me with some regret that he was going to sell his motorcycle.

## *Acknowledgments*

Our greatest debt of gratitude is owed to the Black men in the class of 1963. We hope we have done them justice; not only this book but also our lives have been profoundly enriched by knowing them, back in the day or now, or both. We also thank the many who gave generously of their time in sharing the memories that made this book possible: Emmie Schrader Adams, Jim Anderson, Terry Bannister, Frank Bardacke, Leslie Butler Barron, Alison Wardle Basile, Susan Basu, Chas Bickel, Ron Blau, David Branon, Charles Breyer, Alden Briscoe, Rick Butler, Roni Butler, Olivia Castor, Ned Chase, Linda Clave, Art Dahl, Sarah Davidson, Peter deLissovoy, Dick Diehl, Astrid Dodds, Valerie Epps, Lena Frazier, Fred Gardner, Kent Garrett Sr., Carol Garvey, Otis Gates, Todd Gitlin, Fred Glimp, Milford Graves, Bobo Gray, Harvey Hacker, Jack Hammond, Joan Harris, John Hartman, Michael Joseph, Spencer Jourdain, Lou Kaden, Jerome Karabel, Martin Kilson, David Kronenfeld, Beverly Butler Lavergneau, Stephen Leff, Velma Lewis, Connie McDougald, Ken Manaster, David McGregor, Taylor McLean, Mason Morfit, Joe Morris, Lance Morrow, David Othmer, Jay Pasachoff, Harvey Pressman, Tony Robbins, Dave Schmalz, Karl Singer, Eliot Stanley, Joan Strasser, Bill Strickland, Brandon Terry, Pat Tovatt, Chuck Turner, Fred Wacker, Mary Vogel Walton, Michael Walzer, Napoleon Williams, Carter Wilson, Susi Wilson, and Eliza Woodford.

Our early attempts to shape mountains of data into a readable book were skillfully and insightfully guided by our literary agent,

Gary Morris of David Black Agency. Elinor Burkett provided a few astute pointers as we got under way, and Donna Ellsworth Brand and Andrew Walker read earlier versions of the book and made dozens of valuable comments. Our editors at Houghton Mifflin Harcourt, Susan Canavan and Jenny Xu, and our copyeditor Cynthia Buck provided expertise and encouragement at various points along the way. We also thank Mass Humanities for the grant that allowed us to do the initial interviews, Justina Jordan for organizing some of our data, Jessica Vecchione for helping with video processes, and the staff at the Harvard University Archives for their patient assistance.

Over the decade that we've been at this, we've been fortunate to have wonderful friends and family to cheer us on. So finally, we thank all of them and in no small measure, we congratulate each other for hanging in there.

# *Notes*

## *Preface*

page

ix *"Don't define me":* Malcolm Gladwell, "Getting In: The Social Logic of Ivy League Admissions," *New Yorker,* October 10, 2005, https://www.newyorker.com/magazine/2005/10/10/getting-in.

xiii *personal Negro servant:* Lauren E. Baer, "The Ku Klux Klan at Harvard," *Harvard Crimson,* February 18, 1999.

*burned a cross:* Philip M. Cronin, "'Cross Burners' Disciplined, Say No Malice Was Implied," *Harvard Crimson,* February 27, 1952.

xiv *"many changes":* Taylor Branch, *Parting the Waters: America in the King Years, 1954–1963* (New York: Simon & Schuster, 1988), xii.

## *1. New Boys: Fall 1959*

3 *"The official view":* Morton Keller and Phyllis Keller, *Making Harvard Modern: The Rise of America's University* (New York: Oxford University Press, 2001), 61, 284–285.

*"there was no Black visibility":* John D. Spooner, "John D. Spooner, '59," in *Our Harvard: Reflections on College Life by Twenty-Two Distinguished Graduates,* ed. Jeffrey L. Lant (New York: Taplinger Publishing, 1982), 220.

4 *the booklet's claim: Information about Harvard College for Prospective Students* (Cambridge, MA: Harvard College, 1958), 8.

7 *"the architecture":* George Santayana, "The Harvard Yard," in *The Harvard Book: Selections from Three Centuries,* rev. ed., ed. William Bentinck-Smith (Cambridge, MA: Harvard University Press, 1982), 65.

12 *"a testament to the failure":* "Metropolis in a Mess," *Newsweek,* July 27, 1959, 29.

29 *"might be inspired":* Office for the Arts at Harvard, "History of Memorial Hall," https://sites.fas.harvard.edu/~memhall/history.html.

## 2. *Curiosities*

39 *front-page* Crimson *item:* "CRIME Competition Rolls Onward; Free Beer, Good Cheer Undepleted," *Harvard Crimson,* October 8, 1959.

40 *"luxury brands":* Malcolm Gladwell, "Getting In: The Social Logic of Ivy League Admissions," *New Yorker,* October 10, 2005, https://www.newyorker.com/magazine/2005/10/10/getting-in.

44 *"horse fairs":* Connaught O'Connell Mahoney, "Jolly-Ups and a 'New Look' at Radcliffe," *Harvard Crimson,* June 3, 2002.

*disapproved of interracial marriage:* Frank Newport, "In US, 87% Approve of Black-White Marriage, vs. 4% in 1958," *Politics,* July 25, 2013, https://news.gallup.com/poll/163697/approve-marriage-blacks-whites.aspx.

*One Black graduate:* E. J. Kahn Jr., *Harvard through Change and through Storm* (New York: W. W. Norton, 1969), 116–117.

48 *"I sought no friendships":* W. E. B. Du Bois, *The Autobiography of W. E. B. Du Bois* (1968) (reprint/ebook, Diasporic Africa Press, 2013), locations 1664, 1682, 1694, 1706.

49 *"I had my 'island within'":* W. E. B. Du Bois, "A Negro Student at Harvard at the End of the Nineteenth Century," in *Blacks at Harvard: A Documentary History of African American Experience at Harvard and Radcliffe,* eds. Werner Sollors, Caldwell Titcomb, and Thomas A. Underwood (New York: New York University Press, 1993), 254.

## 3. *Integrators: Spring 1960*

54 Crimson *poll:* Carl I. Gable Jr., "Local Prejudice against Harvard Students Based in Stereotypes, Social Aggression," *Harvard Crimson,* February 26, 1950.

56 *"quickening":* Taylor Branch, *Parting the Waters: America in the King Years, 1954–1963* (New York: Simon & Schuster, 1988), 272.

*As the new decade opened:* S. Swirski, "Changes in the Structure of Relations between Groups and the Emergence of Political Movements: The Student Movement at Harvard and Wisconsin, 1930–1969," PhD diss., Department of Political Science, Michigan State University (1971), 172, quoted in Seymour Martin Lipset and David Riesman, *Education and Politics at Harvard* (New York: McGraw-Hill, 1975), 198.

*"suspicious":* A. James Reichley, "Young Conservatives at Old Harvard," *The Reporter,* June 16, 1955, quoted in Lipset and Riesman, *Education and Politics at Harvard,* 199.

*"the thing is":* Ibid., 200.

*A* Crimson *poll:* Craig K. Comstock, "'Moderate Liberals' Predominate Politically: Lectures and Assigned Reading Influence Student Shift to Left," *Harvard Crimson,* June 11, 1959.

57 *"welcome sign":* "Dimestore Picket," *Harvard Crimson,* February 26, 1960.

58 *"hadn't accepted admission":* John Woodford, "My Years at Harvard," draft

manuscript, published in Jesse A. Rhines, ed., *Black Harvard, Black Yale* (Jesse Rhines, PhD, 2012), location 1095.

59 *"a grand new world":* Ibid., location 213.

61 *"moral idealism":* Michael Walzer, "The Northern Student Movement, 1960," unpublished manuscript, October 1960, 7.

65 *picketers told a* Crimson *reporter:* "Record Blizzard Hits Cambridge; Several Colleges Cancel Classes," *Harvard Crimson,* March 5, 1960.

67 *talked to Woolworth's managers:* "Store Managers React to Protest," *Harvard Crimson,* March 22, 1960.

*economic impact:* "Woolworth Official Attacks Picketing," *Harvard Crimson,* March 1, 1960.

*psychology professors:* "Psychologists Say Picketing Aids Negroes: Quickened Integration Predicted for South," *Harvard Crimson,* March 7, 1960.

68 *"totally new situation":* "Racial Issue Unavoidable: Handlin Emphasizes Importance of Strong Stand for Civil Rights," *Harvard Crimson,* March 12, 1960.

*William Y. Elliott:* "Gradual Integration Advocated by Elliott," *Harvard Crimson,* March 22, 1960.

*"to make haste slowly":* Ibid.

*long letter in reaction:* Spencer Jourdain '61, "Voice of Dissent," *Harvard Crimson,* March 22, 1960.

69 *a notice went out:* "All Harvard and Radcliffe Students," *Harvard Crimson,* May 6, 1960.

*"The Second Shot":* "Students March for Civil Rights," *Harvard Crimson,* May 17, 1960.

70 *a crowd of some 1,500:* Frederick H. Gardner, "Integration Rally Draws 1,000 Student Marchers to Hail Court Decision," *Harvard Crimson,* May 18, 1960.

*"Integrated Minutemen": Life,* May 30, 1960, 36.

72 *Spencer Jourdain would tell:* Monica M. Dodge and Erika P. Pierson, "Activism Quiet on Mostly White Campus," *Harvard Crimson,* May 23, 2011.

## *4. Bright Shadows*

74 *Riesman was concerned:* Seymour Martin Lipset and David Riesman, *Education and Politics at Harvard* (New York: McGraw-Hill, 1975), 328–329.

86 *Lowell presided:* William Wright, *Harvard's Secret Court: The Savage 1920 Purge of Campus Homosexuals* (New York: St. Martin's Press, 2005).

*Before the purge:* Ibid.

87 *in my own Eliot House:* Douglas Shand-Tucci, *The Crimson Letter: Harvard, Homosexuality, and the Shaping of American Culture* (New York: St. Martin's Press, 2004), 196.

88 *Two weeks later:* "Virginius Douglass Johnston," *New York Age Defender,* September 3, 1955.

91 *he did so brilliantly:* Ralph Ellison, "*An American Dilemma:* A Review" (1944), Teaching American History, http://teachingamericanhistory.org/library/document/an-american-dilemma-a-review/.

92 *The next source:* Abram Kandiner and Lionel Ovesey, *The Mark of Oppression: A Psychological Study of the American Negro* (New York: W. W. Norton, 1951), 65, 66, 70.

*"no possible basis":* Ibid., 297.

93 *"shut out":* W. E. B. DuBois, *The Souls of Black Folk* (Mineola, NY: Dover Publications, 1994), 2.

94 *questions of whites:* Ibid., 1.

*"a peculiar sensation":* Ibid., 2.

## 5. House Negroes: Fall 1960, Spring and Summer 1961

98 *"center of social": Information about Harvard College for Prospective Students* (Cambridge, MA: Harvard College, 1958), 16.

*"informal, friendly":* Ibid., 15.

99 *"Where else would you find":* "Eliot Shield, Tradition, and Legacy," Harvard University website, https://eliot.harvard.edu/brand.

101 *One of his reasons:* A. Lawrence Lowell, "Dormitories and College Life," *Harvard Graduates' Magazine,* June 1904, http://collegiateway.org/reading/lowell-1904/.

105 *"the tacit ban":* Herbert H. Denton Jr., "Behind the Velvet Curtain: A Look at Harvard's Final Clubs," *Harvard Crimson,* May 25, 1965.

111 *Three reporters:* Douglas S. Crocket, "3 Harvard Men Scoop the Press," *Boston Globe,* January 9, 1961, 11.

112 *"plain and positive obligation":* Executive Order 10925, Establishing the President's Committee on Equal Employment Opportunity, https://www.eeoc.gov/eeoc/history/35th/thelaw/eo-10925.html.

## 6. So-Called Negroes: Fall 1961

114 *Harvard tradition of hissing:* R. D. Fisher, "Malcolm X—After 31 Years," *Harvard Crimson,* December 3, 1992.

*The agent estimated:* Clayborne Carson, *Malcolm X: The FBI File* (1991; reprint, New York: Skyhorse Publishing, 2012).

*The forum moderator:* Fisher, "Malcolm X."

116 *"We thank you":* All quotes from Malcolm X's March 1961 speech at Harvard are from Archie C. Epps III, *The Speeches of Malcolm X at Harvard* (New York: Morrow, 1967).

117 *"the greatest boon":* "Carrington—'Black Muslims Boon to Klan,'" *Boston Globe,* March 25, 1961, 16.

118 *Malcolm was dazzled:* William Strickland, *Malcolm X, Make It Plain* (New York: Penguin, 1994), 13.

*"shiny black jackets":* Bill Strickland, "Remembering Malcolm: A Personal

Critique of Manning Marable's Non-Definitive Biography of Malcolm X," James and Grace Lee Boggs Center to Nurture Community Leadership, May 12, 2012, http://boggscenter.org/remembering-malcolm-by-bill-strickland/.

119 *"raised many eyebrows":* Spencer C. D. Jourdain '61, "Black Muslim," *Harvard Crimson,* March 28, 1961.

*"the white audience":* Manning Marable, *Malcolm X: A Life of Reinvention* (New York: Viking, 2011), 187.

*Malcolm's grasp of history:* Fisher, "Malcolm X."

120 *documentary series:* Marable, *Malcolm X,* 162.

*improve their image:* Ibid., 184.

*Americans were complacent:* Strickland, *Malcolm X,* 2.

123 *Diploma Riots:* Bruce L. Paisner and Joseph M. Russin, "2000 Riot against Diploma Change after Protest on Widener Steps," *Harvard Crimson,* April 27, 1961; Bruce L. Paisner and Joseph M. Russin, "Police Use Tear Gas, Smoke Bombs to Dispel 4,000 Students in Second Riot over Diplomas," *Harvard Crimson,* April 28, 1961.

*"What's pat":* "Dr. Pusey Cribbed Verse from Bryn Mawr Girl," *Boston Globe,* May 5, 1961, 11. It wasn't Pusey's own writing; it turned out that a Bryn Mawr girl wrote it. Pusey later sent her a thank-you letter.

*The mayhem continued:* "New Riot Rumors Sweep Harvard but All Fizzle," *Boston Globe,* April 29, 1961, 2.

124 *vibrant gay life:* Mark Thomas Krone, "1950s Gay Boston," Boston Queer History, November 21, 2014, https://markthomaskrone.wordpress.com/2014/11/21/1950s-gay-boston/.

128 *the most important frontier:* "Southerner Declares Key to Negro Rights Lies in Voting Reform," *Harvard Crimson,* November 3, 1961.

129 *"the race question":* Strickland, "Remembering Malcolm."

130 *Some eight hundred:* "Bomb Scare Chases 800 at Jordan Hall," *Boston Globe,* October 30, 1961, 1.

*together countered this accusation:* Jack Butler '63 and John Hartman '64, "Black Muslims," *Harvard Crimson,* November 3, 1961.

131 *In his former life:* Richard Lei, "Louis Farrakhan, Calypso Charmer," *Washington Post,* October 14, 1995.

*"The Charmer":* Strickland, "Remembering Malcolm."

132 *pulling no punches:* "Tide of Black Supremacy," *Harvard Crimson,* December 14, 1961.

*"plight of the American Negro":* Ibid.

## 7. *The Lost Negroes*

143 *a fire alarm:* "Loeb Lowell House Hit by Fires: Theatre Stage Curtain Damaged; Lowell Student Felled by Smoke," *Harvard Crimson,* September 27, 1960.

146 *"that will keep listeners guessing":* "Jazz Listening Examples for Percussion," Berklee College of Music, Stan Getz Library, https://library.berklee.edu/browse/subject-guide/principal-instruments-percussion/jazz-listening-examples-percussion.

147 *perennial feeder school:* Lee A. Daniels, "The Halls of Boston Latin School," *New York Times,* April 21, 1985.

*"Running anchor":* "Swimmers Edge Navy to Take 52–43 Win; Trio Sets Relay Mark," *Harvard Crimson,* January 18, 1960.

149 *When he reappeared:* "Trackmen to Face Dartmouth Here; GBI Field Events Set for Tonight," *Harvard Crimson,* February 9, 1962.

## *8. Rising Sons of Darkness: Spring and Summer 1962*

154 *"reach of Jim Crow":* Martin Kilson, "Black Intellectual as Leftist and Freethinker: Martin Kilson's Intellectual Odyssey," unpublished manuscript, 46.

*"status-pretenders":* Ibid., 50.

155 "I would have almost certainly": Ibid., 57.

157 *"increase and broaden":* Richard L. Plaut, "Plans for Assisting Negro Students to Enter and Remain in College," *Journal of Negro Education* 35, no. 4 (Autumn 1966): 393.

159 New York Times *obit:* Richard Severo, "John U. Monro, 89, Dies; Left Harvard to Follow Ideals," *New York Times,* April 3, 2002.

161 *"actively (if quietly)":* Jerome Karabel, *The Chosen: The Hidden History of Admission and Exclusion at Harvard, Yale, and Princeton* (Boston: Houghton Mifflin, 2005), 400.

*"talent search":* Michael Lerner, "Plan Seeks Applications from Southern Negroes," *Harvard Crimson,* February 2, 1963.

162 *"between 1959 and 1961":* Karabel, *The Chosen,* 401.

163 *His adviser:* Ellen Lake, "Thomas F. Pettigrew," *Harvard Crimson,* April 9, 1964.

166 *arrested at a sit-in:* "Two University Students Arrested during Sit-In," *Harvard Crimson,* February 26, 1962.

168 *"shattered the rigid thought structures":* Bernt Lindfors, *African Textualities: Texts, Pre-Texts, and Contexts of African Literature* (Trenton, NJ: Africa World Press, 1997), 56.

*Cambridge changed his life:* Ibid., 68.

*"if we Africans":* Ibid., 81.

169 *"Only in the last five years":* Efrem Sigel, "Harvard Expands Africa Studies with Courses in History, Anthro," *Harvard Crimson,* October 3, 1961.

*no way to evaluate the course:* "Credit Denied Spring Term Swahili Class; Move Inspires Talk of African Program," *Harvard Crimson,* February 8, 1961.

170 *"Come here, you prick":* Larry Grubbs, *Secular Missionaries: Americans and African Development in the 1960s* (Amherst: University of Massachusetts Press, 1960), 116.

## *9. Afro Americans: Fall 1962 and Spring 1963*

176 *executive order:* Bruce L. Paisner, "University Yields to Government on Submission of Employment Data," *Harvard Crimson,* September 25, 1962.

177 *accusing the college of dodging:* John G. Butler '63, Marc J. Roberts '64, and Richard Rothstein '63, "On Discrimination," *Harvard Crimson,* September 26, 1962.

*The Engineers' coach:* Joseph M. Russin, "Crimson Faces Engineers Today; Rains May Mar Season's Opener," *Harvard Crimson,* September 29, 1962.

178 *"lose in interesting ways":* "Fall Sports; Football," *Three Twenty-Seven: The 1963 Harvard Yearbook* (Cambridge, MA: Harvard Yearbook Publications, 1963), 193.

*Coach Yovicsin once remarked:* Boisfeuillet Jones Jr., "John Yovicsin Profile," *Harvard Crimson,* November 19, 1966.

179 *Ole Miss halftime:* William Doyle, *An American Insurrection: The Battle of Oxford, Mississippi, 1962,* ebook ed. (New York: Doubleday, 2003), location 1885.

180 *He spent that night:* James Meredith, with William Doyle, *A Mission from God: A Memoir and Challenge for America* (New York: Atria Books, 2012).

182 New Yorker *article:* James Baldwin, "Letter from a Region in My Mind," *New Yorker,* November 17, 1962.

*long-winded review:* Paul S. Cowan, "A Black Man Talks to the White World," *Harvard Crimson,* November 27, 1962.

*Kilson went back and forth:* Martin Kilson, "James Baldwin," *Harvard Crimson,* December 7, 1962.

183 *Baldwin celebrated:* David Leeming, *James Baldwin: A Biography,* ebook ed. (New York: Arcade, 2015), location 4007.

186 *At a panel discussion:* "Three Students Comment on Role of Meredith's Studies, Muslims," *Harvard Crimson,* January 15, 1963.

187 *tired of the white moderates:* Martin Luther King Jr., "Letter from Birmingham Jail," April 16, 1963, Martin Luther King Jr. Papers Project, https://swap.stanford.edu/20141218230016/http://mlk-kpp01.stanford.edu/kingweb/popular%5Frequests/frequentdocs/birmingham.pdf.

188 *"Africans, Afro-Americans":* Lawrence E. Feinberg, "Africans, Afro-Americans Form Club," *Harvard Crimson,* April 27, 1963.

189 *on record he praised:* Ibid.

*support one another:* Spencer Jourdain, "The Nile Club: The Evolution of a Black Veritas," *Shorefront Journal,* June 13, 2017, https://shorefront journal.wordpress.com/2017/06/13/the-nile-club-the-social-evolution-of-a-black-veritas/; Spencer Jourdain, *Dream Dancers: An American Reflection upon Past, Present, and Future,* vol. 1, *New England Preservers of the Dream, 1620–1924* (Evanston, IL: Shorefront, 2017).

190 *"like that at Harvard":* Feinberg, "Africans, Afro-Americans Form Club."

191 *Black alumnus:* William Harrison '32, "Afro-American Society," *Harvard Crimson,* May 8, 1963.

*Dean Monro called a press conference:* Efrem Sigel, "Monro Supports African Charter Club," *Harvard Crimson,* May 9, 1963.

193 *Armah's argument:* "Afro-American Club," *Harvard Crimson,* May 10, 1963.

*"calm themselves":* Joseph Lee Auspitz, "A Milder View," *Harvard Crimson,* May 10, 1963.

*second minority opinion:* Stephen F. Jencks, "Discrimination: On the Other Hand," *Harvard Crimson,* May 10, 1963.

194 *"Africans in power":* Bernt Lindfors, *African Textualities: Texts, Pre-Texts, and Contexts of African Literature* (Trenton, NJ: Africa World Press, 1997), 83.

*biographical sketch:* Ibid., 84.

195 *"an orgy":* Jane Howard, "Harvard's Commencement Week," memo to Ray Mackland, June 1, 1961, Harvard University Archives, HUA961.2.

196 *The speech was covered:* "Class Presidents Look to Commencement," *Boston Globe,* May 31, 1963, 25.

## *10. Alumni*

205 *the dean argued:* Richard Cotton, "Watson Orders AAAAS to Establish One Price for Baldwin's Lecture," *Harvard Crimson,* January 10, 1964.

*long and strident letter:* "Anochie Replies," *Harvard Crimson,* January 14, 1964.

208 *"a more efficient use":* "Students to Teach at Negro College," *Harvard Crimson,* February 14, 1964.

210 *One biographer:* Bernt Lindfors, *African Textualities: Texts, Pre-Texts, and Contexts of African Literature* (Trenton, NJ: Africa World Press, 1997), 85.

214 *program number one:* That first program can be viewed online at https://www.youtube.com/watch?v=Y7g9ROouhpQ.

216 *NET insisted:* Robert E. Dallos, "11 Negro Staff Members Quit NET Black Journal Program," *New York Times,* August 21, 1968, 95.

219 *"H. Rap Brown was in jail":* John Woodford, "Messaging the Black Man," in *Voices from the Underground: Insider Histories of the Vietnam Era Underground Press,* ed. Ken Wachsberger (Tempe, AZ: Mica's Press, 1993), 81–82.

221 *barely budged:* Jerome Karabel, *The Chosen: The Hidden History of Admission and Exclusion at Harvard, Yale, and Princeton* (Boston: Houghton Mifflin, 2005), 401.

*"tears in their eyes":* Lawrence E. Eichel, "The Founding of the Afro-American Studies Department—The Crisis of 1969," in *Blacks at Harvard: A*

*Documentary History of African American Experience at Harvard and Radcliffe*, ed. Werner Sollors, Caldwell Titcomb, and Thomas A. Underwood (New York: New York University Press, 1993), 379.

*"Four Requests on* Fair *Harvard":* Ruth A. Hailu, "Revisiting the 'Four Demands,' Fifty Years Later," *Harvard Crimson*, May 20, 2018.

222 *"threats of militant":* Eichel, "The Founding," 380.

## *Epilogue*

232 *"singularly clairvoyant":* W. E. B. Du Bois, *Darkwater: Voices from Within the Veil* (New York: Harcourt, Brace and Howe, 1920), https://archive.org/details/darkwatervoicesfooduborich/page/n6.